First World War
and Army of Occupation
War Diary
France, Belgium and Germany

42 DIVISION
Divisional Troops
210 Brigade Royal Field Artillery
1 March 1917 - 11 April 1919

WO95/2649/1

The Naval & Military Press Ltd
www.nmarchive.com
Published in association with The National Archives

Published by

The Naval & Military Press Ltd

Unit 10 Ridgewood Industrial Park,

Uckfield, East Sussex,

TN22 5QE England

Tel: +44 (0) 1825 749494

www.naval-military-press.com

www.nmarchive.com

This diary has been reprinted in facsimile from the original. Any imperfections are inevitably reproduced and the quality may fall short of modern type and cartographic standards.

© **Crown Copyright**
Images reproduced by permission of The National Archives, London, England, 2015.

Contents

Document type	Place/Title	Date From	Date To
Heading	WO95/2649/1		
Heading	210th Brigade R.F.A. Mar 1917-Apr 1919		
Heading	Vol. III War Diary Of 210th Bde. R.F.A. 42nd. Division From-1.3.17. To-31.3.17.		
War Diary		01/03/1917	01/03/1917
War Diary	Marseilles	01/03/1917	01/03/1917
War Diary	Pont Remy	03/03/1917	04/03/1917
War Diary	Marseilles	04/03/1917	05/03/1917
War Diary	Pont Remy	07/03/1917	08/03/1917
War Diary	Marseilles	12/03/1917	12/03/1917
War Diary	Pont Remy	14/03/1917	17/03/1917
War Diary	Caours Drucat	19/03/1917	20/03/1917
War Diary	Caours	23/03/1917	30/03/1917
Heading	Volume II War Diary Of 210th Bde R.F.A. From. 1-4-17 To 30-4-17.		
War Diary	Caours	01/04/1917	03/04/1917
War Diary	Argoeuves	04/04/1917	04/04/1917
War Diary	Fouilloy	05/04/1917	05/04/1917
War Diary	B. Olympe	06/04/1917	21/04/1917
War Diary	Roisel	22/04/1917	29/04/1917
War Diary	St Emilie	30/04/1917	30/04/1917
War Diary	Roisel	30/04/1917	30/04/1917
War Diary	Cappy	22/04/1917	22/04/1917
War Diary	Le Mesnil-Bruntel.	23/04/1917	01/05/1917
Heading	Volume II War Diary Of 210th Bde R.F.A. From 1.5.17 To 31.5.17.		
War Diary	St Emilie	01/05/1917	20/05/1917
War Diary	Vallulart Wood	21/05/1917	22/05/1917
War Diary	Ruyaulcourt	23/05/1917	31/05/1917
War Diary	Ronssoy Wood (F14D81/2 8)	21/05/1917	30/05/1917
Operation(al) Order(s)	210th Bde Order No. 1	03/05/1917	03/05/1917
Operation(al) Order(s)	210th Bde Order No. 2 by Lt. Col A. Birtwistle C.M.G. Commdg 210 Bde RFA	08/05/1917	08/05/1917
Operation(al) Order(s)	210th Bde Order No. 3 by Lt. Col A. Birtwistle C.M.G. Commdg 210 Bde RFA	10/05/1917	10/05/1917
Operation(al) Order(s)	210th Bde Order No. 4 by Lt. Col A. Birtwistle C.M.G. Commdg 210 Bde RFA	13/05/1917	13/05/1917
Heading	Volume II War Diary Of 210th Bde R.F.A. From 1.6.17. To 30.6.17.		
War Diary	Ruyaulcourt	01/06/1917	21/06/1917
War Diary	Quarry Q1a0.9	22/06/1917	30/06/1917
War Diary	Ronssoy (F14D81/2.8)	01/06/1917	30/06/1917
Heading	Vol. II. War Diary 210th. Bde. R.F.A. 1.7.17 To 31.7.17		
War Diary	Havrincourt Wood	01/07/1917	29/07/1917
War Diary	P4a6.9	29/07/1917	31/07/1917
Operation(al) Order(s)	210th Bde R.F.A Order No. 9 by Lt Col A Birtwistle C.M.G Cdg 210th Bde R.F.A. Appx "A"	01/06/1917	01/06/1917
Operation(al) Order(s)	210th Bde R.F.A. Order No. 11 Appx "B"	22/07/1917	22/07/1917
Operation(al) Order(s)	210th Bde R.F.A. Order No. 10 APpx "B" 1	21/04/1917	21/04/1917

Type	Description	Date	Date
Miscellaneous	Amendment To 210th Bde R.F.A. Order No. 12 Appx "C"	23/07/1917	23/07/1917
Operation(al) Order(s)	210th Bde R.F.A. Order No. 12	22/07/1917	22/07/1917
Heading	War Diary of "D" Battery 210th Bde R.F.A. From 1-7-17 To 31-7-17 Vol II		
War Diary	Ronssoy F14D8 1/2 8	01/07/1917	02/07/1917
War Diary	Ronssoy Wood F14D8 1/2 8	02/07/1917	03/07/1917
War Diary	Ronssoy F14D8 1/2 8	04/07/1917	05/07/1917
War Diary	Ronssoy Wood	06/07/1917	09/07/1917
War Diary	Ronssoy	10/07/1917	31/07/1917
Heading	Volume II War Diary Of 210th Bde R.F.A. From 1.8.17. To 31.8.17		
War Diary	P.4a6.9	01/08/1917	05/08/1917
War Diary	P4a6.90	06/08/1917	11/08/1917
War Diary	P4a B5. 95	12/08/1917	15/08/1917
War Diary	P4a85.81	16/08/1917	18/08/1917
War Diary	Royaulcourt	19/08/1917	19/08/1917
War Diary	Bus	20/08/1917	25/08/1917
War Diary	Proven	26/08/1917	28/08/1917
War Diary	L8d1.8	29/08/1917	31/08/1917
Heading	War Diary Of D210 R.F.A. August 1st 1917 to August 26th 1917		
Operation(al) Order(s)	210th Bde Order No. 23	28/08/1917	28/08/1917
War Diary	Ronssoy F14D 81/2 8	01/08/1917	11/08/1917
War Diary	Ronssoy Wood	12/08/1917	19/08/1917
War Diary	Baupaume	20/08/1917	26/08/1917
Operation(al) Order(s)	210th. Bde. R.F.A. Order No. 17	17/08/1917	17/08/1917
Operation(al) Order(s)	210th. Bde. R.F.A. Order No. 18	18/08/1917	18/08/1917
Operation(al) Order(s)	210th. Bde. R.F.A. Order No. 19.	19/08/1917	19/08/1917
Operation(al) Order(s)	210th. Bde. R.F.A. Order No. 20	24/08/1917	24/08/1917
Operation(al) Order(s)	210th. Bde. R.F.A. Order No. 21	27/08/1917	27/08/1917
Heading	War Diary Of 210th Bde R.F.A. From 1-9-17 To 30-9-17		
Heading	Volume II War Diary Of 210th Bde R.F.A. From 1-9-17. To 30-9-17		
War Diary	I8d1.8	01/09/1917	18/09/1917
War Diary	I8d.10.95	19/09/1917	29/09/1917
War Diary	Wormhoudt	30/09/1917	30/09/1917
Operation(al) Order(s)	N. C.2 Sub-Group Order No. 3.		
Operation(al) Order(s)	3rd Div. Arty Order No. 18.	26/09/1917	26/09/1917
Miscellaneous	Addendum 1 to 3rd Div. Artillery Order No. 18.	25/09/1917	25/09/1917
Miscellaneous	No. 2 Group.	25/09/1917	25/09/1917
Miscellaneous	Addendum No. 2 To 3rd Div. Arty Order No. 18.	25/09/1917	25/09/1917
Miscellaneous	Table "A"		
Miscellaneous	9th D.A.O.O No. 153 Is Forwarded Herewith.	18/09/1917	18/09/1917
Operation(al) Order(s)	No. 2 Sub-Group Order No. 2	25/09/1917	25/09/1917
Operation(al) Order(s)	3rd Division Artillery Order No. 18.	24/09/1917	24/09/1917
Map			
Operation(al) Order(s)	No. 2 Sub-Group Order No. 1	18/09/1917	18/09/1917
Operation(al) Order(s)	9th Divisional Artillery Operation Order No. 152.	17/09/1917	17/09/1917
Miscellaneous	Table "B"		
Operation(al) Order(s)	210th Bde R.F.A. Order No. 24	05/09/1917	05/09/1917
Operation(al) Order(s)	210th Bde R.F.A. Order No. 25	11/09/1917	11/09/1917
Operation(al) Order(s)	210th Bde R.F.A. Order No. 26	29/09/1917	29/09/1917
Operation(al) Order(s)	210th Bde R.F.A. Order No. 27	30/09/1917	30/09/1917
Operation(al) Order(s)	210th Bde R.F.A. Order No. 28	01/10/1917	01/10/1917

Type	Description	Date From	Date To
Heading	Volume II War Diary Of 210th Bde. R.F.A. From 1-10-17 To 31-10-17		
War Diary	Wormhoudt	01/10/1917	01/10/1917
War Diary	R30c05.15	02/10/1917	13/10/1917
War Diary	X14.a2.9	14/10/1917	23/10/1917
War Diary	R30.a85.85	24/10/1917	31/10/1917
Heading	Volume II War Diary Of 210th Bde R.F.A. From 1-11-17 To 30-11-17		
War Diary	R30a85.85	01/11/1917	20/11/1917
War Diary	Ghyvelde	21/11/1917	21/11/1917
War Diary	Normhoudt	23/11/1917	23/11/1917
War Diary	Wemaers-Cappel	24/11/1917	24/11/1917
War Diary	Hondeghem	25/11/1917	25/11/1917
War Diary	Witternesse	26/11/1917	28/11/1917
War Diary	Roebecq	30/11/1917	30/11/1917
Operation(al) Order(s)	210th Bde. R.F.A. Order No. 31	22/11/1917	22/11/1917
War Diary	Roebecq	30/11/1917	30/11/1917
Operation(al) Order(s)	210th Bde. R.F.A. Order No. 1.	14/11/1917	14/11/1917
Miscellaneous		20/10/1917	20/10/1917
Operation(al) Order(s)	210th Bde Order No. 30	20/11/1917	20/11/1917
Operation(al) Order(s)	210th Bde. R.F.A. Order No. 32	23/11/1917	23/11/1917
Operation(al) Order(s)	210th Bde. R.F.A. Order No. 33.	24/11/1917	24/11/1917
Operation(al) Order(s)	210th Bde. R.F.A. Order No. 34.	25/11/1917	25/11/1917
Operation(al) Order(s)	210th Bde. R.F.A. Order No. 35.	29/11/1917	29/11/1917
Operation(al) Order(s)	210th Bde. R.F.A. Order No. 36.	01/12/1917	01/12/1917
Heading	Volume II War Diary 210th Bde R.F.A. From 1-12-17 To 31-12-17		
War Diary	F1025.2	01/12/1917	31/12/1917
Heading	Volume III War Diary Of 210th Bde. R.F.A. From 1-1-18 To 31-1-18		
War Diary	F10b5.2	01/01/1918	31/01/1918
Heading	War. Diary. Of 210th Brigade R.F.A. From 1-2-18. To 28-2-18		
War Diary	F10b5.2	03/02/1918	16/02/1918
War Diary	Fouquieres	17/02/1918	28/02/1918
Operation(al) Order(s)	210th Brigade R.F.A. Order No. 37.	12/02/1918	12/02/1918
Miscellaneous	Amendments To 210th Bde R.F.A. Order No. 37.	14/02/1918	14/02/1918
Heading	42nd Division Artillery. 210th Brigade Royal Field Artillery March 1918		
Heading	War Diary. Of 210th Brigade. R.F.A. From 1/3/18 To 31/03/18 Vol III		
War Diary	Fouquieres	01/03/1918	02/03/1918
War Diary	Ham-En-Artois.	03/03/1918	19/03/1918
War Diary	Gauchin Legal	23/03/1918	23/03/1918
War Diary	Adinfer	24/03/1918	24/03/1918
War Diary	Ablainzevelle	25/03/1918	25/03/1918
War Diary	Essarts	26/03/1918	31/03/1918
Operation(al) Order(s)	210th Brigade Order No. 38.	02/03/1918	02/03/1918
Heading	Headquarters, 210th Brigade, R.F.A. April 1918		
Heading	210th Brigade R.F.A. War Diary From 1-4-18 To 30-4-18		
War Diary	Essarts Les-Bucquoy	01/04/1918	01/04/1918
War Diary	Essarts.	02/04/1918	11/04/1918
War Diary	E23c.6.7.	14/04/1918	15/04/1918
War Diary	E.10.d.8.8.	16/04/1918	18/04/1918
War Diary	E11.a.2.2.	19/04/1918	30/04/1918

Heading	Vol III War Diary 210th Brigade R.F.A. From 1-5-18 To 31-5-18		
War Diary	Hannescamps	01/05/1918	14/05/1918
War Diary	Bienvillers	17/05/1918	30/05/1918
Heading	War Diary Of 210th Brigade R.F.A. For The Month Of June 1918 Volume IV		
War Diary	Bienvillers	02/06/1918	30/06/1918
Heading	War Diary Of 210th Bde. R.F.A. Period-Month Of July. 1918. Vol. III		
War Diary	Bienvillers	04/07/1918	04/07/1918
War Diary	Bus	05/07/1918	30/07/1918
Heading	War Diary Of 210th Brigade, R.F.A. From 1st August 1918 To 31st August 1918. Volume XX.		
War Diary	Bus	01/08/1918	04/08/1918
War Diary	Bertrancourt	06/08/1918	18/08/1918
War Diary	Chalk Pits K32A41	19/08/1918	23/08/1918
War Diary	Mirau Mont	24/08/1918	26/08/1918
War Diary	Lou Part Wood	26/08/1918	28/08/1918
War Diary	K32a41	21/08/1918	21/08/1918
War Diary	Loupart	27/08/1918	27/08/1918
War Diary	Thilloy	29/08/1918	31/08/1918
Heading	Vol VIII War Diary 210th Bde R.F.A. From 1.9.18 To 30.9.18		
War Diary	Thilloy	01/09/1918	03/09/1918
War Diary	Bus	04/09/1918	04/09/1918
War Diary	Ytres	05/09/1918	07/09/1918
War Diary	Metz-En-Couture	08/09/1918	13/09/1918
War Diary	Ytres	14/09/1918	16/09/1918
War Diary	Trescault.	26/09/1918	29/09/1918
War Diary	Couillet Wood.	30/09/1918	30/09/1918
Heading	War Diary Of 210th Bde R.F.A. Period-Month of Oct 1918 Vol VIII		
War Diary	Vaucelles	01/10/1918	08/10/1918
War Diary	Longsart	09/10/1918	09/10/1918
War Diary	Fontaine	10/10/1918	10/10/1918
War Diary	Viesly	12/10/1918	16/10/1918
War Diary	Prayelle	17/10/1918	19/10/1918
War Diary	Briastre	20/10/1918	20/10/1918
War Diary	Solesmes	21/10/1918	23/10/1918
War Diary	Romeries	23/10/1918	24/10/1918
War Diary	Beaudignies	25/10/1918	31/10/1918
Heading	War Diary Of 210th Brigade R.F.A. Nov 1918		
War Diary	Vertigneul	01/11/1918	02/11/1918
War Diary	Ruesnes	03/11/1918	04/11/1918
War Diary	Herbignies	05/11/1918	30/11/1918
Heading	War Diary Of 210th Brigade R.F.A. For The Month Of December 1918		
War Diary	Hautmont	01/12/1918	13/12/1918
War Diary	Jeumont	14/12/1918	14/12/1918
War Diary	Thuin	15/12/1918	17/12/1918
War Diary	Montignies Sur-Sambre	18/12/1918	31/12/1918
Heading	War Diary Of 210th Brigade, R.F.A. From 1st January 1919. To 31st January 1919. Volume XXV		
War Diary	Montignies Sur-Sambre.	01/01/1919	31/01/1919
Heading	War Diary. Of 210th Brigade R.F.A. From 1st February 1919. To 28th February 1919.		

War Diary	Montignies-Sur-Sambre	01/02/1919	28/02/1919
Heading	War Diary Of 210th Brigade R.F.A. From 1st March 1919. To 31st March 1919 Volume XXVI.		
War Diary	Ontingies-Sur-Sambre.	01/03/1919	31/03/1919
War Diary	Montignies-Sur-Sambre.	01/04/1919	11/04/1919

WO 95
2649/1

42ND DIVISION

210TH BRIGADE R.F.A.
MAR 1917 – APR 1919

CONFIDENTIAL

Vol 2.

VOL. III

WAR DIARY

OF

210TH. BDE. R.F.A.

42ND. DIVISION

FROM — 1.3.17.
TO — 31.3.17.

Army Form C. 2118

WAR DIARY
or
INTELLIGENCE SUMMARY
(Erase heading not required.)

Instructions regarding War Diaries and Intelligence Summaries are contained in F. S. Regs., Part II. and the Staff Manual respectively. Title Pages will be prepared in manuscript.

Ref 1/100,000 Map ABBEVILLE sheet 14

Place	Date	Hour	Summary of Events and Information	Remarks and references to Appendices
	1 3/17		Composition and distribution of 210th Brigade R.F.A. as follows:—	
			Hdqn A 210 B 210 C 210 } On board S.S. "MANITOU" in MARSEILLES HARBOUR, FRANCE.	
			D 210 210" B.A.C. } At Sea	
			Hdqn A 210 B 210 C 210 } In EGYPT.	
MARSEILLES 1/3/17		10 p.m. 10 p.m. 2 p.m. 9 a.m.	Disembarks from S.S. "MANITOU" and entrains for PONT REMY.	CSD Lt.
PONT REMY 3/3/17			B 210 arrived PONT REMY, detrained and proceeded to CAOURS. C 210 " " " " " ST. NICOLAS des ESSARTS.	CSD Lt.
PONT REMY 4/3/17		11 a.m.	Headquarters, 210"Bde R.F.A arrived PONT REMY, detrained and proceeded to CAOURS.	
		11 a.m.	A 210 arrived PONT REMY, detrained and proceeded to CAOURS.	
MARSEILLES			D 210 arrived MARSEILLES in H.M.T. "KINGSTONIAN", disembarked and proceeded to Rest Camp, MARSEILLES.	CSD Lt.

Army Form C. 2118

WAR DIARY
or
INTELLIGENCE SUMMARY

(Erase heading not required.)

2

Place	Date	Hour	Summary of Events and Information	Remarks and references to Appendices
MARSEILLES	5/3/17	5.30 p.m.	D 210 entrains for PONT REMY.	See 1st
PONT REMY	7/3/17	6 p.m.	D 210 arrives PONT REMY	See 1st
do	8/3/17	2 a.m.	D 210 proceeds by march route to billets at L'HEURE.	See 1st
MARSEILLES	12/3/17		210" B.A.C. disembarks at MARSEILLES from H.M.T.s "MENOMINEE" and "KALYAN", and entrains for PONT REMY	See 1st
PONT REMY	14/3/17		210" B.A.C. arrives PONT REMY and proceeds by march route to billets at DRUCAT.	See 1st
	14/3/17		210 "Bde A.F.A. Advance Party, consisting of the following, returning to units from attachment to 1st Division. H.Q. Lieut. C.G. DUFF and 2 O.R.s A 210 Lieut. H.B. ECCLES and 3 O.R.s B 210 Lieut. E.N. GREENWOOD and 3 O.R.s C 210 Lieut. R.L.C. LOWCOCK and 3 O.R.s D 210 Capt. H.N. MARKS and 3 O.R.s (detached D 210 from 142nd D.A.C.)	See 1st

Army Form C. 2118

3

WAR DIARY
or
INTELLIGENCE SUMMARY
(Erase heading not required.)

Place	Date	Hour	Summary of Events and Information	Remarks and references to Appendices
CAOURS / DRUCAT	19 3/17		2/Lt. L.R. HALLETT attached to D 210 from 211th Brigade R.F.A. 210th B.A.C. dissolved. Personnel, vehicles and horses taken to form a Divisional Ammunition Column.	4.
	19 3/19 20 3/19	08/15	A 210 - 2 guns, B 210 - 1 gun, C 210 - 1 gun sent to RIBEMONT for overhaul. 2/Lt. N.T. COOKE attached to C 210 from 210th Bde R.F.A. H.Qrs Staff. 2/Lt. H. FINCH attached to B 210 from 42nd D.A.C.	
		8 am	Following complete sections (personnel only) proceeded to 1st Division for instructions :—	
			A 210 { Major R. YATES and 32 O.R.s Lt. H.G. CLAPHAM	
			B 210 { Capt. A.G. HALL and 32 O.R.s 2/Lt. C. MACKRELL	
			C 210 { Capt. H.H. SIMON and 32 O.R.s Lt. C. HARTLEY	
			D 210 { Major D.T. MASON and 32 O.R.s Lt. H.B. BARCLAY	
		4 pm	Following six horse teams, complete with harness, transferred to 42nd D.A.C.	5.
			A 210 — 2 teams B 210 — 2 teams D 210 — 2 teams	

WAR DIARY or INTELLIGENCE SUMMARY

Army Form C. 2118

Place	Date	Hour	Summary of Events and Information	Remarks and references to Appendices
CAOURS	23/3/17		MAJOR B.P. DOBSON, C2IO, appointed to temporary command of HQ" D.A.C.	C2g 4
CAOURS	24/3/17	0700	MAJOR J.C. BROWNING, 210" Bde R.F.A. " " " C2IO.	
			10 Details section, who proceeded to join 1st Division on 20th inst. returned to unit, with exception of the following, who were transferred for instruction to 48th Division:—	C2g 4
			A 210 — Major R. YATES and 1 O.R.	
			D 210 — " D.J. MASON and 1 O.R.	
CAOURS	25/3/17	0649	Following proceeded on ten days leave to ENGLAND:—	C2g 4
			210" Bde H.Qrs — 1 O.R.	
			B. 210 — 3 O.R.	
			C. 210 — 2 O.R.	
			Lt. G.H. COOPER attached to HQrs 210 Bde from BASE DETAILS	Sw 94.
			MAJOR. J.C. BROWNING proceeded on three weeks leave to ENGLAND.	
CAOURS	26/3/17		The following proceeded to VAUX EN AMIENS for Artillery Course.—	Sw 94.

Army Form C. 2118

WAR DIARY
or
INTELLIGENCE SUMMARY
(Erase heading not required.)

Instructions regarding War Diaries and Intelligence Summaries are contained in F. S. Regs., Part II. and the Staff Manual respectively. Title Pages will be prepared in manuscript.

5

Place	Date	Hour	Summary of Events and Information	Remarks and references to Appendices
CAOURS	27/3/17		(Major) Lt. C.G. DUFF (A 210) Lt. H.B. ECCLES and ONE NCO (B 210) Lt. G.W. GREENWOOD and ONE NCO (C 210) Lt. R.L.C. LOWCOCK and ONE NCO D 210 - Lt. R.A. SMITH The following proceeded on ten days leave to ENGLAND. A 210 - 2 O.R. B 210 - 2 O.R. C 210 - 2 O.R. D 210 - Lt. R.A. SMITH. The following horses drawn to complete establishment of the Brigade. From REMOUNT DEPOT - 44. " 42nd D.A.C. - 34.	
CAOURS	28/3/17		The following proceeded to Signalling School at DRUCAT Hqrs. - 2 O.R. A 210 - 5 O.R. B 210 - 11 O.R. C 210 - 7 O.R. D 210 - 5 O.R.	

Army Form C. 2118

WAR DIARY
or
INTELLIGENCE SUMMARY
(Erase heading not required.)

Instructions regarding War Diaries and Intelligence Summaries are contained in F.S. Regs., Part II. and the Staff Manual respectively. Title Pages will be prepared in manuscript.

Place	Date	Hour	Summary of Events and Information	Remarks and references to Appendices
CROUVS	29/3/17		2nd Lt B. H. HORNER proceeded on ten days leave to ENGLAND. 2nd Lt W. J. COOKE proceeded to VAUX-EN-AMIENS for TRENCH MORTAR Course.	
CROUVS	30/3/17		The following proceeded on ten days leave to ENGLAND. A 210 — 2 O.R B 210 — 2 O.R C 210 — 2 O.R D 210 — 1 O.R Guns sent to RIBEMONT for overhaul on the 19-3-17 returned. A 210 — 2 pm, B 210 — 5 pm, C 210 — 1 pm.	

A. Bulivant
Lt. Col.
OC. 210th Bde. R.F.A.

Vol 3

VOLUME II

WAR DIARY

of

210TH BDE R.F.A.

From 1-4-17
To 30-4-17.

WAR DIARY
INTELLIGENCE SUMMARY

Army Form C. 2118

Instructions regarding War Diaries and Intelligence Summaries are contained in F.S. Regs., Part II. and the Staff Manual respectively. Title Pages will be prepared in manuscript.

(Erase heading not required.)

Place	Date	Hour	Summary of Events and Information	Remarks and references to Appendices
CAOURS	1/4/17		Distribution of 210" Bde R.F.A. as follows :— (Ref. Map 1/100,000 - ABBEVILLE)	
			H.Q. ⎫	
			A 210 ⎬ CAOURS	
			B 210 ⎭	
			C 210 ST NICOLAS	
			D 210 L'HEURE.	
		5 p.m.	H.Q. Lt. C.G. DUFF	
			A 210 " H.B. ECCLES ⎫ Returned from Artillery Course at VAUX-EN	
			B 210 " G.N. GREENWOOD ⎬ AMIENS (Ref. map 1/100,000 - AMIENS.)	
			C 210 " R.L.C. LOWCOCK ⎭	
			4 O.R. proceed on ten days leave to U.K.	
CAOURS	2/4/17		Preliminary orders received for move forward.	C.Reg 14.
CAOURS	3/4/17		Following officers arrived :—	C.Reg 4.
			2/Lt. A. AINSWORTH attached to A 210	
			" R. COOKE " C 210	
			" R. JONSTON " D 210	

WAR DIARY or INTELLIGENCE SUMMARY

(Erase heading not required.)

Army Form C. 2118

Ref. map 1/100,000 - AMIENS.

Place	Date	Hour	Summary of Events and Information	Remarks and references to Appendices
CAOURS	3/4/17		Capt. F.X.S. CARUS transferred & attached to 42nd D.A.C. from A 210.	C220 4r
ARGOEUVES	4/4/17	8.30 a.m.	210" Bde R.F.A. moved to ARGOEUVES and billetted the night.	
		2 a.m.	Temp. Lt. C.C. REES arrived from 53rd D.A.C. and attached to 210 Bde H.Q. B 2.0.	
			" " H. STOKER " " " " " " " B 2.0.	C220 4r
			4 O.R. proceeded on 10 days leave to U.K.	
FOURNOY	5/4/17	9 a.m.	210" Bde R.F.A. moved to FOURNOY and billetted the night.	
		4 p.m.	Batteries drew unserviceable ammunition from dump at FOURNOY to cart to MERIGNOLLES.	C20 4r
B. OLYMPE	6/4/17	9 a.m.	210" Bde R.F.A. moved to BOIS OLYMPE, unloading on route at MERIGNOLLES the ammunition drawn on 5.4.17.	
			2/Lt. H. FINCH (attached B 2.0) and 14 O.R. proceeded on 10 days leave to U.K.	C220 4r
B. OLYMPE	7/4/17		Lt. H.B. ECCLES (attached 42nd D.A.C.) rejoined A 2.0.	
			2/Lt. G.R. HARTLEY (" " ") " B 2.0.	
			Following officers arrived:—	
			2/Lt. V. WARE - - - - attached A 2.0	
			" R.C. ANDERSON - - " C 2.0	
			" N.F. ADENEY - - - - " B 2.0	
			210 Bde R.F.A. inspected by M.G.R.A. 4th Army	C20 4r

Army Form C. 2118

3

WAR DIARY
or
INTELLIGENCE SUMMARY
(Erase heading not required.)

Instructions regarding War Diaries and Intelligence Summaries are contained in F.S. Regs., Part II and the Staff Manual respectively. Title Pages will be prepared in manuscript.

Place	Date	Hour	Summary of Events and Information	Remarks and references to Appendices
B. OLYMPE	8/4/17		Battery drew ammunition to complete to establishment. 2/Lt. G. R. HARTLEY (B) } Lt. A. BROOKS. (C) } Temporarily attached to 42" D.A.C. " A.S.E. RICHARDSON(D) }	CRA ur
B. OLYMPE	9/4/17		Gas Lectures given to unite by the Divisional Gas Officer. 19 O.R. proceed on 10 days leave to U.K.	CRA ur
B. OLYMPE	11/4/17		Major D.T. MASON, D 210. Returns from 48" D.A. Lt. R.A. SMITH - D 210 } Returns from 10 days leave in U.K. 2/Lt. B.H. HORNER- A 210 } Major J.N. OGILVY attached to 210" Bde H.Q. from Scottish Horse 19 O.R. proceed on 10 days leave to U.K.	CRA ur
B. OLYMPE	12/4/17		Capt. A.G. HALL B 210 temporarily attached to 42" D.A.C. H.N. MARKS (attached D 210) rejoins 42" D.A.C. POSTINGS 2/Lt. L. R. HACKETT } " A. AINSWORTH } A 210 " V. WARE } Temp Lt. H. STOKER } " C.C. REES } " H. FINCH } B 210 " N.F. ADENEY }	

1875 Wt. W5593/826 1,000,000 4/15 J.B.C. & A. A.D.S.S./Forms/C. 2118.

WAR DIARY
or
INTELLIGENCE SUMMARY

Army Form C. 2118

Place	Date	Hour	Summary of Events and Information	Remarks and references to Appendices
B. OLYMPE	12/4/17		POSTINGS (cont'd)	
			2/Lt. R. COOKE ⎫	
			" R.C. ANDERSON ⎬ C 210 Temp.Lt. G.H.COOPER ⎫ D210	
			2/Lt. R. JONSTON ⎭	
			2/Lt. H.J. COOKE from 210 Bde R.F.A. Supernumerary to 42nd Div. T.M. Battery	CGHr
			ATTACHMENTS	
			2/Lt. R. HALLETT to B 210.	
			Major R. YATES, A 210 returned from H.8" D.A.	
B. OLYMPE	13/4/17		Capt. A.G. HALL returned from H2"D.A.C. to B 210.	
			Lt. A.S.E. RICHARDS " " " D 210	
			Lt. R.A. SMITH temporarily attached to 42nd D.A.C.	
			Major W. BIRTWISTLE, B 210. to hospital.	
			62 Sgt. MOULDING, E.J. A 210 to U.K. for commission	CGHr

Army Form C. 2118

WAR DIARY
or
INTELLIGENCE SUMMARY
(Erase heading not required.)

Instructions regarding War Diaries and Intelligence Summaries are contained in F.S. Regs., Part II and the Staff Manual respectively. Title Pages will be prepared in manuscript.

Place	Date	Hour	Summary of Events and Information	Remarks and references to Appendices
B. OLYMPE	14/4/17		Capt. H.H. LORD (A.V.C) attached to 210" Bde H.A. from 3rd E.L.F. Amber. " R.L. ARMOUR (M.V.C.) " " 126" Bde from 210" Bde H.A. Lt. A.S.E. RICHARDS and 9 O.R. proceeded on 10 days leave to U.K.	C89 H. C90 H.
B. OLYMPE	16/4/17		4 O.R. proceeded on 10 days leave to U.K.	
B. OLYMPE	17/4/17		Ref. in ch/ 40,000 - 62 c. Reconnaissance of line ROISEL - FRÉCHIN carried out Capt. R.F. BRADLEY (chaplain) proceeded to ABBEVILLE for dental treatment. 2 guns of A 210 sent to Brigmur for fitting of self contaning oil buffers and recoil indicators.	C91 H.
B. OLYMPE	19/4/17		Capt. A.A. GUNN (R.A.M.C.) and 12 O.R. proceeded on leave to U.K. } 10 days Major J.C. BROWNING D.S.O. C 210 2/Lt. FINCH H. B 210 } returned from leave in U.K. Capt. R.F. BRADLEY (chaplain) returned from dental treat[ment] went at ABBEVILLE.	C92 H.
B. OLYMPE	20/4/17		2 guns of A 210 sent to I.O.M. PERONNE to be fitted with self containing oil buffers and recoil indicators. Capt. R.F. BRADLEY (chaplain) proceeded to join 127 Inf. Bde.	C.B.

Army Form C. 2118

WAR DIARY
or
INTELLIGENCE SUMMARY
(Erase heading not required.)

Instructions regarding War Diaries and Intelligence Summaries are contained in F. S. Regs., Part II. and the Staff Manual respectively. Title Pages will be prepared in manuscript.

Place	Date	Hour	Summary of Events and Information	Remarks and references to Appendices
B. OLIMPE	21/7/17		2/Lt. S. WILSON, Major Lt. C. HARTLEY, B 210, and 6 O.R. proceeded on 10 days leave to U.K.	
			Lt. Col. A. BIRTWISTLE. C.M.G. Major R. YATES A 210 Capt. A. G. HALL B 210 Major D. J. MASON D 210 } proceeded to 295 Bde R.F.A. to reconnoitre battery positions.	
			Order received from "42" Div. Arty. for move of A, B and D 210 into position.	
			2/Lt. G. P. HARTLEY, B 210 and Lt. A. BROOKES, C 210 returned from temporary attachment to 42 "D.A.C."	App 9
ROISEL	22/7/17		210" Bde R.F.A. moved to the following villages (Ref. map 1/40,000 - 62c.) H.Q. - ROISEL A 210 } B 210 } - BOUCLY C 210 - LE MESNIL-BRUNTEL D 210 - HAMELET.	
			2 guns A 210 returned from T.O.M. PERONNE.	
			Major T. H. pursonnel attached to rest of A. B. and D 210.	

1875 Wt. W593/826 1,000,000 4/15 J.B.C. & A. A.D.S.S./Forms/C. 2118.

Army Form C. 2118

WAR DIARY
or
INTELLIGENCE SUMMARY
(Erase heading not required.)

Ref. map 1/40,000 Sheet 62c

Place	Date	Hour	Summary of Events and Information	Remarks and references to Appendices
ROISEL	22/4/17		2/Lt. C. MACKRELL, B210 and 2Lt. H.B. BARCLAY, D210 returned from Artillery Course at VAUX.	CSS
			2/Lt. H. FINCH, B210 and 2Lt. G.H. COOPER, D210 proceeded to Artillery course at VAUX.	
ROISEL	23/4/17		A210, B210 and D210 took up battery positions as under in support of 59th Division, the Batteries being under the tactical command of O.C. Left Group, 59th Division: On our right 296 Bde R.F.A. On our left 48th Division.	
			A210 - 1 section relieved 1 section A295 in CARPEZA COPSE L15 c 2.5.	
			B210 - moved into position L15 d 6.1	
			D210 - " " L2 b 6.2.	
			1396 Cpl. WYNNE, E. C210 proceeded to U.K. r/c commission.	CSS
ROISEL	24/4/17		A210, B210 and D210 registered targets.	CSS
			A210 - 1 section relieved 1 section A295 at L15 c 2.5.	
ROISEL	25/4/17		Two guns of A210 being not ready for removal from I.O.M PERONNE A210 drew 2 guns from C 210 at LE HESNIL BRUNTEL.	CSS
			A210 - Remaining section relieved remaining section of A295 at L15 c 2.5.	
			D210 - 2/Lt. R. JOHNSTON wounded	
			B210 - 1 OR. shot at wound in face, slight.	

1875 Wt. W593/826 1,000,000 4/15 J.B.C. & A. A.D.S.S./Forms/C. 2118.

WAR DIARY
INTELLIGENCE SUMMARY

(Erase heading not required.)

Ref map 1/40,000 — 62c.

Army Form C. 2118

Place	Date	Hour	Summary of Events and Information	Remarks and references to Appendices
ROISEL	26/9/17		A210 2/Lr. A. AINSWORTH } returned from signalling course at MERICOURT. B210 Temp. Lt. H. STOKER	C59
ROISEL	27/9/17	3.55 a.m.	59" Divisional attacked on their front via L5, with their front objective on their own line in L5d 8.4, and the second objective COLOGNE FARM in L6c 3.6. They were supported by 295 Bde R.F.A. and A 210, B210 and D210. Both objectives were gained, but enfilade fire from both flanks forced the infantry to evacuate COLOGNE FARM. The Queries were captured and the position consolidated. No counter-attack was delivered by the enemy, but a counter barrage was put up.	C59
ROISEL	29/9/14		Orders received for relief of 48th Division by 42nd Division. 1 Section A 210 moved to F28 a 5.2 and relieving 1 section of A 211. 1 " B 210 " " F27 a 1.6 " " " B 211 1 " C 210 " " F20 c 9.8 " " " A 240 1 " D 210 " " " " " A 240	C61
STEMINE	30/9/17		H.Q. 210 F.A. BDE moved to STEMINE. 1 section A 210 moved to F28a 5.2 and relieved 1 section of A 211. 1 " B 210 " " F27 a 1.6 " " " B 211 1 " C 210 " " F20 c 9.8 " " " A 240 1 " D 210 " " F14 d 9.6 " " " D 240	

WAR DIARY
or
INTELLIGENCE SUMMARY

Army Form C. 2118

Place	Date	Hour	Summary of Events and Information	Remarks and references to Appendices
ROISEL	30th		Remainder of C210 moved from LE MESNIL-BRUNTEL to VILLERS-FAUCON at E23 c 9.4. Two guns C210 drawn from I.O.M PERONNE. Major B.R. DOBSON assumed temporary command of B210 from 42" D.A.C.	
			Composition and distribution of 210 "F.A." Bde as follows:-	
			H.Q. 210 "F.A.Bde - STEHINE	
			A210 — 2 Sections at F28 a 5.2 } wagon lines at BOUCLY with 59" Div. Arty.	
			B210 — 2 Sections at F27 a 1.6 } " " " 1 " " " with 59 Div. A/y	
			C210 — 2 Sections at F20 c 9.8 } Remainder at VILLERS FAUCON.	
			D210 — 1 Section at F14 d 9.6 } wagon line at HAMELET. 1 " " " with 59" Div. Arty.	

Staff Lieut. A88
210 Bde RFA

Army Form C. 2118.

C 210 Bde RFA
(whilst detached)

WAR DIARY or INTELLIGENCE SUMMARY.

(Erase heading not required.)

Instructions regarding War Diaries and Intelligence Summaries are contained in F.S. Regs., Part II. and the Staff Manual respectively. Title pages will be prepared in manuscript.

Hour, Date, Place		Summary of Events and Information	Remarks and references to Appendices
9. a.m. 25/4/17	CAPPY.	Map 1/40,000 62.C	
		Battery moved from CAPPY to LE MESNIL-BRONVIEL.	
		Lieut A. Brooks with servant, groom & 2 horses found Battery at Artillery School (L"Army) VAUX. 1 NCO to "Army Artillery School VAUX. 5 ASC Horses (HD) & Driver attached. 4 NCO's men returned from England from leave. 1 man returned from hospital.	
26/4/17	Le Mesnil Bronvill	4 Lies R Cooke temporarily attached to D/210 Bde RFA	J.B.
27/4/17	do	No 1596 Cpl Warne L to ENGLAND for commission. 1 Man to 3rd Sqdn RFC for courses in wireless. P.H. helmets ordered to be carried on all occasions.	J.B.
28/4/17	do	5 NCO's & men returned from leave in ENGLAND.	J.B.
29/4/17	do	3 NCO's & men returned from leave in ENGLAND.	J.B.
30/4/17	do	Received orders to move to line in Sections. Right Section moved at 4. P.M. Centre Section moved to line.	J.B.
1/5/17	do 6. 0 A.M.	Left Section moved to line. Positions of A/240 of Bde RFA taken over. Remainder of outgoing battery completed move at 9. 0 P.M.	J.B.

J. Brownrigg Major
C/210 Bde RFA

(73989) W4141—463. 400,000. 9/14. H.&J.Ltd. Forms/C. 2118/10.

Confidential

VOLUME II

WAR DIARY

of

210TH Bde R.F.A.

From 1-5-17
To 31-5-17.

Army Form C. 2118

WAR DIARY
or
INTELLIGENCE SUMMARY

Ref. map 1/20,000
62 C. N.E.

(Erase heading not required.)

Place	Date	Hour	Summary of Events and Information	Remarks and references to Appendices
ST EMILE	1/5/17		Strength of 210" Bde RFA at beginning of month :—	1
			TOTAL 37 officers 751 OR. 660 horses	
			" 34 " 731 " 653 "	
			EFFECTIVE	
			Composition and distribution of 210" Bde R.F.A. as follows:—	
			210" Bde R.F.A. H.Q. ST EMILE. ⎫	
			A 210 — F 28 a 5.2 ⎪	
			B 210 — F 26 c 7.2½ ⎬ In the line	
			C 210 — F 20 c 9.6 ⎪	
			D 210 — F 14 d 8½.8 ⎭	
			In addition B 240 at F 14 c 9.8 and C 240 at F 15 c 3.7 attached to this Brigade under tactical command of Lt. Col. A. BIRTWISTLE Q.H.Q.	
			1 section A 210 moved to F 28 a 5.2 to relieve 1 section of A 211.	
			1 " B 210 " " F 26 c 7.22 " " " B 211.	
			1 " C 210 " " F 20 c 9.6 " " " A 240.	
			1 " D 210 " " F 14 d 8½.8 " " " D 240.	
			2 guns of C 210 removed from I.O.M. PERONNE.	
			D 210 heavily shelled while leaving TEMPLEUX-LE-GUERARD.	
			7/546 Dr. MC ARDLE D 210 flesh wound in both legs, one horse killed, four wounded and G.S. wagon destroyed.	1 hr.

Army Form C. 2118

WAR DIARY
or
INTELLIGENCE SUMMARY
(Erase heading not required.)

Ref. maps. 1/20,000
62 C N.E. & 62 B N.W.

2

Place	Date	Hour	Summary of Events and Information	Remarks and references to Appendices
ST EMINE	2/5/17	10 am	210" Bde R.F.A. having relieved 240" Bde R.F.A. Lt Col. A. BIRTWISTLE, C.M.G. Assumed Command of Right Group, 42nd Division. O.P. on our left 211 Bde R.F.A. at D.29.5 " " " right 295 " " " 59 " " O.P. of C.240 or F.15 b.8.0 destroyed by direct hit. No casualties.	CRA 4r
ST EMINE	3/5/17	11.30 p.m.	Capt A.A. QUINN (R.A.M.C.) returned from ten days leave in U.K. 148th Inf. Bde, 59th Division attacks COLOGNE and MAKAROFF FARMS, supported by 295" Bde R.F.A. and B.210, D.210 and B.240. To simulate an attack A.240, C.240 and C.210 fired on Right Brigade, 42nd Div. front from 11.25 p.m. to 11.35 p.m.	Pete Spinster War no 1 attached CRA 4r
ST EMINE	4/5/17	9 pm	148th Inf. failed to capture COLOGNE FARM, but captured MAKAROFF farm. Enemy counter attacks and drove our troops from MAKAROFF farm back to trench running from L.6 a.2.0 to F.29 d.8.2	
		5.30 pm	One of our observation balloon on ROISEL destroyed by enemy aeroplane. I.O.R. proceeded on 10 days leave to U.K. 2/Lt. S. WILSON. HQrs Staff and Lt. C HARTLEY. C.210 returned from 10 days leave in U.K.	CRA 4r

Army Form C. 2118

WAR DIARY
or
INTELLIGENCE SUMMARY
(Erase heading not required.)

Ref. map 1/40,000
6 & N.E. 62 S N.W.

Instructions regarding War Diaries and Intelligence Summaries are contained in F. S. Regs., Part II. and the Staff Manual respectively. Title Pages will be prepared in manuscript.

3

Place	Date	Hour	Summary of Events and Information	Remarks and references to Appendices
STEENJE	5/5/17		1295 Pr CRANSHAW. H. A210 shrapnel wound in left arm.	CGY
STEENJE	7/5/17	9am to 11am	5.9" gun battery fired with aeroplane observation on A210 at F28a5.2. About 100 rds fired. No guns put out of action but minor damage done to equipment. No casualties to personnel. The shoot was carried out by observation from an enemy aeroplane.	
		9/am	In consequence of above, A210 moved 3 guns to new position at F21 & 6.0.	CGY
STEENJE	8/5/17	9.50 pm	The 176" Inf. Bde, 59" Div attacked with two objectives:— (1) Russian Trench from the "ENFILADE TRENCH" (L52 9.5.4.5 to 9.12 1.6) northwards to F30c 2.7 (approx) (2) The "UNNAMED FARM" at L6a 2.0. The 126" Inf. Bde endeavoured to push down "RIFLE PIT TRENCH" from the north end as far as F30c 2.7. B210 and B240 put down the following barrage in support:— (a) L6a 5.5 to F30c 2.7 (b) F30c 3.2 to F30c 2.7 (c) F30c 7.2 to F30c 6.7 The attack on objective 1 failed. Objective 2 was captured.	vide operation order no 2 attached

1875 Wt. W593/826 1,000,000 4/15 J.B.C. & A. A.D.S.S./Forms/C. 2118.

WAR DIARY or INTELLIGENCE SUMMARY

(Erase heading not required.)

Army Form C. 2118

Ref. map 1/40,000
62 NE, 62B NW

Place	Date	Hour	Summary of Events and Information	Remarks and references to Appendices
SEMINE	8/5/17		A210 moved 3 guns to F21b6.0. A240 moved into pos'n F22b2.6 " " F22c7.2 and came under tactical command of Lt.Col.R.A. BIRTWISTLE, C.M.G.	C29 4
SEMINE	10/5/17	3pm to 3.15pm	Bombardment of enemy front line defences by 42nd Div. Arty. to simulate an attack. Orders received for B240 and C240, A.T.1 attached to Right Group 42nd Div. to be relieved by A240 and D240. B240 and C240 sent one section each to wagon lines	C29 4 vide operation order no 3 attached
SEMINE	11/5/17	9am to 11am	A210 at F21b6.0 heavily shelled by 5.9" gun battery with balloon observation. A210 at F21b6.0 heavily shelled by three guns to B240 post in at F14c 9.8 Orders received for battery of 45th Div. Arty. attached to Right group 42nd Div. to return to their wagon lines, in compliance with which A240, C240, D240 and B240 (less 1 section) pulled out and returned to wagon lines at HARVAUX. 400132 Cpl. KENTON A210 shrapnel wound left arm 700155 a/Bdr HARSDEN " " back	C29 4

Army Form C. 2118

WAR DIARY
or
INTELLIGENCE SUMMARY
(Erase heading not required.)

Ref. map. 1/40,000
62B N.W. 16 c N.E.

Place	Date	Hour	Summary of Events and Information	Remarks and references to Appendices
ST EMILIE	12/5/17	5.10 am to 1.30 am	A210, B210, and D210 fired in support of 5th Essex counter attack on post near GILLEMONT FARM at A13 b 3.4, which had been captured by the enemy the previous afternoon. The post was recaptured. 2/Lt. H. FINCH B210 Lt. G. H. COOPER. D210 } returned from Artillery Course at VAUX. 2/Lt. A. AINSWORTH. A210. took up duties of Intelligence Officer at Brigade H.Q.	eSp
		9.30 pm	A 210 moved their gun to B210 position at F 14 c 98. In response to infantry report that enemy were massing in "rifle pit trench" (F29 c 8.3 to F30 c 4.2) B210 fired for 5 mins on F30 a 6.0 to F24 c 7.1. 295 Bde R.F.A. on our right co-operated	
ST EMILIE	13/5/17		T/Lt. STOKER H.B. B210 D/Lt. COOKE. R. C210 } proceeded to Artillery Course at VAUX.	

WAR DIARY
or
INTELLIGENCE SUMMARY

(Erase heading not required.)

Ref. maps 1/40,000 62 c N.W. 62 c N.E.

Army Form C. 2118

Place	Date	Hour	Summary of Events and Information	Remarks and references to Appendices
SENLIS	13/5/17	2pm	A210 registered enemy trench just east of GINCHONT with balloon observation.	Wrote operation order not issued
		3pm	D210 registered above target with aeroplane observation.	
		6.30 to 6.40 pm	A210 and D210, in conjunction with 60 pdrs. and C.211, bombarded above trench. 30 or 40 of the enemy ran from the trench which was badly knocked about.	C.S.O. H.
SENLIS	14/5/17	10am	Warning order received of move of 4th "D.A." to join XV "Corps".	
		5pm	Director of Signals, III Corps inspected Brigade communication. Gun no. 1358, A210, burst by a premature and completely disabled. The cause of premature believed to be the use of fuze 101, Z.Z. O.R. provided on 10 days leave to U.K.	C.S.O. H.
SENLIS	15/5/17	12.30 am	Enemy drove our men out of small advanced post on S.W. corner of GINCHONT FARM. A210 and D210 fired in support of counter attack which resulted recapture the post. Gun no. 1358, A210, burst on 14th unit by a premature, was returned to I.O.M. PERONNE.	

Army Form C. 2118

WAR DIARY
or
INTELLIGENCE SUMMARY
(Erase heading not required.)

Ref. maps 1/20,000
62 c N.E. 9 62 B N.W.

Place	Date	Hour	Summary of Events and Information	Remarks and references to Appendices
STEENJE	16/5/17	3.45 am to 4 am	2/Lt. J.R. TOMMIS, 112"Div. Signals returned from hospital. B 210 fired 141 rounds on line F30 a 6.0 to F24 c 7.1 in response to call for fire from Infantry, who stated that the enemy were massing in the vicinity.	CRS
		During the night	112 "Div. Infantry relieved by 2nd and 3rd Cavalry Divisions. Lt. C. C. REES, H.Q. Staff, to hospital.	CRS
STEENJE	18/5/17		Lt. C. HARTLEY, C 210, proceeded on six weeks course of signalling. Major B.P. DOBSON, B 210, Lt. H.B. BARCLAY, D 210, and 6 O.R. proceeded on 10 days leave to U.K. Heavy intermittent bombardment of GINCHONT FARM all day. B 210 & B R.F.A. retaliated on wood in A 14 & and enemy trench east of GINCHONT FARM.	CRS
STEENJE	19/5/17	8 am to 10 am	B 210 (F 26 & 4.22) been bombed with "4.2". About 100 rounds fired from 10 am to 11 am. The bombardment was continued with gas shells. No casualties and no damage to equipment resulted from above. During the morning gas shells were put into GINCHONT FARM.	
		5 pm	Major, W. BIRTWISTLE, B 210 returned from hospital.	
		9 pm	1 section each of B 210 and C 210, and 1 gun of A 210 pulled out and returned to major line, being relieved by sections of R.H.A. batteries of 2nd & 3rd Cavalry Division.	CRS

WAR DIARY or INTELLIGENCE SUMMARY

Army Form C. 2118

Ref. maps 1/20,000 G 2 c N.E., 1 G 2 c N.W.
57 c S.E.

Place	Date	Hour	Summary of Events and Information	Remarks and references to Appendices
ST EMILIE	20/5/17	3 a.m. to 6 a.m.	Enemy attacked GINNEMONT FARM, attack being preceded by a very heavy bombardment. 210 "B" Bde R.F.A. put down a barrage in defence. Enemy attacked three times but did not succeed in entering the farm. He captured two prisoners.	
		9 p.m.	Remainder of A, B, C 210 pulled out to Wagon lines, being relieved by R.H.A. of 2nd and 3rd Cavalry Divisions.	C 20
		11.30 p.m.	210 "B" Bde H.Q. handed over command of Right Group R.A. A 210 remainder in position, being under the tactical command of the R.H.A.	
VALLULART WOOD	21/5/17	11.30 a.m.	210 "B" Bde R.F.A. (less D 210) marched to VALLULART WOOD, via VINERS - FAUCON, LIERAMONT, NURLU and ETRICOURT and arrived about 3 p.m.	C 21
VALLULART WOOD	22/5/17	9 p.m.	One section of A 210 relieved one section of A 92 at Q 4 a 2.3 One " " B 210 " " B 92 " Q 1 a 3.2 One " " C 210 " " C 92 " Q 22 d 4.4	C 24
RUYAU- COURT	23/5/17	10 a.m. 12 noon	210 "B" Bde H.Q. moved into position at P 10 a 2.8 210 "B" Bde H.Q. assumed command of Left Group R.A. 42nd Div.	

Army Form C. 2118

WAR DIARY
or
INTELLIGENCE SUMMARY
(Erase heading not required.)

Ref. maps 1/20,000 57c N.E. & 57c S.E.
1/57c S.E. 9.

Instructions regarding War Diaries and Intelligence Summaries are contained in F.S. Regs., Part II. and the Staff Manual respectively. Title Pages will be prepared in manuscript.

Place	Date	Hour	Summary of Events and Information	Remarks and references to Appendices
RUYAULCOURT	23/5/17	8 a.m.	MAJOR. N. BIRTWISTLE, B210, proceeded on three weeks leave to U.K. with 9 O.R. on 10 days leave.	
		9 p.m.	Remainder of A210 relieves remainder of A92 at A4 a 2.3 " B210 " " B92 " A1 a 3.2 " C210 " " C92 " A22 d 4.4 C210 becomes under tactical command of O.C. Ryr. Group 1st Div.	C27
do	26/5/17	10.30 p.m.	Rocket sent up and Stromba horns sounded for gas alarm, but no information received as to discharge of gas by enemy.	C28
do	28/5/17		Major R. YATES, A210 } went up in observation balloon to register. Capt. A.G. HALL, B210 } 1 O.R. proceeded on 10 days leave to U.K. New gun arrived for A210, to replace that burnt by premature on 14-5-17. In action C210 moved into position to P12 d 3.3. 2/Lt. A.R. HALLETT } B210 to hospital. " R. JOHNSTON } D210	C29

Army Form C. 2118

WAR DIARY
or
INTELLIGENCE SUMMARY
(Erase heading not required.)

Ref. maps 1/20,000
57cNE.75/cS.E.
10.

Place	Date	Hour	Summary of Events and Information	Remarks and references to Appendices
RUYAULCOURT	29/5/17	9 pm	2/Lt. J.R. TOMMIS, H.Q. Div. Signal Coy. to hospital. Remaining two sections C210 moved into position to P12d 3.3. One Section D211, moved into position to Q4c 1.4. One Section D211 remained in position at Q8d 5.6.	
		10 pm	C210 and D211 came under tactical command of 210 & 218 RFA. 10 O.R. proceeded on 10 days leave to U.K.	ce9
RUYAUCOURT	31/5/17		Lieut. G.W. GREENWOOD, B210 and 9 O.R. proceeded on 10 days leave to U.K.	
		11 pm to 1.40 am	Information having been received that the enemy were attempting to establish a line of posts from K33 central to K34d central, 210/B de RFA (Lieut D210) descended this area between 11 pm and 1.40 am. One patrol thus advanced and found the enemy holding the line of posts mentioned. We captured one wounded prisoner. Several enemy dead were seen.	ce9

Army Form C. 2118

WAR DIARY
or
INTELLIGENCE SUMMARY
(Erase heading not required.)

Ref. maps 1/40,000
57c N.E. & S.E.

Place	Date	Hour	Summary of Events and Information	Remarks and references to Appendices
	31/5/17		Composition and distribution of 210 "Bde RFA as follows.	11

H.Q. 210 Bde RFA — P10 a 2.8

A 210 — Q7 a 1.4 ⎫
B 210 — Q1 a 3.2 ⎬ covering 42nd Divisional front
C 210 — P12 d 3.3 ⎭

D 210 — F14 d 9.6 (Ref. 1/20,000 62c N.E.) under tactical command of R.H.A. 2nd Cavalry Divn.

TOTAL STRENGTH   38 Officers   758 O.R.   642 horses
EFFECTIVE STRENGTH   36 "   745 "   635 "

DRAFTS RECEIVED
1-5-17 — 11 OR
18-5-17 — 22 OR
28-5-17 — 16 OR

War diaries of C 210 and D 210 for periods during which they were detached, are enclosed herewith.

J.E. Browning
(temp) Comm'dg Major
210 Bde. RFA

WAR DIARY
or
INTELLIGENCE SUMMARY

Army Form C. 2118.

D 210 Bde R.F.A
(when detached)
SHEET 1.

Place	Date 1917	Hour	Summary of Events and Information	Remarks and references to Appendices
RONSSOY WOOD (F14 D 8½ 2)	May 21	12.6 1am	Fired with QUENNEMONT FARM and the Sunken Road in A14c and A14d.	All references are to FRANCE Sheets 62c N.E and 62 B NW 1/20,000
		11.45am	Fired at working party in HINDENBURG LINE in A21A dispersing enemy and obtaining direct hits.	
		1.45 to 3pm	Fired at trench from A25 B2½ to F30 C 8½, and in A25 B and cross roads F30 C	
		3pm		
		4 pm	Registered Cupola in G1 D15	
		4.30pm	Registered Junction Trenches G1 D36	
		5pm	Registered Railway G1 B½ 5½	
		4.51pm	Fired at and dispersed a party of German Officers A26 B83	
		5.30pm	Fired at Ross in A26 B.	
			Fired 81 Rounds in all today.	
	May 22		Received orders from 3rd Bde RHA that on the SOS signal we are to Rate for Gun Pits to for 5 minutes follows by fire for 2 min for 5 rounds for 20 min if not stopped previously.	
		4.45	Fired at new work and working party at A27 B49.	
		5.15pm	Fired 30 rounds fired today.	
	May 23	12 to 2pm	In support of orders to lay to knock down the wire at dangerous post at sunken road in A20c. Fired when at broken trenches down bit turned round rounds for longfires first.	
		11.30pm	Fired at & at dugouts working party at A27 B49 Fired on A19D26, A25B34, A20C40, A25B21 on Missings block front from about MALAKOFF FARM Fired 130 rounds today.	

WAR DIARY
or
INTELLIGENCE SUMMARY

Army Form C. 2118.

D 210 Bde RFA
(where attached)
SHEET 2

Place	Date 1917	Hour	Summary of Events and Information	Remarks and references to Appendices
RONSSOY WOOD (F14 D & 8)	May 23		Relations 715483 Sad Sgt MORE A. G. Hospital; 715261 Dr TAYLOR H. L. U.K on 10 days leave 715389 Dr KAY J. G. U.K on demobilisation.	All references are to maps :- FRANCE sheets 62c NE and 62 B NW 1/20000
	May 24 4.45/	6/pm	Registered with Balloon observation fire in A14 B and cross roads at A14 D 91	
		10.30/p	On receipt of S.O.S signal from GUILLEMONT FARM fired on barrage as follows :- A 19 D 29, A 19 C 39, A8C td and A7 B82. Fired 164 rounds Total. Consol. 2 inches operations and brumless intelligation LIEUT RA. SMITH and 715193 G. STRAUGHTON. T reported from D92. 20s 29mm RA.	
	May 25 8 am		Fired on digits in F30C and broke up work when being dropped.	
		9.30 am	Fired on Factory G115±5½.	
		4.30/-	Fired at cross rds A20C14. Expended 55 rounds Total.	
	May 26		In reply to enemy gas shell reports (-1 Bde Mkg as following number of men to be sent not last dive to U.K for two 2 years :- 80 : 18 months - 8 ; 9 months - 18 ; 715193 Gr STRAUGHTON. T sounds 6 3-5 Bde RHA for Camp duty	
		6.30 am	715205 Sgt CROSSMAN R to Hospital	
		2.30	Fired at wood in A26 by way of retaliation	
		3 pm	-- do --	
		5 pm	Fired at enemy signals in A20C14. Expended 54 rounds Total. Henry L Major R Germans wept down friendly lines in A20 C14. Genl SELIGMAN BGRA Enemy aircraft machine gunning line in A20 C14.	
	May 27 11.45am		Fired at working parties in A11 Central.	
		5.45 pm	2 inches at cross roads A2L C. 65a. (retaliation)	
		9 pm	-do- at Cross Rds A2L C.65a. E1 D.35½. militia	

Army Form C. 2118.

WAR DIARY
or
INTELLIGENCE SUMMARY
(Erase heading not required.)

D 210 Bde R.F.A.
(sheet attached)
(SHEET 3)

Place	Date Hour	Summary of Events and Information	Remarks and references to Appendices
RONSSOY WOOD (F14 D&5)	May 27 1917 11.55 am	Fired at A26 Central, A7yB82 and A8A (valley). Expended 58 rounds today.	All references are to map FRANCE sheet 62 C N.E. and 62 B N.W. 1/20000
	May 28 12.30 am	Fired salvo on valley at A8A (retaliation). Expended 10 rounds today. Received orders for new S.O.S. lines in case of an attack on CLEMONT FARM namely A14 A20 & A73 D88. Bombardiers 715647 Sgt HALLETT E and 715142 Gnr RYAN R. to hospital. 715649 Bdr NOBEE G. to hospital U.K. on 10 days leave.	D.W.
	May 29 10.15 am	Fired into Lines A14A Central (retaliation). Expended 15 rounds today.	
	May 30 10.30 am	Fired at enemy post (obtaining 3 direct hits) at F30 C 42.	
	11 am	Fired into valley A8A Central and road junction A9C11 (retaliation).	
	11.30 am	Engaged Germans at A15A01	Balloon and
	12.30 am	Fired on Sunken Road in A14D and S Lines running NE the reform observation.	aeroplane
		Barrage of bursts in lines to lay Boyau Squantun.	
	11.50 am	Fired at Boy A15A07 and Sunken Road in A14 D 4, army of retaliation. Expended 81 rounds today.	D.W.
	May 31	Excellent installation and morning operation left the battery. 715113 Cpl KENDALL J. to U.K. on 10 days leave.	
	12 noon	Fired on German trenches in A8A. Trenches were fully manned and many direct hits obtained.	
		Orders received that in case of resilience being my rounds by Division to CANOTE, we are to barrage X30 A89 & X30 A66, A13 B68 and GAL C22 (the enveloping/preparing orders).	

Fired 64 rounds today.

Army Form C. 2118.

WAR DIARY
or
INTELLIGENCE SUMMARY.
(Erase heading not required.)

Reference map FRANCE 1/5000 57 C S.E.

Place	Date	Hour	Summary of Events and Information	Remarks and references to Appendices
	25.2.17	9 P.M.	Left Section of Battery moved into position N of Gouzeaucourt Wood at Q35.a.95.60.	
	25.3.17	9 P.M.	Remainder of Battery moved into position N of Gouzeaucourt Wood Q35.a.95.60. Major J.C. Browning D.S.O. having been detached from Battery, the command temporarily taken over by Capt A. Simon. The O.P used was at Q18.d.5.5 + F.O.O was chosen + a telephone line laid. The Lt. was registered on Daion Point. [F.O.O at R19.a.5.5 in an infantry post in front of the trenches.]	
	26.8.17	9 P.M.	Left Section of Battery was relieved by a section of A/151 R.F.A + moved to a position in Havrincourt Wood at P19.d.81.80.	
	29.1.17		The Left Section was registered on a Daion Point.	
	30.1.17	9 P.M.	Remainder of Battery moved from Q35.a.95.60. to position at P19.d.81.80. The whole Battery was registered on Daion Point. The O.P used by the Battery was at Q16.b.4. and in the infantry trenches a F.O.O was chosen at K33.d.8.0 (map sheet 57 c N.E.) A telephone line was laid to it during the night.	

210th Bde ORDER No 1

by

Lt. Col. A. Birtwistle. C.M.G. Commdg 210th Bde RFA

Ref. Maps 1/20,000 - 62 c N.E
and 62 B N.W.

Copy No 6

3-5-17

1. In accordance with 59th Div. Order No 34, the 178th Infantry Brigade will, on the night 3/4th May, attack and capture COLOGNE and MALAKOFF FARMS.

2. In support of these operations, B210, B240 and D210 will carry out the following programme.

3. B210 and B240 will carry out the left Barrage.

4. LEFT BARRAGE (vide attached sketch map):—

B210
Zero to zero+8 — F30c 4½.0 to L6a 4½.5½.
Zero+8 to zero+15 — F30c 9.2 thro' G1 b1.8½ to G1 b½.6½
Zero+15 to zero+60 — A25d 3½.3½ to G1 b 3.7

B240
Zero to zero+8 — F30c 3½.5½ to F30c 4½.0
Zero+8 to zero+15 — F30c 5½.7½ to F30c 9.2
Zero+15 to zero+60 — A25 b 0.0 to A25d 3½.3½

5. LEFT BARRAGE - Rates of Fire

Zero to zero+5   — 1 rd per gun per minute Shrapnel
Zero+5 to zero+8 — 3 "   "   "   "   "   H.E.
Zero+8 to zero+15 — 2 "   "   "   "   "   H.E.
Zero+15 to zero+30 — 1 "   "   "   "   "   Shrapnel
Zero+30 to zero+60 — ½ "   "   "   "   "   Shrapnel

6. D210 will bombard wood S.W. of MALAKOFF FARM, F30c 6½.2 from zero+4 min. to zero+8 min.
At zero+8, D210 will lift to trench A25d 3½.0 - A25d 1.7

Rates of Fire

Zero+4 to zero+8 — 2 rds. per gun per minute
Zero+8 to zero+30 — 1 "   "   "   "   "
Zero+30 to zero+60 — ½ "   "   "   "   "

7. Fire from all 18 pdr and 4.5" How. Batteries will stop at zero + 60 minutes, unless specially asked for by G.O.C. 178" Inf. Bde.

8. Zero hour will be 11.30 pm 3rd May.

9. Watches will be synchronized under arrangements to be made later.

10. Copy of 59" Div. Arty. Order No 33 attached hereto.

11. ACKNOWLEDGE.

Issued by orderly at 2.30 pm 3rd inst.

C.G. Duff / Lieut. Adjt.
210 Bde RFA

Copy No 1 — O.C. B 210
2 — " D 210
3 — " B 240
4 — Hdqrs 42" Div. Arty
5 — File
6 — War Diary
7 — " "

Copy No 5

210th Bde R.F.A. ORDER No 2
by
Lt. Col. A. Birtwistle. C.M.G. Commdg 210 Bde RFA

Ref. maps 1/20,000
62 c NE, 62 B.N.W.
and
Map No 63.

8-5-17

1. The 176th Inf Bde will, on night 8/9th May.
   (a) Capture and consolidate the German trenches in L6a and F30c from the "ENFILADE" trench (L5b 95.45 – G12 1.6) northwards to F30c 2.7 (approx)
   (b) The "UNNAMED FARM" at L6a 2.0.

2. The 2/6th N. Staffs Regt. supported by 2/6th S. Staffs Regt. will carry out the operation.

3. Batteries of this Group will fire as under:—
   (a) <u>Zero + 4 to Zero + 6</u> (Red line on sketch)
   B 210 – L6a 5.5 to F30c 4.1
   B 240 – F30c 4.1 to F30c 2½.6½
   Rate of fire 4 rds. per gun per minute HE
   (b) <u>Zero + 6 to Zero + 8</u> (Red line on sketch)
   B 210 – F30c 3½.2 to F30c 3½.4
   B 240 – F30c 3½.4 to F30c 2.6½
   Rate of fire 4 rds. per gun per minute Shrap.
   (c) <u>Zero + 8 to Zero + 60</u>
   At Zero + 8 the barrage on the objective will lift 100x per 2 minutes until reaching the Final Barrage line marked green on Map A, where it will remain till Zero + 60, when fire will cease.

   FINAL BARRAGE
   B 210 – F30c 4½.3½ to F30c 7.4½
   B 240 – F30c 7.4½ to F30c 6.7
   Rates of Fire
   Zero + 8 to Zero + 12 – 3 rds per gun per minute Shrap.
   " + 12 "   " + 30 – 2 "   "   "   "   "   "
   " + 30 "   " + 60 – 1 "   "   "   "   "   "   HE

4. In the event of hostile counter-attack the S.O.S. lines will be the Final Barrage Line (Green line)

5. Heavy Artillery are assisting with fire on strong points.

6. Zero hour will be at 9.50 p.m. 8° inst. today.

7. An officer will attend at this HQrs to synchronize watches at 7 p.m. today.

8. Copy of 295 Bde RFA Operation order No 2, with sketch attached is enclosed herewith.

9. ACKNOWLEDGE by code word "FOOT"

10. During 8° inst up to zero, a desultory fire will be kept up on objectives detailed above

Issued by orderly
at 3.30 pm

C.G. Duff / Lieut. Adjt.
210 Bde RFA.

Copy No 1 — O.C. B210
       2 — "   B240
       3 — HQrs 42 Div. Arty
       4 — File
       5 — War Diary
       6 — War Diary

Copy No 12

210th BDE R.F.A. ORDER No 3

by

Lt. Col. A. Birtwistle, commdg 210th Bde RFA

Ref. Maps 1/20,000, 62 C N.E.
and 62 b N.W.

10 - 5 - 17

1. 42nd Divisional Artillery, including all Field Batteries in the Divisional Area will carry out a bombardment on the hostile front line defences from 3 pm to 3.15 pm today 10th May, to simulate an attack. Corps Heavy Artillery and Divisions on right and left will co-operate.

2. Objectives will be as follows:—
   A210 - Wood in A19d
   B210 - Wood at A25 b 1.2
   C210 - QUENNEMONT FARM, A20 c 4.0.
   D210 - 1 how. Sunken road in A14 c
        - 1 "   "   "   in A14 d
        - 1 "   QUENNEMONT FARM
        - 1 "   Wood in A14 b.
   B240 - Road from A7 b 8.2 to A2 d 0.0
   C240 - The KNOLL from A7 b 2.8 to A1 d 0.5
   A240 }
   D240 } - Wood in A 26 b and d

3. RATE of FIRE - 1 round per gun per minute H.E. for all batteries except B240 who will use shrapnel.

4. Watches will be synchronised by telephone from this office at 1 pm today.

5. ACKNOWLEDGE by code word "DOOR"

Issued by orderly
at 12.15 pm.

C. G. Duff Lt. Adjt.
210th Bde RFA

Copy No 1 - O.C. A210   Copy No 7 - O.C. C240
       2 - " B210   8 - " D240
       3 - " C210   9 - Hdqrs 42nd Div. Arty.
       4 - " D210   10 - Hdqrs 126 Inf. Bde
       5 - " A240   11 - File
       6 - " B240   12 - War Diary
                               13 - War Diary

Copy No 5

210° Bde R.F.A. Order No 4
by
Lt. Col. A. Birtwistle C.M.G. Commdg 210° Bde RFA.

Ref. Maps 1/20,000 sheets
62 c N.E. and 62 b N.W.

13-5-17

1. There will be a bombardment of the trench east of GILLEMONT FARM running from A13b7.0 through A14a2.6 to A7d9.3 this afternoon 13th inst.

2. Batteries of this Brigade will fire as under on the above trench:—

   ZERO to ZERO + 10

   A210 — A13b7.0 through A14a2.6 to A7d9.3
   (night lines as registered with captive balloon today.)

   D210 — A13b7.0 through A14a2.6 to A7d9.3
   (as indicated in aeroplane photograph)

   Above co-ordinates are approximate only.

3. Rate of fire 18 pdrs. 3 rds per gun per minute shrapnel. 4.5" How. 2 rds per gun per minute H.E.

4. Batteries will cease fire at ZERO + 10 minutes.

5. ZERO hour will be notified later.

6. Watches will be synchronized by telephone from this office when zero time is notified.

7. ACKNOWLEDGE by code word "RIPE" by telephone.

Issued by special orderly at 3.30 p.m.

C. G. Duff Lieut. Adjt
210° Bde RFA

Copy No 1 — O.C. A210
  "   " 2 — " D210
  "   " 3 — File
  "   " 4 — War Diary
  "   " 5 — War Diary

CONFIDENTIAL

Volume II

War Diary

of

210th Bde R.F.A.

From 1.6.17.
To 30.6.17.

WAR DIARY or INTELLIGENCE SUMMARY

Army Form C. 2118

Ref. Maps 20,000
54c N.E. 9 S.E. 1

Place	Date	Hour	Summary of Events and Information	Remarks and references to Appendices
TYAUCOURT	6/6/17		Composition and distribution of 210th Bde R.F.A. as follows :-	
			H.Q. 210th Bde R.F.A. — P10a 2.8 } Covering 42nd Divisional front	
			A 210 — Q 7 a 1.4	
			B 210 — Q 1 a 3.2	
			C 210 — P 12 d 3.3	
			D 210 — F 14 d 9.6 (Ref. map 20,000 62c N.E.) under tactical command of 2nd Cav. Division	
			TOTAL STRENGTH 38 officers 758 O.R. 642 horses	
			EFFECTIVE STRENGTH 36 " 745 " 635 "	
		4 p.m.	Lt Col A. BIRTWISTLE C.M.G. assumed temporary command of 42nd Div. arty. during absence of CRA on leave.	
		4 p.m.	Major J. C. BROWNING, D.S.O., C 210, assumed temporary command of 210th Bde R.F.A.	
		10.45 p.m.	"S.O.S." received from left flank of Divisional sector. 210th Bde R.F.A. put down barrage, but no enemy attack developed. "S.O.S." signal believed to have been put up by enemy	

WAR DIARY or INTELLIGENCE SUMMARY

Army Form C. 2118

Ref. Maps 1/20,000
57c N.E. & S.E.

(Erase heading not required.)

Place	Date	Hour	Summary of Events and Information	Remarks and references to Appendices
RUYAULCOURT	2/6/17	9 p.m.	Our guns A210 sent to I.O.M. LECHENE for repair of breech. 126 Inf. Bde attempted to establish two advanced posts in G.H.a & b. Posts established, but not a few forward in the vicinity owing to presence of strong German posts in the vicinity to O.P. of D 2.11. left Theton, at G/d 3.6 had to be abandoned owing to enemy shell fire.	C 50
Do.	3/6/17	11.25 p.m.	Gas Alarm sounded, but no discharge made. Alarm seems to have been started by enemy.	C 50
	5/6/17		10 O.R. proceeded on 10 days leave to U.K. 344 Gr. BOOSTAND. J. 8210. Wounded by shrapnel in own plane. Capt. M.A. GUNN. R.A.M.C. posted to H.1. Stationary Hospital. F.W. SCHOFIELD. R.A.M.C. attached from 1/1st Field Ambulance (F.A.) as M.O. to 210 Bde R.F.A.	
			5 O.R. proceeded on 10 days leave to U.K.	
Do.	8/6/17	1.45 a.m.	Gas Alarm sounded, but no discharge made. Alarm seems to have been started by enemy.	C 50

WAR DIARY
or
INTELLIGENCE SUMMARY.

Army Form C. 2118.

Ref. a Maps 1/20,000
54 c N.E., S.E.

Place	Date	Hour	Summary of Events and Information	Remarks and references to Appendices
RIVAUCOURT	8/6/17	10 p.m.	127 Inf. Bde commenced digging a new front line trench from R26 c 8.1 thro' R32 b 4.0, R32 d 8.7 to K33 c 4.0. 210 "Bde R.F.A. stood by to protect digging parties if required.	C.G.S
Do	10/6/17		2/Lt. G.P. HARTLEY, B210, promoted Lieutenant as from 1-6-16. 5 O.R. forwarded on 10 days leave to U.K. 4 O.R. forwarded on 10 days leave to U.K.	C.G.4
Do	11/6/17		One gun B210 returned from I.O.M. LE CHENE. One gun C210 sent to I.O.M. LE CHENE.	C.G.50
Do	13/6/17 10 p.m.		A concentrated bombardment lasting two minutes was carried out on RIBECOURT by 40, 42, 59 Divisional Artillery and by Heavy Artillery.	C.G.60
Do	14/6/17 1.30 a.m. to 1.53 a.m.		C210 carried out bombardment of enemy advanced post at K34 c 9 d, in conjunction with Stokes Mortars M.G. of 125 Inf. Bde	
	11.30 p.m.		III & IV Corps Artillery carried out a four minute bombardment spread in K22 a & c with a view to destroying enemy cook carts.	

Army Form C. 2118.

Ref. map. 1/20,000
5⅞ c N.E. & S.E.

WAR DIARY
or
INTELLIGENCE SUMMARY.
(Erase heading not required.)

Place	Date	Hour	Summary of Events and Information	Remarks and references to Appendices
RUYAULCOURT	14/6/17	11.50 p.m.	Carts etc. which were reported to use the road at that hour. Each gun and howitzer taking part in above fired one round on same target.	App.
Do	15/6/17		Major W. BIRTWISTLE, B.210, returned from three weeks leave in U.K. 6 O.R. proceeded on 10 days leave to U.K.	App.

Do	16/6/17		Capt. F.X.S. CARUS, A.210 and 6 O.R. proceeded on 10 days leave to U.K.
			Temp. Lieut. H.G. CLAPHAM - A.210
			        " G.H. COOPER - D.210
			        " R.L.C. LONCOCK - C.210
			        " H.B. BARCLAY - D.210
			promoted full lieutenant with seniority as from 1-6-16.	

Do	14/6/17		In conjunction with the 48th Divisional Artillery bombardment on enemy front line trenches during the day D.211, left section, fired 200 rounds on trench N.24 c.12.4 to N.26 d 4½.8.	
		4 p.m.	D.211 R⁺¹ section fired on N.16 d.6.4 with aeroplane observation.	App.

WAR DIARY
or
INTELLIGENCE SUMMARY.
(Erase heading not required.)

Army Form C. 2118.

Ref. Map 1/20,000 57c N.E. & S.E.

Place	Date	Hour	Summary of Events and Information	Remarks and references to Appendices
RUYAUCOURT	18/6/17	11 midn to 12.7 a.m.	III Corps Artillery carried out bombardment on area K28 B.1.7, K28 a.4.2.45. K28 a.6.8. along Road to K22 d.0.2 - K28 B.1.1.4. with a view to inflicting casualties on enemy personnel. Lt. Col. A. BIRTWISTLE. C.M.G. proceeded on 10 days leave to U.K.	C29
Do.	19/6/17		2/Lt. E.G. WARNER, H.Q. D.A.C. attached to B210. 4443 B.S.M. BEAVEN, G.T. proceeded to 35th Division for commission. Y.O.R. proceeded on 10 days leave to U.K.	C29
Do.	20/6/17		One gun B210 sent to I.O.M. LECHELLE for fitting of buffer tank. One gun C210 returned from I.O.M. LECHELLE. Capt. G.O. CONNELL. R.A.M.C. attached a M.O. to C210 vice R.M. from My Man. Regt. 6 O.R. proceeded on 10 days leave to U.K.	C29
Do.	21/6/17	7 a.m to 1.30 a.m.	C210 heavily shelled with 4.2" How shell. H.E. direct, H.E. delay and misving shell used. This shoot appeared to be by wind. No damage to equipment.	

WAR DIARY
or
INTELLIGENCE SUMMARY.

Army Form C. 2118.

Ref. Maps 1/20,000 57 e S.E. , N.E.
6

Place	Date	Hour	Summary of Events and Information	Remarks and references to Appendices
RUYAULCOURT	21/6/17		CASUALTIES	
			405849 Gr. H.DINTER, H.H. C210 } killed by shell fire	C⁵⁰⁸⁸
			406311 " TOMLINSON. J. " } wounded " "	
			63284 Bt. COUPE. R. " } wounded " "	
			B210 Bde H.Q. moved to new position in Quarry at Q1a0.9	
			Capt. H.W. SCHOFIELD R.A.M.C. returned to duty with 1/1" W.E.L. Field Ambulance.	C⁵⁰⁸⁸
Quarry Q1a0.9	22/6/17		LT. G.P. HARTLEY, B210 + 6 O.R. proceeded on 10 days leave to U.K.	
do	23/6/17	12 noon to 11 pm	B210 at Q1a.3.2 heavily shelled by 4.2.5. About 400 rounds sent over. Direct hit obtained on one gun and trail blown off. 14.89m wireless set also blown up. Two direct hits being obtained on the wireless dugout. Damaged gun of B210 sent to I.O.M. LECHELLE.	C⁵⁰⁸⁸
do	24/6/17	3 pm	D.211 Right Section carried out Thermite shoot on dump in RIBECOURT at L.25 b.H.6. Shoot commenced with aeroplane observation, but continued visually owing to breakdown of communication. Some fires were caused.	

Army Form C. 2118.

WAR DIARY
or
INTELLIGENCE SUMMARY
(Erase heading not required.)

Refs Maps 1/20,000 57c S.E., N.E.

Place	Date	Hour	Summary of Events and Information	Remarks and references to Appendices
Quarry Q/a.0.9	24/6/17		2/Lt. R.E. Anderson, C210, proceeded on course to Artillery school at Vaux-en-Amiénois. Lt. R.F. Newton, Signalling Officer 125 Inf. Bde., temporarily attached to 210th Bde. RFA.	Sgd.
do	25/6/17		New wireless mast installed at Q/a.0.9. 6 O.R. proceeded on 10 days leave to U.K.	Sgd.
do	26/6/17	5:30 am. 5pm	Raiding party of 1 officer and 20 O.R. from 10th Man. Regt. raided elephant huts at K34 c.1.3. The raiding party met with strong opposition and were forced to withdraw. Q210 stood by ready to fire, but were not required. D.211 Right lantern carried out Thermite shoot. direct observation on German in Havrincourt. Several direct hits were obtained, but only slight fire caused.	Sgd.
do	27/6/17		2/Lt. J.R. Tommis, R.E. Sig., attached 210 Bde RFA, returned from 10 days leave in U.K. 20 O.R. proceeded on 10 days leave to U.K.	Sgd.

Army Form C. 2118.

WAR DIARY
or
INTELLIGENCE SUMMARY

Refer Maps 1/20,000 57c SE & N.E.

(Erase heading not required.)

Instructions regarding War Diaries and Intelligence Summaries are contained in F.S. Regs., Part II. and the Staff Manual respectively. Title pages will be prepared in manuscript.

8.

Place	Date	Hour	Summary of Events and Information	Remarks and references to Appendices
Quarry Q.1.d.9	28/7	4.45 p.m.	C210 carried out successful shoot with aeroplane observation on hour K.28.a.8½.9½, and road from K.22.c.2.2 to K.22.a.4.0.	
			Lt. R.F. NEWTON, temporarily attached 210 Bde R.F.A, returned to duty with 125 Inf. Bde.	
			Capt. H.K.S. CARUS, R210, returned from 10 days leave in U.K. 1 O.R. returned on 10 days leave to U.K.	
			405004 Sgt. F.R. STEPHENSON C210 Awarded Military Medal for services while Battery position was being shelled on 21-6-17.	C.F.Y.
			406351 Gr. G. BOAST C210	
do	29/7	9 p.m. to 9.30 p.m. at 10.30 & 10.33 p.m.	III & IV Corps carried out bombardment of enemy route to trench, information having been received that a relief was in progress. 210 Bde R.F.A. fired on road junction K.28.d.2.0, K.34.a.1.9, K.34.a.1.7 and trench K.28.c.6½.4 and K.34.a.1½.6½.	
		10 p.m.	D211 fired 40 lethal shell on enemy Battalion H.Q. at K.28.c.2.7, and suspected Company H.Q. at K.34.a.8½.8½.	

A5834 Wt. W4973/M687 750,000 8/16 D.D. & L. Ltd. Forms/C.2118/13

Army Form C. 2118.

Ref e Maps 1/40,000
54 e N.E. + S.E.

9

WAR DIARY
or
INTELLIGENCE SUMMARY
(Erase heading not required.)

Instructions regarding War Diaries and Intelligence Summaries are contained in F. S. Regs., Part II. and the Staff Manual respectively. Title pages will be prepared in manuscript.

Place	Date	Hour	Summary of Events and Information	Remarks and references to Appendices
Quarry G.10.9.	29/6/17		Gun No.106, B.210, returned from I.O.H. LECHELLE. Lt F.C. WOODWARD, 42nd D.A.C. temporarily attached to C.210.	C.S.O.
do	30/6/17		Capt. A.G. HALL, B.210, Lt A. BROOKS, C.210 and 1 O.R. proceeded on 10 days leave to U.K. Lt Col. A. BIRTWISTLE C.M.G. Returned from 10 days in U.K.	C.S.O.

	Officers	O.R.	Horses
Total Strength	34	847	643
Effective Strength	33	836	638

Drafts Received during the month.

23-6-17	1	58	—	(16 D 210 from C 332 (B.R.) RFA)
25-6-17	—	—	20	
30-6-17	—	25	—	(from hand D.A.C.)

Army Form C. 2118.

WAR DIARY
or
INTELLIGENCE SUMMARY.
(Erase heading not required.)

Ref. u Map 1/20,000
57c S.E. & N.E.

Place	Date	Hour	Summary of Events and Information	Remarks and references to Appendices

Composition and distribution of 210th Bde R.F.A. as follows:—

H.Q. 210th Bde R.F.A. — Q.1.a.0.9.

A 210 — Q.4.a.1.4. ⎫
B 210 — Q.1.a.3.2. ⎬ Covering 42nd Divisional front.
C 210 — P.12.d.3.3. ⎭

D 210 — F.14.d.9.6. (Ref. Map 1/20,000, 62e N.E.) under tactical command of 2nd Cavalry Division.

War Diary for D 210, at present detached, is rendered herewith.

A. Birtwistle
Lt. Col.
Commdg 210th Bde R.F.A

Army Form C. 2118.

WAR DIARY
or
INTELLIGENCE SUMMARY.
(Erase heading not required.)

Instructions regarding War Diaries and Intelligence Summaries are contained in F. S. Regs., Part II. and the Staff Manual respectively. Title pages will be prepared in manuscript.

Place	Date	Hour	Summary of Events and Information	Remarks and references to Appendices
RONSSOY (FWD H.Q.)	1917 Jan 1	3 pm	Reported from our junction A7F77. Expended 29 rds H.E. Firing. Deserter — Corporal Banko 413 IR Regt came to O.K.	
	2	1.30 pm	Registered N.E. Barrage in A13D	62°VE 662
		2 pm	Fired on working Parties in Hindenburg Line A27c 697	2 NW corner 1 E corner
		4 pm	Fired on A14D Reservation. Sunken Road in A14D Reservation	
		6 pm	Expended 39 rounds today. Firing at B15A 67	
	3	2 pm	Fired on Werkheit in reservation B. Shelling of CP. E HY	
		6 pm	Went on A14D Front Trenches at F24 C.P.S. and A192 14. Expended 123 rds today.	
			Harassed H.B. Barrage firing from line UK	
			39045 shelled	
	4	1:20 am	Fired on Machine Gun position F 20 C 77.	
		11:55	Triangle wood F20 C 792.	
			Animals — 4 L.L. Cases from Artillery behind Vaux with Capt McKay vestb Lieuts Fd. W. Departures — Lts Ridyard H.C.C. Douglas A.H. and Lawson J. to UK on leave	

Army Form C. 2118.

WAR DIARY
or
INTELLIGENCE SUMMARY.
(Erase heading not required.)

Instructions regarding War Diaries and Intelligence Summaries are contained in F. S. Regs., Part II. and the Staff Manual respectively. Title pages will be prepared in manuscript.

Place	Date	Hour	Summary of Events and Information	Remarks and references to Appendices
Ronssoy Fwd O.P.	1917 June 5	3.25 am to 3 am	Fired on junction of trench and road in A.14.9 near GILLEMONT FARM	Reference from 1st Major 6.C.W.L. + 62 B.I.W
		10.35 am	Fired on Wood in A.2.6 central	None
		12.10 pm	" Jungle Wood A.25.13	1/5000
		12.20	" Wood in A.2.6 central	
			S.2.9.11	
		12.40	" Factory S.1.13.2.5½	
		12.45	" Ebmes in QUENNEMONT FARM	
		3.5.10	" Wood in A.2.6 central	
		10.20	" A.25.B	
			" Quarry A.20.C.13.	
	6	12 noon AM	" on QUENNEMONT FARM. Expended 107 Rounds today	
		9.10 to 10.30	" QUENNEMONT FARM OP LINE (40)	
		9.5 am	" Wood in S.1.D.15 (4)	
		11.45	" Trench from S.1.D.15 to crossroads L.6.A.9.2 (20)	
		12 noon		
		12.5 pm	" Wood F.30.C.6.1 (4)	
		12.5 to 6.45		
		1.40 pm	" Cross Roads in F.30.C (20)	

Army Form C. 2118.

WAR DIARY
or
INTELLIGENCE SUMMARY.
(Erase heading not required.)

Instructions regarding War Diaries and Intelligence Summaries are contained in F. S. Regs., Part II. and the Staff Manual respectively. Title pages will be prepared in manuscript.

Place	Date	Hour	Summary of Events and Information	Remarks and references to Appendices
Romsey Hin ALP	1917 June 6	pm 7.6 9.20	Fired on trenches in rear of (202). Registration of Barrage for support of B.patt Linden Road in P4 (30) QUESNOYMONT F4H (10)	Appendices 2 from G62C near 0123 HW trenches
		4.20 to 11.20	Fired on trenches in A13D on receipt of F.O.O. message (24) Expended 215 rounds today	
			Ammunition in gun G.H. COOPER to C240 R.E.A. for temporary duty.	
	7	Am 11.10 12	Fired on O.P. in QUESNOYMONT F4HM (258)	
		2-10.25	Trench S.1 D 45 — E 69 Outline (19)	
		pm 6.20.40 11.30	QUESNOY MONT TRENCH F.2 + C on line of trenches at 10 pm (327) Fired 119 rounds today.	
	8	Am 10-20 Noon	Fired on sentry A 14c 77.30 / Retaliation for shelling / Support post 0050.1030 Trench A 14 a 60	
		12.20 pm	G" gun in A3D	
		1-5	Coury Post L.F.4.4.2 L Blowing in the trench supposing hormel (42)	
		8	La Souil	
			Fired 110 rds today	

Army Form C. 2118.

WAR DIARY
or
INTELLIGENCE SUMMARY.
(Erase heading not required.)

Instructions regarding War Diaries and Intelligence
Summaries are contained in F. S. Regs., Part II.
and the Staff Manual respectively. Title pages
will be prepared in manuscript.

Place	Date	Hour	Summary of Events and Information	Remarks and references to Appendices
RONSSOY 1917 FHDR.P. 9 June P.			Dispositions - POST P DI CREMATORIES to ANZOLAS - SNELEN	References L.T. Maps 62cNE an 62S.W. Trench Maps F.20
	9	AM 10.30 11.30	Orders issued to support unit on SUPPORT FARM by 2 guns on REMISE (MSSSRD REFSH 17 F 20 2nd gun 2.15 AM M 10 M. Shot at 2 Junction in L.E.A F. 9.	
		PM 4.20 5.25	Shot on the shed dugouts	SH
			Dispositions - HC 2nd column plus for guns for troops to be for from 3. 30. 70.c 2d	
	10	AM 2.45 to 2.50	Subjected the wind until 2 guns BATT'n A 1 at 25 and A 9.50 m support of raid on SUPPORT FARM Expended 250 to other fire (including ½ PM) 295.25 rounds ammunition.	
		PM 12.15 4.25 6.45	Received SOS regime. to support SALEEMENT FARM post a fresh on number M15 E fired 28 guns on the shed found on road in 11.4 D & 9 rounds at M15A 058 by order of DC, SA. sec. 4HA.	NW

A 5834 Wt. W.4973/M657 750,000 8/16 D. D. & L. Ltd. Forms/C.2118/13.

Army Form C. 2118.

WAR DIARY
or
INTELLIGENCE SUMMARY.
(Erase heading not required.)

Place	Date	Hour	Summary of Events and Information	Remarks and references to Appendices
RONSSOY	1917			
Sh P.S.S	June 9	p.m.	Searched and swept MAGQUINCOURT VALLEY in M8a south & section and	Reference to My C NE and G.3 NW Squares
	10	10 gr	CLAYMORE WOOD in A.14 with 4 inch new pattern	
	11	12 noon		
		12.20 p.m.	Fired alarm on BONY	
		12.26		
		12.26 to 1.5	S.O.S. signal reported from Sidgemont near Pat's bombarded trenches in A.13.D	
			Arrivals - Lt Taylor 4 from furlough	
	10		Fired at Factory SIB's 5 & 7 searched & swept Ntnorcoss'ment in L.6.A	
	12	noon	for Joseph Mortars (?)	
		2 pm	Fired on VENDHUILE Stations for bombardment of G & pad.	
		3 pm	Factory G.18.2.5.5, Triangle Wood, A.26 Rges and Trenches F.30.C	
		3 pm	Tnches L.6.A	
		5 pm	Fired 140 rounds today	
			Arrivals - 9/5/17 Lieut Ryan R from Edinburgh UK 7/5 2 13 2d Cornell	
			and 9/5/17 2nd Lieut Fortman R from signal school.	

Army Form C. 2118.

WAR DIARY
INTELLIGENCE SUMMARY.
(Erase heading not required.)

Instructions regarding War Diaries and Intelligence Summaries are contained in F. S. Regs., Part II. and the Staff Manual respectively. Title pages will be prepared in manuscript.

Place	Date	Hour	Summary of Events and Information	Remarks and references to Appendices
RONSSOY P14D6 P14D6	Jan 13	AM 11.45 2pm 4pm 7pm	Fired at:- Trenches A13D & A14C (33) Cross Roads and dug outs about L68 9.0 (15) Triangle Street & Junction N/ MALAKOFF FARM F20 G (12) Factory S1.B3½ S2 (23), N.W.t. L6A 9.0. Junction S1.D2.6 - S1 D 2.8 (12) Main 9.500 (4) Fired 147 rds today	References to plates 6. CM2 and 6. BMS Enclosed hereunto DNA
	14	AM 10 5-7pm	Fired at the knoll (10) Fired at junction A15A.07 Complaint observation (61) Fired 71 rds today	DNA
	15	3.40 to 5pm	Fired at:- Sal L6A 4.4 Blaybury personnel & trucking approached (31) Dugout A2L D 29 – Alarm up 6 (21) Slot S1.D1.5 (6) Junction L6A 8½.12 (6) Fired 54 rds today	DNA

A5834 Wt W4973/M687 750,000 8/16 D. D. & L. Ltd. Forms/C.2118/13.

WAR DIARY
or
INTELLIGENCE SUMMARY.
(Erase heading not required.)

Army Form C. 2118.

Instructions regarding War Diaries and Intelligence Summaries are contained in F. S. Regs., Part II. and the Staff Manual respectively. Title pages will be prepared in manuscript.

Place	Date	Hour	Summary of Events and Information	Remarks and references to Appendices
RONSSOY F14d 8.8	1917 June 15		Arrivals :- 715156 Cpl Banks JB from leave, Departures 715041 Sergt Hallett R to Hospital, absence from	References Maps 62 C NE & 62 B NW France 1/20000.
	16	a.m. 10.15 to 11.30	Fired on Trenches in A14 C (30)	
		noon	A27A (14)	
		pm 12.45 to 3.30	Gun position in A22A with aeroplane observation (144)	
		9.15	Trenches in A20 C & A26 B (11)	
			Fired 199 rds today.	
			Departures :- 715147 Dr McCready S, 715347 Dr Sinclair J to Signalling School. 715304 Dr Kelly T to Hospital Gastritis. 715328 131 Ward W, 715184 Dr Hav J, 715151 Dr Bush J.S at 9/6 on 10 day furlough.	
			Arrivals 715129 Dr Mackin W from Hospital.	

A5834 Wt. W4973/M687 750,000 8/16 D. D. & L. Ltd. Forms/C.2118/13.

Army Form C. 2118.

WAR DIARY
INTELLIGENCE SUMMARY.
(Erase heading not required.)

Instructions regarding War Diaries and Intelligence Summaries are contained in F. S. Regs., Part II. and the Staff Manual respectively. Title pages will be prepared in manuscript.

Place	Date	Hour	Summary of Events and Information	Remarks and references to Appendices
RENINGHE/ Fr d 92 c 6.9	1917 June 17		NIL	Reference 62 c NW 62 d NW France
	18	12.15 pm	Fired on Ruby Wood S 24.2 (18)	
		12.20	" Trenches E of SILLEMONT FARM (20)	
		5.15	" MACQUIN COURT FARM A 3d 26 (12)	
		11.20 to 1.23	" Sunken Road F 24 c on S.O.S. signal to support B Bat.	
	19	12.15 am	" Triangle Wood F 20 a 95	
		12.20 12.40 1.20 am	" Cross Roads F 26 c 67 } Fired 144 rounds Today 19/6/17.	
			" Trench F 24 c 92 c	
		During day (?)	" GUERNET COPSE (?)	

Army Form C. 2118.

WAR DIARY
or
INTELLIGENCE SUMMARY.
(Erase heading not required.)

Instructions regarding War Diaries and Intelligence Summaries are contained in F. S. Regs., Part II. and the Staff Manual respectively. Title pages will be prepared in manuscript.

Place	Date	Hour	Summary of Events and Information	Remarks and references to Appendices
RONSSOY East Pt 6	1917 June 20	from 2.10 to 4.20	Fired 26 rds at GUEPPE T COPSE } fired 33 rds lachry	Reference to Maps 62 C N E T 62 B N W France 1/40000
		11–15 p.m.	F.2 O.C. 5.6	
			Crossroads – 715-208 S.E.O.C. Dugouts 715-28 E.&N. Dugouts 715-240	
			Ex. By Lawson from V.K. fartbergh	
	21 Jun	3	Fired at Sunken road in A.14.D (4) Cutting A.14 C (5) Trench Mortar A.14a F.O (3) A.14a 2.0. (3)	
			fired 19 rounds	
	22 1.5 am		Fired on trench in A.13A in support of Etinhem Farm post – S.O.S signal	
			fired 93 rounds	
		11 am	Fired on Queunemont Farm 10 Rounds	

WAR DIARY
or
INTELLIGENCE SUMMARY.

Army Form C. 2118.

Place	Date	Hour	Summary of Events and Information	Remarks and references to Appendices
RONSSOY FWD O.P.	1917 June 23.	from 4/9.15 to 4/9.20	Registered S25 D 8 6 ②	Ref. Maps 62 C N.E. 62 E N.W. France 1/20,000
		4.30 to 4.45	Do S25 D 9 3 ⑩	
		5.20 6.40	Do 15 rounds on German front line trench around and to East of STRATPOINT FARM (- A13A 3½ 9, A13 D 3½ 9½, A13A 4.0, A13A 5½ 1½, A13A 8½ 3 (51)	
		7.10 7.15	Do Suspected Trench Mortar position in A 14 A ②	
			All above rounds registered one of Bn Obs. observation —— Fired 81 rounds Today.	
			Defensive — G. SIMPLE W.T. Hospital dress Batavia, 17/5 2 Lt Bn CURRIE W.T. J H/15 (Permanent) Cpt 1327 A DERRIE. R. all to O.R. on 100 yard Learn, 7/15 141" spr CARRUTHERS R. to Chobley School VAUX.	
			Barrosa C. 2nd Lt SANDUMAN and 51 other ranks from 212 BDE R.F.A. being prepared if additional billets to make 6 gun Battery.	
			Received orders to support Raid on 25/6/17 by 3rd Cavalry Division between X 27 c 2.2 & X 24 × 2.4 and distance X 24 c 09 × X 25 A 6.0. Zero determined on S 21 A 56 × 25 c 9.7 Rob 1 rd per elm for 5 minutes for 10", 2 rds per thm for fire for 10" X 1 rd per thm for 10 mm.	

Army Form C. 2118.

WAR DIARY
or
INTELLIGENCE SUMMARY.
(Erase heading not required.)

Instructions regarding War Diaries and Intelligence Summaries are contained in F. S. Regs., Part II. and the Staff Manual respectively. Title pages will be prepared in manuscript.

Place	Date	Hour	Summary of Events and Information	Remarks and references to Appendices
RAMSCAPPELLE FIELDS	1917 June 24	p.m. 3.20 to 4	Fired mate quarry in A13A (10 r.s.) in Retaliation for Enemy shoot. Received orders for destruction shoot and fired on trenches E of GILLEMONT FARM in reply thereto.	Reference Trace 62.0/5 Mar. 525 P.M.
	25	a.m. 7.10 & 7.40	Fired 50 rounds at S.25 c 7.6 and S.25 c 9.3 in support (firing by 3rd Cavalry Division) (Venus & Royals Raid)	
		a.m. 5.30	" 5 " A14 A13 retaliation	
		p.m. 4.30	Fired 6 rounds on N.E. corner of GILLEMONT FARM in reply from Cavalry at GILLEMONT FARM POST	
		6	" 3 " " "	
		7.15	Fired shots at enemy construction from A13 d 6.5 to A7 a 9.0 destroying any traps - this is possibly AP.20 Registered trenches about A13 D 5.2.6 - Balloon observation. (2) projectiles bural on 7.28	
			Expended 64 rds today.	
			Arrivals: 71520 DR KELLY T. from hospital.	

A5834 Wt. W4973/M687 750,000 8/16 D. D. & L. Ltd. Forms/C.2113/13.

WAR DIARY
or
INTELLIGENCE SUMMARY
(Erase heading not required.)

Army Form C. 2118.

Place	Date	Hour	Summary of Events and Information	Remarks and references to Appendices
Roussoy Fd. 2.2.	1917 June 26	from 6.50 to 7.20	Fired 14 rds. at trench A13a 2.5. – A13a 2.5. – Ballon formation. Orders for projected raid tonight cancelled. 6" Hows. not having been able to complete their preliminary destruction shoot.	References Maps 62C WeWire 6.3.8.56 Bonnin Yeeros
	27	12.20 pm	Arrivals – 7/5250 Br. CURRIE J, 7/5141 P/Br STRAIGHTON JS and 7/8170S SINTON E. from Army to O.R. Registered trench mortar position A25 B.4.4. getting 3 hits, 14 rounds. Departures – Sergt Settles Armourer & Bombardiers S, Sgt Arthur S, Zee N, Armstrong J/F, & William H, Farleigh Telford H, Gr. Hamilton A, Wynne B, & Connell H. Bro Thornberry J Allan W. Lewis J, Armstrong S. To U.K. on 10 days leave.	DK
	28	am 12.15	Fired 20 rds, 14" at sunken road in F 24 C and 6 x 6 trench mortar A 25 B 4.4 in support of B/Frd.	
		1 pm	" 4 rounds at road from A 20 c 5.6. to A 20 A 9 5 6.	
		1.20 pm	" Trench F 24 C 9.2.6.	DK

WAR DIARY
or
INTELLIGENCE SUMMARY.
(Erase heading not required.)

Army Form C. 2118.

Place	Date	Hour	Summary of Events and Information	Remarks and references to Appendices
Ruins of FM D p² 9	1917 June 29	6am 10:30	Fired 12 rounds at trenches. An H.A.2.D. in retaliation for hostile shelling. Received orders for intermittent shelling of roads and trenches between 10:45 pm to night and 3:4 am 30/6/17; Consequent information that enemy aircraft relay now taking place	Reference 1/1000 62 C NE and 62 B NW FRANCE 1/100000
		pm 10:45 to 10:45 11:30–35 11:30 11:50–55 11:54 PM 12:14–15 12:14 1–1:45 1:15–1:19 2:5–15 2:9 3:2:4	Fired at Ay D6.5, A15C 4.6, A27a 52.15, A27A 1.5, A26A 23.3	
	30		Fired 267 rounds.	
			Departures Sergt Tinn W, Watson W, Bmr Heslop J and St Barnes H a leave for 10 days to UK	

CONFIDENTIAL

VOL. II.

WAR DIARY

210TH. Bde R.F.A.

1.7.17 to 31.7.17.

Army Form C. 2118.

Ref" Map 1/20,000
54c N.E. + S.E.

WAR DIARY
or
INTELLIGENCE SUMMARY.
(Erase heading not required.)

Place	Date	Hour	Summary of Events and Information	Remarks and references to Appendices
HAVRIN-COURT WOOD	1/7		Composition and distribution of 210th Bde R.F.A. as follows:-	1

H.Q. 210th Bde R.F.A. - Q.1.a.0.9. ⎫
        A 210   - Q.4.a.1.4. ⎬ Covering H.2nd Divisional
        B 210   - Q.1.a.3.2. ⎬ Front.
        C 210   - P.12.d.3.3. ⎭

        D 210   - F.14.d.9.6. (Ref. Map 1/20,000. 62cN.E.)
under tactical command of 2nd Cavalry Division

	O.	O.R.	HORSES
TOTAL STRENGTH	34	847	643
EFFECTIVE STRENGTH	33	836	638

Lt.Col. A. BIRTWISTLE. C.M.G. resumed command of 210th Bde. R.F.A.
Major J.C. BROWNING D.S.O. relinquished command of 210th Bde
R.F.A. and resumed command of C 210.

CD

WAR DIARY
INTELLIGENCE SUMMARY

Army Form C. 2118.

Ref. Maps 1/20,000
57c N.E. & S.E.

Place	Date	Hour	Summary of Events and Information	Remarks and references to Appendices
HAVRINCOURT WOOD	2/17	10 a.m. to 2 p.m.	4.2" How. Bty bombarded C.2.10 at P.12.d.3.3. Rate of fire, about 1 round every two minutes. Two guns sent to I.O.M. QUINCOVRE for minor repairs.	
		9.30 p.m. to 11.30 p.m.	D.2.11 RTMor. fired 20 rds. BCBC (lethal) into Batt. H.Q. at K.28.c.2.7. Enemy retaliated with 90 shells on A.4 Central. D.2.11 RTMor., a minute retaliation, fired 20 rds BCBR into Chapel Wood and 20 BX into K.28.c.2.7.	
			One gun B.2.10 returned from I.O.M. LECHELLE.	
			L/M.B. ECCLES, A.2.10, LT. E. NUTTALL, C.2.10, and LT. E. NUTTALL, C.2.10, and 15 O.R. proceeded on 10 days leave to U.K.	Copy with Appendices A
do.	3/17	1.8 a.m.	127 Inf. Bde carried out raid on DEAN COPSE and WIGAN COPSE assisted by 48th D.A. and Heavy Artillery fire in support. Two prisoners (and 1 unwounded) captured in WIGAN COPSE. Raid on DEAN COPSE failed.	
		5.14 p.m.	2.10 Bde R.F.A. bombarded CHAPEL wood for two minutes. Two guns of C.2.10 placed in new position at Q.Y.a.3.2.	Copy with Appendices

Army Form C. 2118.

WAR DIARY
or
INTELLIGENCE SUMMARY.
(Erase heading not required.)

Ref eHaq 1/20.000
57c N.E. & S.E.
3

Place	Date	Hour	Summary of Events and Information	Remarks and references to Appendices
HAVRINCOURT WOOD	4/7/17	5.34 p.m. 15 6.7 p.m.	210 Bde RFA engaged 11 enemy O.Ps to provide covering fire for heavy T.M. firing on X roads K32.2.8.7½.	
		10.34 p.m.	2 minute bombardment of every T.M. at K33d 97.9½.	
		11.17 p.m.	2 minute bombardment of enemy Rifle Pits in FEMY WOOD.	egl
			Two guns, C210, flooded in new position at R7 a.30.25. Lt G.P. HARTLEY, B210, Returned from 10 days leave in U.K. Lt C. HARTLEY, C210, returned from Sig walking Course.	
do.	5/7/17	2 am 11 p.m.	2 minute bombardment of enemy Rifle Pits in FEMY WOOD. 210 Bde R.F.A. Co-operated with heavy T.M. bombardment of DEAN COPSE. 18 e.R. proceeded on 10 days leave to U.K.	cgl

Army Form C. 2118.

Ref & Map 1/20,000
57 c. N.E. & S.E.

WAR DIARY
or
INTELLIGENCE SUMMARY.
(Erase heading not required.)

Instructions regarding War Diaries and Intelligence Summaries are contained in F. S. Regs., Part II. and the Staff Manual respectively. Title pages will be prepared in manuscript.

Place	Date	Hour	Summary of Events and Information	Remarks and references to Appendices
HAVRINCOURT WOOD	6/7/17	4 p.m. to 6 p.m.	Heavy T.M.s carried out bombardment of BOGGART HOLE (K33 c.1.65) and the barricade at K33 c.9.8 & K33 c.85.65.	
			210 Bde R.F.A. co-operated with fire on K33 b.75.40 to K33 b.35.35	
		10.30 p.m. to midnight	Medium T.M.s carried out bombardment of ELEPHANT HUTS at K33 d.9.1.	
			210 Bde R.F.A. co-operated with fire on RIFLE PITS, K34 c.2.4 to K34 c.80.35.	CSy
do	7/7/17		18 O.R. proceeded on 10 days leave to U.K.	CSy
do	8/7/17	5.34 a.m.	2 minutes bombardment of K34 a.1.5 to K34 a.3.2	
		11.23 p.m.	2 " " every T.M.s from K33 c.5.2 to K33 b.65.05	
			2 guns of C/210 returned from I.O.M. Quinconce.	CSy
do	9/7/17	10 a.m.	210 Bde R.F.A. came under tactical command of 58th Division.	
		10.17 p.m.	2 minutes bombardment of cyst at K33 b.0.2.	CSy

A5834 Wt. W4973/M687 750,000 8/16 D. D. & L. Ltd. Forms/C.2118/13

Army Form C. 2118.

Ref eu 1/20,000
57c N.E. & S.E.

WAR DIARY
or
INTELLIGENCE SUMMARY.
(Erase heading not required.)

Instructions regarding War Diaries and Intelligence Summaries are contained in F. S. Regs., Part II. and the Staff Manual respectively. Title pages will be prepared in manuscript.

Place	Date	Hour	Summary of Events and Information	Remarks and references to Appendices
HAVRINCOURT WOOD	10/1/17	3.13 p.m.	Short bombardment carried out on TRIANGLE WOOD, K35a.	
		10.43 p.m.	Short bombardment carried out on GRAND RAVINE from K33 a 25.50 to K33 a 40.55.	
			19 O.R. proceeded on 10 days leave to U.K. One gun A20 sent to I.O.M. QUINCONCE. 2/Lt. K. WARE, A20, attached to 42nd D.A.C. 2/Lt. R. HARTNEY, H1 D.A.C. attached to A20.	C&D
do.	11/1/17		D21 R.T. Sec. answered GF call from aeroplane on K18 d 2.2. One gun of B20 burst by N.E. preventive. Condemned at Brigade. 12 O.R. proceeded on 10 days leave to U.K.	C&D
do.	12/1/17	8.30 a.m.	Lt.Col. A. BIRTWISTLE. C.M.G. founded TRIANGLE WOOD minutely by the King.	
		noon to 2 a.m.	5.9" How. Bty fired 150 rds at A20 at Q 9 a 1.4.	
	12 Jan 16	12.37 a.m.	Bombardment of ETNA DRAW COPSE by Medium and Heavy T.M.'s. 210 43rd R.F.A. co-operated by placing their barrage round, & flanking roads in the vicinity.	

Army Form C. 2118.

Ref. e Map 1/20,000
5 y & N.E. & S.E.

6

WAR DIARY
or
INTELLIGENCE SUMMARY
(Erase heading not required.)

Place	Date	Hour	Summary of Events and Information	Remarks and references to Appendices
HAVRINCOURT WOOD	12/7/17	6 p.m.	D2/11 fired 40 rounds BX on hostile battery at R22.c.6.8.	
		11.22 p.m.	Short bur. bombardment of suspected T.M. and M.G. emplacements in vicinity of VESUVIUS.	
			Capt. A.G. HAM, B2/09 & Lt. A. BROOKS, C2/10, returned from 10 days leave in U.K.	CSP
			T/Lt H.B. STORER, B2/10, rejoined from 42 D.V. Sig sch.	
			23 O.R. proceeded on 10 days leave to U.K.	
do	13/7/17	1.13 a.m.	Short burst bombardment of suspected T.M. at R34.2.3.2.	
		3.25 a.m.	D2/11 RT section fired with BCBC (kettle) on battery position at R.18.d.1.6 and R.18.d.25.3 in co-operation with Corps Heavy Artillery.	
		3.55 a.m.		
		10.15 a.m.	Short bombardment of square in HAVRINCOURT.	
		2 p.m.	42" D.A. Horse Show held at BUS.	CSP
do	14/7/17		Lt H.B. ECCLES, A2/10, returned from 10 days leave in U.K.	CSP
			B2/10 Cpl. ROBINSON R. killed by shrapnel.	

Army Form C. 2118.

Ref & Map 1/20,000
57c N.E. T.E.

WAR DIARY
or
INTELLIGENCE SUMMARY.
(Erase heading not required.)

Place	Date	Hour	Summary of Events and Information	Remarks and references to Appendices
HAVRINCOURT WOOD	15/1/17		Short band advance on Dumps and Cadrip at K23 a 4.4. 2/Lt R.C. ANDERSON, e210, returned from Artillery course at VAUX Capt.H.H. LORD, A.V.C., Capt H.H. SIMON, e210, L/H.G. CLAPHAM, A210, and 25 O.R. proceeded on 10 days leave to U.K.	CRO
do	16/1/17		Heavy T.M. bombarded BOGGART HOLE, K33 b 1.6. Group operated.	CRO
do	17/1/17	10.15 p.m. 10.25 a.m.	Short bombardment of Dumps at K9 c 9.3 " " " " K15.2.5.2 x roads	CRO
			One gun A210 returned from Ordnance QUINCONCE " " " " sent to "	
do	18/1/17	2 a.m.	Medium T.M's bombarded Rifle Pits in FERN WOOD, in co-operation with the Group.	CRO
		9.25 p.m. to 11.5 p.m.	Short burst of fire on road in HAVRINCOURT, and track junction K29 c 4½.2.	
			L/T.H. ROBEY, D210, and 26 O.R. proceeded on 10 days leave to U.K.	CRO

WAR DIARY
or
INTELLIGENCE SUMMARY.
(Erase heading not required.)

Army Form C. 2118.

Ref. Map 1/20,000
54/c N.E. + S.E.

8

Place	Date	Hour	Summary of Events and Information	Remarks and references to Appendices
HAVRINCOURT WOOD	19/7/17	11.10 a.m. 11.15 a.m. 11.20 p.m.	Shot bursts of fire on dumps and railway sidings, L25 c 8.8, Rail Junctions L20 d 7.4 + L25 d 3.0.	CS.1.
		3 a.m.	Shot burst of fire on works in HAVRIN COURT.	
do.	20/7/17		One gun A 210 sent to BRAINCUM, QUINCONCE.	
		10.32 p.m.	After heavy shelling on the whole sector throughout the day, the enemy raided our trenches in the vicinity of S.P. in K33c, and succeeded in getting into our ungarrisoned portion of our front, from which he retired, having failed to get an identification. 210 Bde R.F.A. barraged in support of our infantry.	
		1 p.m. to 3 p.m.	D211, RT Station barraded PUSCH TRENCH from Q6 c 7.1 to Q6 c 55.25.	CS.2.
do.	21/7/17		Detached gun of A 210 at J36 d 9.7.9.7 moved into main position 97 c.R. Proceeded on 10 days leave to U.K. One section B210 moved to J35 c 9.2 and relieved one section O/6" Bty. R.F.A. One section A 211 moved into position by B210. 3rd Division of Division relieved by	CS.3.

WAR DIARY or INTELLIGENCE SUMMARY

Army Form C. 2118.

Ref: Map 1/20,000
57c N.E. & S.E.

Place	Date	Hour	Summary of Events and Information	Remarks and references to Appendices
HAVRINCOURT WOOD	22/9/17		M.G.R.A. 3rd Army visited 210 Bty R.F.A.	
		4.15 am	D211 fired on Motor transport at K18d 5.3 in response to G.F. Call from aircraft.	
		4.37 pm	As above, in K18d 3.2.	
		8.41 pm	D211 & B210 fired 3 rds. Gun fire on active hostile battery at K18d 6.3 in response to N.F. call from aeroplane.	* Note: 2/9/9.14 B
		10.30 am	2/9 Bn. Q.V.R. raided chalk pit at K33d 5½.1.* Raid successful and two prisoners captured. 210+Bty R.F.A. fired in support from R34c0.12 to K33d 3.4.	
			Renaissance of B210 moved known position at J36a 8.2.	Afy/x B/1
		" A211 " " " position vacated by B210.	
			B210 came under orders of 3rd D.A. A211 came under orders of O.C. left Group, 58 D.A.	
			2 guns of A210 returned from Arcluam, Quinconce.	
			2/Lt. E. C. REES, B210 Returned from hospital.	S.W.

Army Form C. 2118.

Refs:Map 1/20,000
57cNE.T.S.E
10

WAR DIARY
or
INTELLIGENCE SUMMARY.
(Erase heading not required.)

Place	Date	Hour	Summary of Events and Information	Remarks and references to Appendices
HAVRINCOURT WOOD	23/7/17	9 a.m. to 10 a.m.	D 2/11, Rt section carried out a deliberate bombardment of PLUSH TRENCH from R.1.d.1.4 to R.1.d.3.2.	
		11.10 p.m.	2/12th Bn Rangers raided WIGAN COPSE. R.26.d.2.4. * 20+B & R.77. 240 Bde R.F.A. & Heavy Artillery fired in support. Fire of the enemy killed, various identification obtained. We had no casualties. A.2.10. 40 & 013. A/B.S.M. GRIFFITHS. R.A.B. injured by recoil of gun.	NOE APPENDIX C
do	24/7/17	5 am	O.C. D 2/10 Bde R.F.A. assumed command of Right Group R.A. 3rd Division. A 2/11 came under command of O.C. D 2/11 +Bde R.F.A.	
		12 nt	Shot howitzer spent from K.14.d.12.2 to K.14.b.12.1. No direct casualties on enemy working party.	
			1 section C 2/10 relieved one section 23rd Bde R.F.A. at J.34.a.0.6 D 2/11 Rt Sn. ,, ,, ,, 130th Bde R.F.A. " J.35.a.5.2	
do	25/7/17	During day	Burst opposite an enemy working party in K.14.b.1.d. 1 section C 2/10 relieved one section 23rd Bde R.F.A. at J.34.a.0.6 One gun C 2/10 sent forward for overhaul of carriage.	

WAR DIARY
or
INTELLIGENCE SUMMARY.
(Erase heading not required.)

Army Form C. 2118.

Refer Map. 1/20,000
57/c N.E.

11

Place	Date	Hour	Summary of Events and Information	Remarks and references to Appendices
HAVRINCOURT WOOD	26/7/17	During the night	Short bombardment of road junction K.27.c.7.4. Bursts of fire on enemy working parties in K.14.b & d. LT C. MACKRELL B.210. and 14 O.R. proceeded on 10 days leave to U.K.	C.B.D.
do	27/7/17	During the night	Short bombardments of tracks in K.9.c & 9.3, road junction K.9.c.6.1. and X road. K.15.b.5.2. Capt. L. HIGHTON, 211 +Bde R.F.A. posted to 210 +Bde R.F.A. LT T.H. ROBEY, 210 +Bde R.F.A. posted to 42nd D.A.C. Capt. H.H. LORD, A.V.C. Capt. H.H. SIMON, C.210 and LT H.G. CLAPHAM, A.210. returned from 10 days leave in U.K.	C.B.D.
do	28/7/17	2.5 am 2.45 am	Bursts of fire on enemy working parties in K.14.b & d. 31 O.R. proceeded on 10 days leave to U.K.	C.B.D.
do	29/7/17	1.15 am 1.50 am 10 p.m.	Bursts of fire on enemy working parties in K.14.b & d. Short bombardment of Army and Siding at K.23.a.7.4. 1 gun C.210 returned from Ordnance.	C.B.D.

Army Form C. 2118.

Ref. Map 1/20,000
57 C N E.
12

WAR DIARY
or
INTELLIGENCE SUMMARY.
(Erase heading not required.)

Instructions regarding War Diaries and Intelligence Summaries are contained in F.S. Regs., Part II. and the Staff Manual respectively. Title pages will be prepared in manuscript.

Place	Date	Hour	Summary of Events and Information	Remarks and references to Appendices
P4a.6.9	29/7/17	—	210 Bde H.Q. moved from Quarry at Q.1.a.0.9. to P4a 6.9	C.g.g.
do	30/7/17		One gun B210 sent to Ordnance. Major R. YATES, A210, Lt R.R.E. KNOCKER, C210, and 25 O.R. proceeded on 10 days leave to U.K.	C.g.g.
do	31/7/17	Early morning	Burst of fire carried out on enemy working parties in R14 b. d. Lt C.G. DUFF, Hdqrs. & 12 O.R. proceeded on 10 days leave to U.K. Composition & Distribution of 210 Bde R.F.A. as follows. H.Q. 210th Bde. — P4a.6.9. A 210 — Q7a.1.4 B 210 (4) — J36a.9.2 (2) — J35a.9.2 C 210 (4) — J34a.0.6 (2) — J07a.5.1 D 210 — F14d.9.6 (Ref 1/20,000 62c N.E.) under tactical command of 35th Div. Arty.	A.B.E.

WAR DIARY
or
~~INTELLIGENCE SUMMARY.~~ Ref. map 20,000 57c N.E.

Army Form C. 2118.

13

Place	Date	Hour	Summary of Events and Information	Remarks and references to Appendices
P4a 6.9	31/7/17		TOTAL STRENGTH. 35 officers 838 o.r. 708 horses	
			EFFECTIVE STRENGTH 34 " 827 " 708 "	
			DRAFTS RECEIVED 15-7-17 4 O.Rs.	
			War Diaries of D/210 for periods during which they were detached are enclosed herewith.	A32.

A. Briturth.
LT. COL.
COMMDG. 210TH. BDE. R.F.A.

Appx. "A"

SECRET

Copy No. 11.

210th, Bde R.F.A. Order No 9.

by

Lt Col A Birtwistle CMG cdg 210th, Bde RFA

Reference Map Blue Print July 1st 1917.
Part of 57c G.M 3
1/10000 df. 28-6-17

1. On the night 2/3rd July, the 127th Infantry Brigade will carry out a raid on WIGAN COPSE K 26 d 2. 4½ and DEAN COPSE. K 32 b. 8½. 7.

2. In support of above. 210th Bde RFA will fire as under.

ZERO to ZERO + 15 minutes

A.210
3 guns Trench K 26 d 4.9 to K 26 d 9 8.
3 "   "   K 27 c 0 3 to K 27 c 3 2

C.210   Trench K 26 d 9 8 to K 27 c 3½. 4½

D.211   1 How. VESUVIUS – K 27 c 2 8
Rt. Sec. 1 "   CINDER TRACK – K 33 a 4 5.

ZERO to ZERO + 20 minutes

D.211
Lt Sec. 2 Hows ETNA – K 26 d 9. 1.

3. The Divisional Artillery on our left will fire as under.

ZERO to ZERO + 15 minutes

8 - 18 pdrs Trench K 26 b ½.0 to K 26 d 4.9.
1 How Suspected MG. K 26 d 6 8½
1 "   "   "   K 26 d 9 8
1 "   "   "   K 26 b 4 5
1 "   "   "   K 27 a 1. 8½.

4. Rates of fire 18 pdrs 4 rounds per gun per minute (50% Shrap 50% H.E.)
4.5 Hows. 2 rounds per gun per minute

5. ZERO HOUR will be at 1.8 am on 3rd inst.

6. An officer from each unit will attend at this headquarters at 6.30 pm. 2nd inst to synchronize watches. A synchronized watch will be despatched from this office to the Headquarters of the R A Group on our left.

7. ACKNOWLEDGE by code word "BOX".

Issued by orderly
at 7 pm

C. G. Duff
Lieut. Adjt
210th Bde RFA.

Copy No 1. — H.Q. 42nd Div Arty
2 — H.Q. 126th Inf. Bde
3 — H.Q. 127th Inf. Bde
4 — O.C. Right Group R.A. 48th Divn.
5 — O.C. A 210
6 — O.C. B 210
7 — O.C. C 210
8 — O.C. D 211 Rt Section
9 — O.C. D 211 Lt Section
10 — War Diary
11 — War Diary ✓
12 — FILE.

Appx "B"

Copy No 12

210th Bde R.F.A. Order No 11

Ref. Map 1/20,000   22-7-17
57c N.E.

1. The 2/9th Battalion Q.V.R. will carry out a raid tonight 22/23rd inst. on the Chalk Pit at K33d 5½.1.

2. In support of above this Group will fire as under:—

   <u>ZERO to ZERO + 3 minutes</u>

   A210 K34c 0.1½   to   K33d 8.2
   B210 K33d 8.2   "   K33d 5½.3
   C210 K33d 5½.3   "   K33d 3.4

   Rate of fire, 3 rounds per gun per minute shrapnel.

   <u>ZERO to ZERO + 30 minutes</u>

   D211   1 how.   K34c 3½.½
   Rt Sec 1 "   K34c 2½.4½
   D211   1 "   K33d 9½.8
   Lt Sec 1 "   K33c 8½.4½ (Barricade)

   Rate of fire. ZERO to ZERO +3, 2 rds per how per minute.
   ZERO +3 to ZERO +30, 1 rd. per how per minute.

3. Heavy Artillery will co-operate with fire on BOGGART HOLE K33 b 1.6

4. To create a diversion, from ZERO to ZERO +3
   1 Heavy T.M. will fire on Enemy trench K32 b 8½.7
   1 Medium T.M.   "   "   "   "   "   BOYAU K26d 9.1
   1   "   "   "   "   "   "   "   X trench K32 b 4½.8

5. ZERO HOUR will be at 10.30 pm today 22nd inst.

6. Upon the signal, three green very lights being sent up by the Infantry, in rapid succession, the support mentioned in para 2 will be repeated, D211 R⁺ & L⁺ Sections firing for 3 minutes only.

The N.O.P. officer will repeat this signal and report at once to this office that the signal has been sent up. Battery lookouts will be specially warned as to its meaning.

7. Units will stand by on the above target until 11.15 p.m. today, 22ⁿᵈ inst.

8. Watches will be synchronized by telephone from this office at 9 p.m.

9. ACKNOWLEDGE by codeword "BAG".

Issued by orderly   C.G. Duff Lᵗ Adjt.
at   210ᵗʰ Bde R.F.A.

Copy No 1 - H.Q. 58. D.A.
        2 - H.Q. 175 Inf. Bde
        3 - H.Q. 14ᵗʰ Heavy Group.
        4 - A 210
        5 - B 210
        6 - C 210
        7 - D211 Rᵗ Sn.
        8 - D211 Lᵗ Sn.
        9 - B.T.M.O.
       10 -
       11 - War Diary
       12 - War Diary
       13 - File

Appx "B/1"

200th Bde R.F.A. Orders No. 9

Ref. Map Armentières 1/40,000   20/7/17

1. 200th Bde R.F.A. R.A.F.A. 3/50 will shortly take over the front occupied by a portion of the 3rd Division on the ...

2. The following moves will take place night 21/22nd inst. Other moves will be notified later.
   1 Section B/200 will relieve 1 section C/159 3rd Division at J.35.b.4.2 (2 gun position) or J.36.a.8.2 (4 gun position).
   1 Section A/200 will move into the position vacated by the section of B/200 mentioned above.

3. Ammunition will be left in the position to be taken over by the incoming unit, when the relief of the whole unit is complete.
   Amounts taken and handed over will be reported to this office by 9 a.m. on the day following completion of relief.
   Further orders regarding the supply of ammunition will be issued in due course.

4. Camouflage in use will be left standing on the position. All camouflage not in use will be taken by the unit and handed over to the C/159.

5. B/200 will continue to find the Brigade and R.T. Liaison Officers tonight 20/21st inst.
   C/200 will find the R.O.C. party until further orders, commencing tonight 20/21st inst.

6. All maps and documents will be handed over to the incoming unit on relief.

7. Communications will be left standing in all cases.

8. B210 after completion of relief will come under the orders of OC. 40th Bde R.F.A. until further orders.

9. Completion of relief will be notified to this office by code word "DUCK".

10. ACKNOWLEDGE.

Issued by orderly at

C.G. Duff Lieut. Adjt.
210th Bde R.F.A.

Copy No 1 — 58th D.A.
2 — 145 Inf. Bde
3 — A210
4 — B210
5 — C210
6 — D211 Rt Sec.
7 — D211 Lt Sec.
8 — War Diary
9 — War Diary
10 — File

SECRET

App^t "C"

AMENDMENT to 210TH BDE R.F.A. ORDER Nº 12

Para 1. NIGHT 25TH/26TH JULY

Delete "Remainder" and insert "one section"
after "J.3.4.a.0.6." add "Remaining two
guns will cover the front from the present
position in HAVRINCOURT WOOD"

E. S. Duff Lieut Adjt.
210TH Bde R.F.A.

23-7-14

Distribution as for
210TH BDE ORDER Nº 12

210th Bde R.F.A. Order No. 12.   Copy No 11.

Ref. Map 20,000   22-7-17
57. N.E. + S.E.

1. In continuation of his Office Order No. — the relief of this Brigade and the taking over of the Right Brigade front of the 3rd Division will be carried out as follows:—

    NIGHT 22/23rd JULY

    Remainder of B/210 will move to the position vacated by 6th Battery, 3rd Division.
    Remainder of A/211 will move to the position vacated by B/210. The above moves will not take place until 11.30 p.m. tonight 22nd inst.

    NIGHT 24th/25th JULY

    One section C/210 will move to the position vacated by 23rd Bty at J.34 a 0.6
    Left Section D/211 will move to the position vacated by the 130 Bty at J.35 a 4.2

    NIGHT 25th/26th JULY

    Remainder of C/210 will move to J.34 a 0.6

2. At 5 p.m. 24th inst, A/210, which remains in its present position will come under the orders of the 3rd Div. Artillery.
    At 5 p.m. 24th inst, O.C. B/211 A/RFA will assume command of the remaining batteries of this Group, pending their move to the new position.
    The hour at which Lt. Col. A. BIRTWISTLE, C.M.G. assumes command of the Right Group, 3rd Division, will be notified in due course, until which time units or portions of units which have moved into the 3rd Divisional area, will come under the orders of the O.C. 40th Bde. R.F.A.
    The composite 4.5" How. Bty, composed of 1 section 130 Bty and Left Section D/211 will come under the Command of O.C.

Left Section D.211.

4. Units will continue to draw ammunition from the 58th Div. A.R.P. at RUYAULCOURT, which will also be used by the Section of 130th Bty attached to D211 Left Section, who will be responsible for the supply of ammunition.

O.C. D.211 Left Section will take on charge all ammunition at the present 130 Bty position as from 9 a.m. 25th inst. All ammunition left by D211 Left Section on present position will be removed by 42nd D.A.C, who will also remove all ammunition left on the present position of C.210.

The usual ammunition returns will continue to be rendered to this office, units under 40 Bde R.F.A. also sending a copy of their returns to that copy H.Q.

5. Units will continue to draw rations & forage as usual.

6. Units whose present positions will remain unoccupied after the move will return their artillery boards to this office.

7. 210th Bde H.Q. will remain in present position pending the construction of new Headquarters.

8. ACKNOWLEDGE.

Issued by orderly at

C.G. Duff Lieut. Adjt.
210 Bde R.F.A.

Copy No 1 - 58th D.A.
       2 - 175 Inf. Bde
       3 - 42nd D.A.
       4 - A 210
       5 - B 210
       6 - C 210
       7 - D 211 Rt Section
       8 - D 211 Lt Section

CONFIDENTIAL.

WAR DIARY.

of

"D" Battery, 210th Bde R.F.A.

From 1-7-17 to 31-7-17

Vol. II.

Army Form C. 2118.

WAR DIARY
or
INTELLIGENCE SUMMARY.
(Erase heading not required.)

Instructions regarding War Diaries and Intelligence Summaries are contained in F. S. Regs., Part II. and the Staff Manual respectively. Title pages will be prepared in manuscript.

Place	Date	Hour	Summary of Events and Information	Remarks and references to Appendices
RONSSOY F14 D 8½ 8	1914 July 1st		Receives orders to support raid on COLOGNE FARM by fire on COLOGNE FARMS and NW quadt of G1A. Rate of fire 5 rounds per min. per minute from Zero -4 to Zero + 2 and 1 round per three per minute from Zero + 2 to Zero + 7 mins	References are to 62c NE & 62B NW FRANCE 1/20000
		from 7c 8.30	Fired at QUENNEMONT FARM 3 rds	
			" COPSE in A26 B 4 "	
			" TRIANGLE WOOD in F30c 3 "	
			" FACTORY in G1 B 2 "	
			" MALAKOFF 2 "	
			" COLOGNE FARMS 4 "	
			Day wet cold and stormy	
			Corporal 4/15328 Bowes, WJ went W. from Furlough.	
	2nd	12.57 pm to 1.2 1.2 " 2.0	Fired on COLOGNE FARMS in support of raid } Fired 334 rounds	
			" " " " NW quadt of G1A " " " " " "	

Departures:- 4/15324 Gnr LIDDELL CR 4/15214 Gnr McKEOWN J 4/15276 Gnr McCLEARY WH } on
4/15333 Gnr MOFFETT EA } Furlough
4/15314 Gnr MASON CS

WAR DIARY
or
INTELLIGENCE SUMMARY.
(Erase heading not required.)

Army Form C. 2118.

Instructions regarding War Diaries and Intelligence Summaries are contained in F. S. Regs., Part II. and the Staff Manual respectively. Title pages will be prepared in manuscript.

Place	Date	Hour	Summary of Events and Information	Remarks and references to Appendices
RONSSOY WOOD FIVE St & 2½	1917 July 2nd	4 am	Fired at dug outs in A20 c & A20 A 90 — 20 rounds	Maps 62c NE 4 62 B NW FRANCE 1/20000
		4.30	" " " A29 c 8 4½ — 4 rounds	
		5	" junction of trenches A14 A 2.2½ Registration by Balloon 60 rounds	
		5.45	" " "	
		6	" MG position A8 c 2.1 Observation by Balloon 25 rounds	
		7	Day fine but hazy	
	3rd	12.50 pm	Fired at Post L6A 4½ 4. 20 rounds	
			Received orders to support raid on enemy trenches E of GUILLEMONT FARM 2 guns in trench at A13 a 2½ 6½. 1 gun west end of communication trench at A14 A 2 2½ and A13 d 6½ 6½. Zero 12.30 a.m. to cease fire at 12.52 a.m.	
			Day fine and warm but hazy.	
			Received 2 howitzers and 4 ammunition wagons but no equipment for them	

WAR DIARY or INTELLIGENCE SUMMARY

Army Form C. 2118.

Place	Date	Hour	Summary of Events and Information	Remarks and references to Appendices
RONSSOY F14D 6¼ 8 4	July 1917 5	a.m. 12.30	Fired on A13 d 2½ 6½, A14 a 2 2½, A15 d 6½ 6½ in support of raid on GILLEMONT FARM. 3 and 212 rounds	Troops 62 & NE & 62S NW FRANCE 1/20000
		12.52		
		3.10 p.m.	Fired at digging party G1 D1 6½ 7 rounds	
		3.40 p.m.	" " G1 D1 6½ 12 rounds	
		8.10 p.m.	Trench Mortar A8 c 21 10 rounds	
			1. Hospital 715342 Dr ORMSTON T F (Rabies)	
	6	6 a.m. 1.20	On receipt of SOS signal from GILLEMONT FARM fired 131 rounds on Barrage A13 d 3 & 6. 4 8	
			Left Horse - Furlough to U.K - 715235 2nd ARMSTRONG J. 715184 Dr ELLIOT J S. 715318 Dr SMITH T	
			9. Hospital - 715839 Gnr SNOWDON J - accidental injury to finger	
			Arrivals - from Signalling School - 715149 Gnr McCREADY S & 715449 D SINCLAIR J	

Army Form C. 2118.

WAR DIARY
or
INTELLIGENCE SUMMARY.
(Erase heading not required.)

Instructions regarding War Diaries and Intelligence Summaries are contained in F. S. Regs., Part II. and the Staff Manual respectively. Title pages will be prepared in manuscript.

Place	Date	Hour	Summary of Events and Information	Remarks and references to Appendices
RONSSOY WOOD	1919 July 6		General STAVELEY G.O.C. R.A. 35th DIV visits Battery	Maps 62C NE 62B NW FRANCE 1/20000
		1/pm	Fired 10 rounds at Trench Mortar A25 c 4 4	
		4.30 to 6 pm	Registered X30 a 6.6, X30 a 8.9, A16 c 8, 526 c 2.2 with balloon observation fired 34 rounds	
			Arrivals from Furloughs. 415251 Pte. CURRIE W. 715193 E. STRAUGHTON T. 715340 D. CURRIE T.	
	7th	1.10 am	Fired 5.15 rounds at Trench Mortar A8 c 2.1.	
		6 pm	Fired 9th rounds on A25 c 4.5 c. A25 c 6. 7½ and A20 c 2. 5 to A20 c 7.9. Very Conciderant of enemy dugouts in conjunction with 6" How and R.H.A. Battery.	
			Fine Sunny warm day	

Army Form C. 2118.

WAR DIARY
or
INTELLIGENCE SUMMARY.
(Erase heading not required.)

Instructions regarding War Diaries and Intelligence Summaries are contained in F. S. Regs., Part II. and the Staff Manual respectively. Title pages will be prepared in manuscript.

Place	Date	Hour	Summary of Events and Information	Remarks and references to Appendices
RONSSOY WOOD	1919 July 7th	8.5 a.m.	Fired 10 Rounds at Road in AIID retaliation for shelling of GILLEMONT FARM Post Arrival from Hospital 9/15342 Driver ORMSTON T F Departures :- 9/15035 Gunner PARKINSON R and 9/15229 Driver ARMSTRONG W R both on Furlough	Maps 62 C NE & 62 I S NW FRANCE 1/20,000
	8th		General W.H. GREENLY commanding 2nd Cavalry Division visits the Battery and expresses high appreciation of its work whilst attached to the Division	
		10 pm	Fired 10 rounds into trenches in A13 c (retaliation)	
		10.10/p to 10.30/p	Fired 12 rounds at A13 d 5.6 and A13 D 9.9 (retaliation)	
			Received 48 rounds light draught Very hot day.	
	9th	3.35 a.m.	Fired 11 Rounds at the KNOLL (F6 A 60) retaliation	
			Departures to Hospital { 9/15/394 Dr. WYLIE W (Scabies) 9/44616 Dr. ALLEN A (boils)	

WAR DIARY
INTELLIGENCE SUMMARY
(Erase heading not required.)

Army Form C. 2118.

Instructions regarding War Diaries and Intelligence Summaries are contained in F. S. Regs., Part II. and the Staff Manual respectively. Title pages will be prepared in manuscript.

Place	Date	Hour	Summary of Events and Information	Remarks and references to Appendices
Upper Bonssoy	6/17		The 2nd Cavalry Division having spread I/Artillerie are now attached to relieving i.e. 35th Division + 157. Bde R.F.A. Details as – 1 V.K. in furlough 2 other ranks	Maps 62cNE and 62cNW France 1/20000
		11 noon	Fired 7 rounds at QUENNEMONT FARM. A 25. B ¾ 4.	
		1 pm	" 6 " " "	
	12 noon		Transferred to 159 Bde R.F.A. for attachment. At LEMPIRE F 10 C 69 41. Arrivals for furlough 4 other ranks	
	13	12.10 am	S.O.S. message received from 157 Bde R.F.A. Fired in villagisation Ay. Arrondissement broken down in + 30 A + C	
		12.30 am	Orders received from 159 Bde R.F.A. to fire on broken road in + 30 A + C	
		1.25 am	Cease firing ordered. Fired 114 rounds on the S.O.S. message.	
		11.43 am & 12.40 pm	Repulsed DONO Wood	

WAR DIARY or INTELLIGENCE SUMMARY

Army Form C. 2118.

Place	Date	Hour	Summary of Events and Information	Remarks and references to Appendices
ROISSOY	1917 July			Maps 62 C.N.E & 62 13 N.W FRANCE 1/20,000
	13	12.50 pm	Fired on Sunken road in +30 A.	
		1.40 pm	Registered 36 c.9750 to 36 c.9050	
		1.50 pm	Fired 32 rounds Enemy exclusive V.T. O.S.	
			Arrivals :- from U.K. for furlough 50 OR. ranks.	
			Departures :- to U.K. 2 OR. ranks — to hospital 1 OR. rank.	SW
	14	3pm	Registered Tombois trench A.15.d.½.8. (9 rounds)	SW
	15		Departures to U.K. on furlough 30 OR. ranks. Arrivals — from U.K. 1 OR. rank — Gunnery School — 1 OR. rank	SW
	16		Arrivals :- from U.K. furlough 50 OR. ranks — from hospital 1 OR. rank 1 Horse arrives by falling into trench.	SW

WAR DIARY
INTELLIGENCE SUMMARY.
(Erase heading not required.)

Army Form C. 2118.

Place	Date	Hour	Summary of Events and Information	Remarks and references to Appendices
RONSSOY	1917 July 17		Onlinestered for bombardment it was from A.1.b.70.80 to S.26.c.0.1. to neutralise hostile opposed enemy artillery.	Maps 62 C NE & 62 B NW FRANCE 1/20000
		10.50 pm	Bombarded area A.1.b.70.80 to S.26.c.00.10. fired 78 rounds	
		11.6	Arrived from hospital 1 other rank	
			" " " " 5.	
			Casualties — 1st W.K. on leave Lieut T. H. ROBEY.	
	18		Casualties — 1st W.K. on leave. 1 other rank. hospital 1 other rank.	
	19	11.5 am	Fired on BOSQUET FARM X.18.A. and on X.23.D & S.30 41 rounds	
		1 pm	" " Trenches A.1.B.2 & 1 57 rounds.	
		11 pm	Arrived from W.K. furlough — 1 other rank	

Army Form C. 2118.

WAR DIARY
INTELLIGENCE SUMMARY.
(Erase heading not required.)

Instructions regarding War Diaries and Intelligence Summaries are contained in F. S. Regs., Part II. and the Staff Manual respectively. Title pages will be prepared in manuscript.

Place	Date	Hour	Summary of Events and Information	Remarks and references to Appendices
RONSSOY	1917 July 20	am 9.30	fired 15 rounds on VENDHUILE Arrivals - from U.K. (furlough) 3 O.Rs tanks. Departures - to Hospital 1 O.R. rank - to U.K. on leave 8 O.R. ranks/[?] ranks	62 C.M.E and 62 B.N.W FRANCE
	21.			[signature]
	21		Brought up 2 limbers from MARQUAIX and occupied positions at FISC 8797 + FIS A 68.02.	[signature]
	22	am 11.20	fired 15 rds at VENDHUILE Arrivals - from Hospital 1 O.R. rank.	[signature]
	23	5pm	Registered trenches ahead X 30 c + 1 with new section — 27 rounds Arrivals from 42? D.A.C. 1 O.R. rank " " " U.K. (leave) 1 " "	[signature]
	24	pm 5.40	Fired on enemy trenches x 24 c 27 rounds Arrivals: from Furlough 1 O.R. rank Departures to Hospital 1 O.R. rank.	[signature]

WAR DIARY or INTELLIGENCE SUMMARY

Army Form C. 2118.

Place	Date	Hour	Summary of Events and Information	Remarks and references to Appendices
ONSSOY	1917 July 25	9.30 am	Fired on Machine Gun position X3dC 10 70. 42 rounds.	62C NE and 62 13 NW FRANCE 1/40,000 map.
		9.0am	Ronssoy Wood shelled by enemy H.E. 8mm — Batty sustained 3 casualties, Lt. SMALLMAN, Gnr. MAKENZIE and Gnr. RINTON E, slight wounds.	
		1 pm	Demolition:— 15 reported wounded. Lieut H.J. SMALLMAN. Lt W.K. Wilson gutta masks.	
	26	6.20 am	Fired 60 rounds on road in X30 A.O.C. in support of attack against Birdcage Trenches in X30 A.O.O.	
	27	7.14 pm	Arrived — 7/Lieut. R COOKE	
		6.30 pm	Registered X30 A 50 45 } 18 rounds	
		7.30	Fired at X6 A 76 80 }	
	28	12-1 pm	Fired on registered FEA 4586, X6 A 9650 & X6 C 70 70	
		2.30 to 3 pm	" " X3dC10	

Army Form C. 2118.

WAR DIARY
or
INTELLIGENCE SUMMARY.
(Erase heading not required.)

Place	Date	Hour	Summary of Events and Information	Remarks and references to Appendices
RUYSSOY	July 28	4.17 am / 4.15 / 4.30	Fired on X30a 5045, A1B 2040 and S25 6065	MAPS 62cNE and 62BNW FRANCE
		7.	" " F6a 4686 registering with air spt. Also shift rounds to neighbourhood.	
			Batteries – Lieut R.A. Smith & 10Ew march to Vaux	
			Ammunition – 2/Lieut N.F. ADENEY to temporary duty.	
	29	am / 2.45 / 3.30	Fired on X+C10 F6a 4581 X30a 5045 and X30c 6080 / Fired h/20. MANCHESTER REGIMENT on trench in X30A & S25 6065 in support / on trench h/20.	
			Fired 115 rounds on 28, 029', h.j.	
			Departures to U.K. on leave 3 ORs ranks	
			Arrival:– Lieut T.H. ROBEY from U.K. leave.	
	30	12.45 am	Fired 172 rounds at F6a 7030, A1B20, F6c 9650 F6c 4686 & S25 6065 in support of raid h/ 20. Lewis Inradus on trench in F6 A. Lieut H.D. BARCLAY accompanied raid commander	

WAR DIARY
or
INTELLIGENCE SUMMARY.

Army Form C. 2118.

Place	Date	Hour	Summary of Events and Information	Remarks and references to Appendices
ROMSSOY	1917 July 30	P.M 10.15 10.55 11 11.25	fired 40 rounds in hasty barrage at MACQUINCOURT FARM.	Maps 62c NE and 62 R.NW FRANCE 1/20,000
	31		Routine. Capn. KENDALL J to Vaux.	

CONFIDENTIAL

Volume II

War Diary

of

210th Bde. R.F.A.

From 1·8·17
To 31·8·17

Army Form C. 2118.

Ref. Map. 1/20,000
57c NE & SE.

WAR DIARY
or
INTELLIGENCE SUMMARY.

(Erase heading not required.)

Place	Date	Hour	Summary of Events and Information	Remarks and references to Appendices
P4a 6.9	1/8/17		Composition and Distribution of 210th Bde R.F.A. as follows:—	
			H. Qrs. 210th Bde R.F.A. — P4a 6.9	
			A210 — Q7a 1.4 ⎫	
			B210 (4) — J36a 9.2 ⎬ Covering ⅔ 3rd Divisional	
			„ (2) — J35a 9.2 ⎭ Front.	
			C 210 (4) — J34 a 0.6	
			(2) — Q7a 5.1	
			D210 — F14d 9.6 (Ref. 20.000 62.c N.E) under tactical command	
			of 35th Div. only	
			O. O.R. HORSES	
			TOTAL STRENGTH 33 835 708	
			EFFECTIVE STRENGTH 32 825 708	
	11 pm to 1 a.m		A210 and B210 called on several times to silence hostile T.M's in K 26 b. and fired 120 A.X.	HBE

Army Form C. 2118.

Ref. map. 1/20,000
57C N.E. & S.E.

WAR DIARY
or
INTELLIGENCE SUMMARY.
(Erase heading not required.)

Instructions regarding War Diaries and Intelligence Summaries are contained in F.S. Regs., Part II. and the Staff Manual respectively. Title pages will be prepared in manuscript.

Place	Date	Hour	Summary of Events and Information	Remarks and references to Appendices
P4a 6.9	2		13 O.R. returned from leave in U.K.	
			2nd Lieut Anderson R.C. & 2/Lr. Ware V. transferred to 282nd and 342nd Bde R.F.A respectively	
			Left Section D/211, forming half Coy. How. Bty relieved in personnel by 51st Bde R.F.A	H.B.E
	3.		Left X D/211 relieved in personnel by Section D/51 Bde.	
			15 O.R. proceeded on 10 days leave in U.K	
		11.30	A210 & B210 called on to silence T.Ms in K26a.	
		11.40	Also on working parties reported in K14b+d	
	4.	11hr	A210 called on 4 times to silence T.Ms in K26a. Observation bad and front extremely quiet all day.	H.B.E
	5.		210 Bde R.F.A. transferred to 9th Div Area, but positions of units unchanged	H.B.E
			G.O.C R.A IV Corps visited Bde H.Qrs.	
			25 O.R. proceeded on 10 days leave to U.K.	
		10am	A210 and B210 fired 60 Rounds on Sap Heads in K14b+d to prevent working parties	
		1:30 a.m. 9.30pm 3 a.m.	B210 & C210 fired 100 Rounds on HAVRINCOURT- FLESQUIERES ROAD.	H.B.E

Army Form C. 2118.

Ref Chart 1/20,000
57c N.E. + S.E.

WAR DIARY
or
INTELLIGENCE SUMMARY.
(Erase heading not required.)

Instructions regarding War Diaries and Intelligence Summaries are contained in F. S. Regs., Part II. and the Staff Manual respectively. Title pages will be prepared in manuscript.

Place	Date	Hour	Summary of Events and Information	Remarks and references to Appendices
P14a 85.90	6		Lieut C. HACKRELL returned from 10 days leave in U.K.	
			25 O.Rs returned from 10 days leave in U.K.	
		10 am	A210 fired 36 Rounds and Compt How Bty 10 Rounds to silence T.M.s in K26a and	
		11.15	on Gate K27)C2.8 Road Junction K29c6.7.	
		12.55am	Slow Bombardment by all guns on Cross Roads HAVRINCOURT K29b 75.35	J.H.B.E.
		1.15am	" " " " Road Junction K29b05.20.	
		1.20	A210 + B210 fired 60 Rounds to prevent working parties in K14b + d.	
	7		60 Rs returned from 10 days leave in U.K.	
		6am	Slow bombardment on K29b05.20.	
		11.15	A210 + B210 fired 60 Rounds to prevent working parties in K14b + d.	J.H.B.E.
	8.		10 O.Rs proceeded on 10 days leave to U.K.	
			3 O.Rs returned from 10 days leave in U.K.	
		11am	A210 called on to retaliate on T.M. in K26a.	
		5am	Concentration on K16d.85.50	
		During night	A210 + C210 fired 200 Rounds on Roads in K29 a.4.c. + K20d.	J.H.B.E.
		11.30pm	A + B210 fired 60 Rounds to prevent working parties in K14b + d.	

Army Form C. 2118.

WAR DIARY
or
INTELLIGENCE SUMMARY.
(Erase heading not required.)

Ref Map 20000
57 c N.E + S.E.
4

Place	Date	Hour	Summary of Events and Information	Remarks and references to Appendices
P40.85.90	9.		3 O.Rs returned from 10 days leave in U.K.	
			No 700337 Cpl. GEE. C and No. 700371 Bdr PATE W granted chilling Medal for conspicuous bravery in putting out burning camouflage under shell fire	H.B.E.
			One gun of C210 pulled out & taken to O.Workshops for slight repairs.	
		11pm to 3am	Prepared to put down 10 minutes slow bombardment on K14 & K20 in support of gas cloud, but did not fire owing to change of wind.	
	10.		Lieut. H.B. STOKER and 9 O.Rs proceeded on 10 days leave to U.K.	
			2 O.Rs returned from leave in U.K.	
			1 18 pdr B210 returned from Ord Works & put in action	
		10.20 am	Short bombardment of cross Roads & tracks K15 & K5.2	
		11pm to 1am	Prepared to cooperate with gas cloud - did not materialise for reasons of wind	H.B.E.
	11.		Very wet, but quiet for a week	
			Major R. YATES A210 & Lieut R.L.C. LOWCOCK C210 & 6 O.Rs returned from leave in U.K.	
			Capt. J. x S. CARUS A210 proceeded to B Co course at HAUTEOQUE near ST POL	
		10.30 am	A210 fired 18 rounds on being called to silence hostile T.M's K26.6 on K14 & Yd to prevent working parties	H.B.E.
		10.30 pm	A200 & B210 fired 60 Rounds on K14 & Yd	

Army Form C. 2118.

Ref 1/6 of 1/20,000
57C NE & S.E

WAR DIARY
or
INTELLIGENCE SUMMARY.
(Erase heading not required.)

Place	Date	Hour	Summary of Events and Information	Remarks and references to Appendices
PHQ 85.95	12		6 O.Rs. proceeded on 10 days leave to U.K. 11 O.Rs. returned from 10 days leave in U.K.	CRA
do	13/8/17	8am to 9am	B210 position shelled with 150 rounds. Two casualties caused.	
do		11pm	Fired burst on road junction K27 d 4.7.	
			1 gun C210 returned from Ordnance	
do	14/8/17		Lt. C. G.D. DUFF. H.Q. Returned from 10 days leave in U.K. Lt. C. H. COOPER. C210 2/Lt A. AINSWORTH. HQ. } and 7 O.R. proceeded on 10 days leave to U.K	CRA
		6am	B210 fired a burst on converging tracks N9 c 95.55.	CRA
		During the night	400 A. & A.X. fired on roads and tracks in K28 a, c & d. 150 B.X. fired on K28 d 1.0.	CRA
do	15/8/17	12.30 am	27 Inf. Bde discharged gas. 210 438 R.F.A. fired for 10 minutes in support	
		4 am	One minute burst on VESUVIUS, K27 c 2.8.	
		10pm	Two minute burst on Sap K8d 95.25 to K9c 00.15	
		11.30 pm	" " " Road K9 d 55.20 to K9 d 55.40.	CRA

WAR DIARY
OR
INTELLIGENCE SUMMARY.
(Erase heading not required.)

Army Form C. 2118.

Ref.e Map 1/20.000
57c N.E. and S.E.

6

Place	Date	Hour	Summary of Events and Information	Remarks and references to Appendices
Pt a 85.81.16	16/8/17	9pm to 9.5pm	Searched out WIGAN COPSE – BELLEVUE TRENCH area. Composite Hows. road B.C.B.R.	C.R.S.
			Our gun A210 sent to endeavour. Our gun from detailed position of C210 placed in A210 position	
do	17/8/17	1.45am to 1.50 am	Searched out WIGAN COPSE – BELLEVUE TRENCH area. Composite Hows. road B.C.B.R.	C.R.S.
		9.15 pm	One minute bombardment as above	
			Our gun C210 blown up by premature.	
do	18/8/17	10.55 pm	26th Inf Bde raided Quarry on YORKSHIRE BANK at K32 c 3.9, Eastern edge of YORKSHIRE BANK and DEAN COPSE. 210 Bde R.F.A. fired in support of raiding party. One prisoner was captured and many casualties caused. Enemy artillery shelled his own trenches after the raid.	C.R.S.
		9am	A raid on the enemy sap at K14 b.1.2 had to be abandoned owing to presence of enemy post at road junction K14 b 0.5. 5.5.	e.R.S.
			1 O.R. Proceeded in 10 days leave to U.K.	

Army Form C. 2118.

Refs Map 1/20,000
57c N.E. & S.E.

WAR DIARY
or
INTELLIGENCE SUMMARY.
(Erase heading not required.)

Instructions regarding War Diaries and Intelligence Summaries are contained in F. S. Regs., Part II. and the Staff Manual respectively. Title pages will be prepared in manuscript.

Place	Date	Hour	Summary of Events and Information	Remarks and references to Appendices
ROTAUCOURT	19/8/17	—	210th Bde R.F.A. relieved by one battery 50th Bde R.F.A. and one battery 293rd Bde R.F.A. Brigade relieved & began journ. HQ. to RUTAUCOURT and remainder to BUS.	CSJ
BUS	20/8/17	10 a.m.	Hdqrs moved to BUS. All guns of Brigade sent to I.O.M. BAPAUME for overhaul. D210 moved by road route from HARAUUX to BAPAUME. 3 O.R. proceeded on 10 days leave to U.K.	CSJ
BUS	21/8/17		Major J.C. BROWNING. D.S.O. C210 proceeded to 41st Stationary Hospital for Heart treatment.	CSJ
BUS	23/8/17		B210. 400337. Cpl. GEE.E.C. awarded bar to Military Medal for gallantry during bombardment of battery position on 13th inst. B210 400139. Gr ARMITSTEAD. W. awarded M.M. for gallantry during bombardment of battery position on 13th inst.	CSJ
			H.O.R. proceeded on 10 days leave to U.K.	
BUS	24/8/17		2/Lt. R. COOKE. D210 and 1 O.R. proceeded on 10 days leave to U.K.	CSJ

WAR DIARY
or
INTELLIGENCE SUMMARY.
(Erase heading not required.)

Army Form C. 2118.

Ref: Maps 1/20,000 { 28 SE, 28 NE, 28 NW } France and Part of Belgium

Place	Date	Hour	Summary of Events and Information	Remarks and references to Appendices
	25/8/17 & 26/8/17		210th Bde RFA proceeded by train from BAPAUME to PROVEN.	
	26/8/17		Lt C. HARTLEY C 210 } returned from Artillery Course at VAUX. Lt R.A. SMITH D 210 } Lt H.B. STOKER B 210 } Lt G.H. COOPER C 210 } Returned from 10 days leave in U.K. 2/Lt J.A. AINSWORTH H.B.T.	
PROVEN	26/8/17		210th Bde RFA detrained at PROVEN and marched into camp at WATOU. Capt. F.X.S. CARUS, A 210 Returned from B.E.F. course at ST POL. Lt C.R. proceeded on 10 days leave to U.K.	C.99
	27/8/17		210th Bde RFA, proceeded by march route to temporary wagon lines in the vicinity of H 7c	C.99
	28/8/17		One section A 210 relieved one section A 70 at I 3 d 45.75 " " B 210 " " B 70 " I 3 d 45.80 " " C 210 " " C 70 " I 3 a 50.10 " " D 210 " " D 70 " I 3 d 80.40 A 210 Capt. F.X.S. CARUS A 210 slightly wounded A 210 700236 D. PARKINSON, J. severely wounded.	C.99

Army Form C. 2118.

WAR DIARY
or
INTELLIGENCE SUMMARY.
(Erase heading not required.)

Ref: Map 1/20,000
28 SE ⎫ France &
28 NE ⎬
28 NW ⎭ part of Belgium

Place	Date	Hour	Summary of Events and Information	Remarks and references to Appendices
I8d1.8	29/8		210th Bde R.F.A. H.Q. relieved 50th Bde H.Q. at I8d1.8 (Ramparts at YPRES)	
			Remainder of A210 relieved remainder of A70	
			" " B210 " " B70	
			" " C210 " " C70	
			" " D210 " " D70	
			90th Bde R.F.A. came under command of 91st Regt. Art. Group, 15th D.A.	
			A210 104799 G/Teale G. wounded	
			B210 405189 Dr Worsley. S. Severely wounded	CRB
I8d1.8	30/8	9 p.m.	S.O.S. Sent up by Division on our Right. Brigade co-operated for 5 minutes.	CRB
I8d1.8	31/8	4.20 a.m.	S.O.S. Sent up and barrage put down	
		4 p.m. to 6 p.m.	D210 heavily shelled. Carriage of gun no 2099, D210 rendered unserviceable by direct hit from 5.9" How	
			D210 Lt H.B.Barclay. wounded	CRB

Army Form C. 2118.

WAR DIARY
or
INTELLIGENCE SUMMARY.
(Erase heading not required.)

Refer Map 1/20,000 France and
20 S.E. part of Belgium
28 N.E.
28 N.W.

Place	Date	Hour	Summary of Events and Information	Remarks and references to Appendices
	31/8/17		Composition and distribution of 210th Bde R.F.A. as follows:—	10
			H.Q. 18 d 1.8	
			A 210 13 d 45.75	
			B 210 13 d 45.80 } In Right Sub Group 42nd Division.	
			C 210 13 a 50.10	
			D 210 13 d 80.40	
			Officers. O.R. Horses	
			TOTAL STRENGTH 39 806 665	
			EFFECTIVE STRENGTH 32 495 665	
			DRAFTS received Nil	
			War diary of D 210 for period during which that unit was detached is enclosed herewith.	C.S.S.

A. Birtwistle, Lt Col
Commdg 210th Bde R.F.A

Confidential

War Diary

of

D 210 RFA

August 1st 1917 to August 26th 1917

Secret   210th Bde Order No 25
                          Copy No. 8
                    Lt Col H.B. Powell CRA 40g
                                    28-8-17

1. Relief of remaining Batteries
of each Brigade to be carried out as
follows
(a) 70th Bde will furnish gun teams
[illegible] to 210th Wagon Lines at
5 p.m tomorrow 29th inst. Batteries
will have transport limbers etc
in readiness to move at this time
As limits Wagons will not be taken
(b) Command of batteries will pass
over on completion of relief

2. Ammunition will be taken over at
12 noon tomorrow 29th inst, a
return of amounts taken over
furnished to this office.

3. 210th Signal Subsection will
proceed by march route to XPO
at 9 a.m on the 29th inst
A210, B210 & C210 will each
supply one G.S. Wagon and the

to report at 8.0am to Bde
Office.

4. Each battery will detail one
Officer and 2 O.R. to report to
Lieut S.W./500 at 10 am
tomorrow 29th inst to proceed
to new wagon line and take
over equipment

5. The Wagon Line of the 20th Bde
RFA will be moved from
present position to position now
occupied by the 70th Bde at
G 17 b 8.7 on 30th inst. Parade
at 11 am 30th inst DAC will
furnish transport as follows
H'dqrs — 1 G.S. Wagon
A 210 — 2 G.S Wagons
B 210 — do —
C 210 — do —
D 210 — do —

6 Ten tents and all trench
shelters drawn on arrival at
present position will be
returned to Bde Office by 9am

on the 30th inst. These will be returned to O.O. Corps Troops, Poperinghe, DAC providing transport.

7. Hdqrs 310th Bde RFA will close at present position at 9 a.m. on the 29th inst, and reopen at YPRES at I8d.18 at 12 noon on same day.

8. ACKNOWLEDGE

[signature]
Lieut
For Adjutant
310th Bde RFA

Issued by O.C. by
at

Copy No 1 OC A 210
       2   B 210
       3   C 210
       4   D 210
       5   War Diary
       6   "   "
       7   File
       8   War Diary

Army Form C. 2118.

WAR DIARY
or
INTELLIGENCE SUMMARY.
(Erase heading not required.)

Place	Date 1917	Hour	Summary of Events and Information	Remarks and references to Appendices
RONSSOY FIELD S.W.8	August 1st	2.45 pm to 3.30 pm	Fired 10 rounds at F6 a A6.86 Quiet and normal. Arrivals: Major R.W. BURNYEAT } instr. attached from B/211 RFA. and Lieutenant Balcombe } 5 ORs from furlough * 1 OR's 15 Horses and 2 Ammunition wagons for Section of DAC attached C Battery	Ref to trenches to 62 C NE and 62 B NW FRANCE 1/20000
	August 2nd	11.20 am	Orders received that from 10 am today D210 would be in a Sub group under command of Lieut Col. STEWART OC 296 Bde RFA. Rained incessantly all day. High wind and cold Arrivals: Major Burnyeat Brown and 2 Chargers from B211 1 OR RAMC.	

WAR DIARY or INTELLIGENCE SUMMARY.

Army Form C. 2118.

Place	Date 1917	Hour	Summary of Events and Information	Remarks and references to Appendices
RONSSOY Fld D 8½.8	August 3rd	10.20 pm	Fired 14 rounds at CROSS ROADS in VENDHUILE	References are to 62cNE and 62BNW FRANCE 1/20000
		10.35 pm	Fired 14 rounds — do — do — do —	
		11.0 pm	Fired 4½ rounds — do — do — do —	
			Arrivals: 5 ORs from furlough in UK	fwd
			Departures: 6 NCOs on furlough to UK	
	August 4th		Arrivals: 1 OR from furlough in UK	fwd
	Aug 5th	11pm to 11.3pm	Fired 30 rounds on TINO TRENCH in X 30 C	fwd
			Arrivals: 4 ORs from furlough in UK	

Army Form C. 2118.

WAR DIARY
or
INTELLIGENCE SUMMARY.
(Erase heading not required.)

Instructions regarding War Diaries and Intelligence Summaries are contained in F. S. Regs., Part II. and the Staff Manual respectively. Title pages will be prepared in manuscript.

Place	Date	Hour	Summary of Events and Information	Remarks and references to Appendices
RONSSOY FWD S2.8	August 1917 6th	3.48 am to 4.10 am	On receipt of S.O.S. message fired 112 rounds on trenches in X30A & X30C and A13D	References on t. 62c NE Sub 62B NW FRANCE 1/20000
		4:10 am		
		12.30 to 12.45	Fired 6 rounds at trench crossing road F6A 9025	
		2.30 to 4.0pm	Fired 25 rounds registering TOMBOIS TRENCHES F6c 9540 & A1D 0075	
		4.0pm to 4.30pm	Fired 8 rounds on trenches in X30C 4855 & X30C 5085.	[signature]
	Aug 7th		Casualties:- 1 Sadr Sergt from B.a.c. 5 ors for furlough in UK	[signature]

Army Form C. 2118.

WAR DIARY
or
INTELLIGENCE SUMMARY.
(Erase heading not required.)

Instructions regarding War Diaries and Intelligence Summaries are contained in F. S. Regs., Part II. and the Staff Manual respectively. Title pages will be prepared in manuscript.

Place	Date	Hour	Summary of Events and Information	Remarks and references to Appendices
RONSSOY F14D 8 & 8	August 1917 August 8	2.15pm to	Fired 24 rounds on CROSS ROADS in F6A 4656 and French crossing road in F6.9	References See C. 62C NE and 62D NW FRANCE 1/20000
		3.22pm	Arrivals — 3 ORs from Furlough in UK Departures — 4 ORs on Furlough to UK 3 ORs to Hospital.	
	August 9	12.0 am to 12.5 am	Fired 40 rounds on trenches in X24A.	
		3 am		
		3.54 am	Fired 44 rounds on road in X14B. SW of LESTRANCHEES	
		4.15 pm	Fired 4 rounds on TINO TRENCH F6a 4686	
		10.50pm	Fired 23 rounds on trenches in A14A	
			Few but dull Thunderstorm in afternoon	
			Arrivals — 3 ORs from Furlough in UK	
			Departures — 2 ORs on Furlough to UK	

WAR DIARY
or
INTELLIGENCE SUMMARY.
(Erase heading not required.)

Army Form C. 2118.

Place	Date	Hour	Summary of Events and Information	Remarks and references to Appendices
RONSSOY F14.D 8.7.8	August 10th	4 am	Fired 30 rounds Gas Shell (BTS) into VENDHUILE	Reference are to 62.c NE and 62.B NW FRANCE 1/20000
		3.30pm & 5.20pm	Registered A76 H6 (2 hours) and A76 94 (1 hour). Fired 24 rounds	
			Arrivals – 2 OR's from Hospital. Fine windy day.	
	August 11th	10.40 am & 11.5	Fired 10 rounds on F6A 4686	
		1 pm & 2.15pm	Fired 15 rounds on A7B 6540 and F6(A) 93.	
		4.5pm	Fired 21 rounds at R9.S of Open S9.c obtaining direct hits	
			Fine hot dull day.	

Army Form C. 2118.

WAR DIARY
or
INTELLIGENCE SUMMARY.
(Erase heading not required.)

Instructions regarding War Diaries and Intelligence Summaries are contained in F. S. Regs., Part II. and the Staff Manual respectively. Title pages will be prepared in manuscript.

Place	Date 1918	Hour	Summary of Events and Information	Remarks and references to Appendices
RONSSOY WOOD	Aug 12	from 12.5	Fired at Pleo 4686 Two Rounds	References map G 62 C NE 62 B NW FRANCE 1/20000
		1.14	" do do	
		3.6	Fired at trench X 30 A 5800 & X 30 A 5230	
		3.54	Balloon observation	
		4.5		
		5.18	Registered WEST MACQUINCOURT TRENCH (E of KNOLL) Balloon observation	
		6.29		
		6	Fired at OP in S.21.C.	M
		7.3		
			Expended 59 rounds	
			Arrivals: 1 O.R. from leave in U.K.	
			Departures: 2 O.R.s to Hospital	
	Aug 13	10 hrs		
		10.25	Fired at VENDHUILE 52 rounds	
		10.40		
			Departures 1 O.R. to Hospital	al

A 5834 Wt. W4973/M687 750,000 8/16 D. D. & L. Ltd. Forms/C.2118/13.

WAR DIARY
or
INTELLIGENCE SUMMARY.

(Erase heading not required.)

Army Form C. 2118.

Instructions regarding War Diaries and Intelligence Summaries are contained in F. S. Regs., Part II. and the Staff Manual respectively. Title pages will be prepared in manuscript.

Place	Date	Hour	Summary of Events and Information	Remarks and references to Appendices
RANSSOY WOOD	Aug 14/17	from 6.55 to 7.20	Fired at OP in S21C and on TINO trench in X30 A & C } 53 rounds	References Sheet 62 C NE and 62 B NW FRANCE 1/20000
		9.30 to 9.52	Fired at KNOB WOOD	
			Retaliation – 3 OPs on Evan & UK	
	Aug 15		Defensive – 1 OP on Laban & UK. Ammunition – 1 OP fired on in UK.	
	Aug 16	10am	Fired at OP AID 2.7	
		10.30am	" – Trench FLAM 79 } 25 rounds TOMBEE trench	

WAR DIARY
or
INTELLIGENCE SUMMARY.

(Erase heading not required.)

Army Form C. 2118.

Place	Date 1916	Hour	Summary of Events and Information	Remarks and references to Appendices
BONSSOY WOOD	Aug 17	10 am	Recce at OP A7 B 36	References to LACNE and 62dNW FRANCE 1:20,000
		12.15 pm	" " 52 C	
		2.30 pm	" " A1 D 3.4	} 125 rounds
		6.30 pm	" " 52 D C 14.4	
	Aug 19	6.30 am	Gas Shell bomb. FLA 41, 7 & 6, Y 30 & 4.5 2.2	In support of attack by 35th Division on the KNOLL & GILLEMONT FARM
		8.c		
		11 am	" " do " do "	} 300 rounds
		& 4 pm		
			Defensive. 1 OR to hospital, 1 OR sickness L.U.K	
			Casualties: 1 Sergt from Base, 9 OR's from Base with U.K.	

Army Form C. 2118.

WAR DIARY
or
INTELLIGENCE SUMMARY.
(Erase heading not required.)

Instructions regarding War Diaries and Intelligence Summaries are contained in F.S. Regs., Part II. and the Staff Manual respectively. Title pages will be prepared in manuscript.

Place	Date 1918	Hour	Summary of Events and Information	Remarks and references to Appendices
LONSSOY WOOD	Aug 19	4 a.m.	Sent 8 17 mule teams on point of KNOLL to meet convoys of attacking Battalions	References 62C NE and 62B NW FRANCE 1/20000
		4 a.m.	Sent at junction of roads in A.I.D. and ½ E WEST MACQUINCOURT roads	
		6 p.m.		
		6 p.m.	Orders received to proceed to wagon line tonight and march to BAPAUME tomorrow	
		8.30 p.m.	Sent on roads in A.I.D. and W MACQUINCOURT roads on return to wagon line on KNOLL by convoy	
		11.45 p.m.	Sent on VENDHUILE Expended 1130 rounds today	
	Aug 20	12.50 a.m.	R.W.S. met & taken and marked to join L.A. at MARQUAIS	
		2.30 a.m.		
		9.30 a.m.	March to BAPAUME	
BAPAUME		5 p.m.	Arrived at BAPAUME and left to Headqrs Section & 142 DAC Battn Section & 142 DAC	
			Returning — 1 OR to Hospital	

A5834 Wt. W4973/M687 750,000 8/16 D. D. & L. Ltd. Form/C.2118/13.

Army Form C. 2118.

WAR DIARY
or
INTELLIGENCE SUMMARY.

(Erase heading not required.)

Instructions regarding War Diaries and Intelligence Summaries are contained in F. S. Regs., Part II. and the Staff Manual respectively. Title pages will be prepared in manuscript.

Place	Date 1917	Hour	Summary of Events and Information	Remarks and references to Appendices
Bertrancourt	Aug 21		NIL	AM
	Aug 22		NIL	AM
	Aug 23		Arrivals :- 1 OR from Hospital. Departures :- 2/Lieut R. COOKE on leave to U.K.	AM
	Aug 24		Artillery received instructions that BAPAUME at 5:45 am on 26th inst Arrivals :- Capt K. HIGHTON. 2 ORs and 2 Chargers from D2.11 Departures :- MAJOR KINDERSLEY & 2 ORs and 2 Chargers to B211 1 OR to Hospital.	AM
	Aug 25		Arrivals :- LIEUT R.A. SMITH and 1 OR from Army School VAUX 2 ORs from Hospital. 5 ORs from leave in U.K. 1 horse cast (C.C.D.)	AM

A5834 Wt. W4973/M687 730,000 8/16 D. D. & L. Ltd. Forms/C.2118/13.

Army Form C. 2118.

WAR DIARY
or
INTELLIGENCE SUMMARY.
(Erase heading not required.)

Place	Date	Hour	Summary of Events and Information	Remarks and references to Appendices
BAPAUME	Aug 26 1914	4.30am	Left BAPAUME by train	

for OC D210 RFA

SECRET   Copy No. 9

210TH. BDE. R.F.A. ORDER No. 17

Ref. Map 1/10,000
HAVRINCOURT
part of 57c N.E.

1. 12th. Royal Scots will carry out a daylight raid on enemy sap head at K14b 1·2 tomorrow 18th. inst.

2. In support of above this Group will fire as under:—

   AT ZERO - 3, ZERO - 1½ AND ZERO.

   B210 (5) 1 salvo shrapnel on M.G. at K14b. 1·2
   C210 (4) 1   "   "   " saphead at K8d. 7·2

   ZERO + ½ to ZERO + 12

   A210 ⎰ (3) M.G. at K14b. 95·00
        ⎱ (3) M.G. at K14b. 9·4.
   B210 ⎰ (3) M.G. at K14d. 45·65
        ⎱ (2) M.G. at K20a. 6·0
   C210 ⎰ (2) T.M. at K8d. 7·2
        ⎨ (1) M.G. at K8d. 65·85
        ⎩ (1) O.P. at K8b. 30·05
   Comp. ⎰ 1 How. - O.P. at K8b 30·05
   Howzr ⎱ 2 " - T.M. at K8d 7·2
   Bty.

3. **RATE OF FIRE** - 18 pdr. 3 rds. per gun per minute shrapnel.
                    4·5" Howrs. 2 rds. per how per minute

4. **ZERO HOUR** Zero hour will be at 9 a.m. 18th. inst.

5. Watches will be synchronized by telephone from this office at 8 a.m.

6. ACKNOWLEDGE by code word "MILL"

Issued by Orderly
at 12 noon   C.J. Duff
17.8.17   LIEUT.
                                  ADJT. 210TH. BDE. R.F.A.

210TH. BDE. R.F.A.
———— ORDER NO. 14

Distribution:-

Copy No. 1   27TH. INF. BDE.
       2   9TH. DIV. ARTY
       3   12TH. R. SCOTS
       4   A 210
       5   B 210
       6   C 210
       7   Comp. How. Bty.
       8   War Diary ✓
       9   do.   ✓
      10   F.W.

SECRET   Copy No. 9

210TH. BDE. R.F.A. ORDER No. 18.

Ref. Map 1/20,000   August 18th. 1917
57c N.E.

1. The 26th. Infy. Bde. will carry out a raid on the Quarry in YORKSHIRE BANK at K32b 3.9, Eastern edge of YORKSHIRE BANK & DEAN COPSE tonight 18/19th. inst.

2. In support of above this Group will fire as under:—

A 210		K26d 0.4 to K26d 5.4	
B 210	(2)	K26d 8.4 – K27c 0.4	
C 210	(4)	K26d 5.4 – K26d. 8.4	
Con. How. Bty.	{ 3 Hows. – Trench K26d 3.9 to VESUVIUS K27c 20.75		

3.   AMMUNITION & RATES OF FIRE

(a) 18 pdrs.   ZERO to ZERO + 1

First half-minute 4 rounds smoke shell per gun, second half-minute 2 rounds per gun shrapnel or H.E.

ZERO + 1 to ZERO + 30

One round smoke shell and 2 rds. per gun per minute shrapnel or H.E. A 210 will fire H.E. B 210 & C 210 will fire shrapnel.

(b) 4.5" Hows. ZERO to ZERO + 30

2 rounds per how. per minute, one round of gas and one round of H.E.

4. The Composite How. Bty. will not fire gas shell unless the wind is West or S.W. In the event of wind being unfavourable BX will be fired instead of gas shell.

5. 18 pdr. Batteries will not fire smoke shell unless the wind is West, S.W., or South. In the event of the wind being unfavourable, A 210 will fire H.E. & B 210 & C 210 will fire shrapnel instead of smoke shell.

6. 42nd. Div. T.Ms. will co-operate as follows:-

ZERO to ZERO + 25

2 - 2" T.Ms. on area enclosed by East bank of Canal from Railway Bridge to point K26 b 2.5, and a line 60" further East and parallel to Canal.

RATE OF FIRE   ZERO to ZERO + 25

One round per T.M. per minute.

7. ZERO HOUR will be at 10.55 p.m. tonight 18th inst.

8   Watches will be synchronised by telephone from this office at 9.30 p.m.

9   ACKNOWLEDGE by code word "FISH."

Issued by Orderly
at 1.30 p.m.

C.G. Duff
LIEUT.
ADJT. 210TH. BDE. R.F.A.

Copy No. 1 – 9th. Div. Arty.
      2 – 27th. Inf. Bde.
      3 – 11th. Royal Scots
      4 – A 210
      5 – B 210
      6 – C 210
      7 – Comp. How. Bty.
      8 – War Diary
      9 – War Diary ✓
     10 – File.
     11 – D.T.M.O. 42nd Div.

SECRET.   COPY No. 8

210TH. BDE. R.F.A. ORDER. No 19.

19.8.17

1. 210th Bde RFA (less D/210) will withdraw to Wagon Lines tonight 19/20 Augt on being relieved by units as under
   (a) 210th Bde RFA. H.Q. will be relieved by 50th Bde R.F.A. H.Q. The command of the Left Group will pass on completion of relief.
   (b) A/210 will be relieved by B/50
   (c) B/210 will not be relieved, but will withdraw to its Wagon Line after dark
   (d) C/210 will be relieved by a battery of the 293rd Bde R.F.A.
   (e) The Composite How. Bty will remain in its present position and will come under the command of 50th Bde R.F.A.

2. (a) Batteries will hand over ammunition to incoming units. B/210 ammunition will be left on the ground under charge of two men. This ammunition will be taken over by 50th Bde. R.F.A. on morning of 20th inst.
   (b) Batteries will report by wire to this office, prior to moving out, the amount of ammunition handed over, or, in the case of B/210, left on the ground.

3. All trench maps, artillery boards etc. will be handed over to incoming units. B/210 will return same to this office

4. All communications will be left standing

-/-

5. One officer and four signallers each of Hqrs, A/210 and C/210 will remain behind for 24 hours after completion of relief to assist incoming units. The officer from A/210 will man the Brigade O.P. tonight. The officer from C/210 will act as Left Liaison Officer tonight. The Right Liaison Officer will, commencing tonight, be provided by the Composite How. Bty.

6. Completion of relief, or in case of B/210, notice of marching out, will be wired to this office by code word "SLIDE". A/210 and C/210 will not pull out from their positions until the arrival of the relieving units on the ground.

7. Ten G.S. Wagons and teams from the 42nd D.A.C. will report at Bde. Wagon Lines at BUS at 4.30 p.m. today, 19th inst., and will be allotted as follows:

   Hqrs 210 – 1.   A/210 – 3
   B/210 – 3   C/210 – 3

   Units will send guides and the wagons will be distributed under the instructions of O.C. Wagon Line.

8. Trench Shelters, Tarpaulins, etc. will be taken with units, but all corrugated iron huts, etc. will be left standing.

-2-

9. All guns will be sent to I.O.M, Workshop No. 27 & 31 at BAPAUME, tomorrow 20th inst, for overhaul.

Staff Sgt. Fitter Allan, all Battery fitters, and one limber gunner per gun will accompany the guns to the Workshop.

10. It is expected that the Brigade will remain at the Wagon Lines until 25th inst.

The work of completing equipment, checking of stores and cleaning of all equipment is most important and must be pressed forward with all speed.

11. Hqrs. 210th Bde R.F.A. will be at Hq. Wagon Lines, RUYAULCOURT tonight and will move to BUS tomorrow 20th inst.

12. ACKNOWLEDGE.

Lieut & Adjt
210th Bde R.F.A.

Issued by orderly at- 6.30 pm

Copy No 1 — 9th Div Arty.
       2 — 42nd Div. Arty.
       3 — 2/13 Inf. Bde
       4 — A/210
       5 — B/210
       6 — C/210
       7 — Comp How Bty.
       8 — War Diary ✓
       9 — War Diary
      10 — File.

SECRET   Copy No. 10.

210TH Bde. R.F.A. ORDER No. 20.

24-8-17

1. 210TH Bde R.F.A. will entrain at BAPAUME on 25th and 26th inst, in accordance with 42nd D.A. Order No 16 and attached table.

2. Units except D/210 will move to BAPAUME by march route independently via BARASTRE and HAPLINCOURT, starting at the following times

+ H.Q. 210th Bde R.F.A — 5.45 p.m. 25th inst
+ A/210 — 2.45 p.m. 25th inst
+ B/210 — 8.45 p.m. 25th inst
+ C/210 — 11.30 p.m. 25th inst.

+ With troops mentioned in attached 42nd D.A. Order No 16.

Starting point in each case will be the cross roads in BUS

D/210 will move under battery arrangements to be at BAPAUME Station at 5.45 a.m. 26th inst.

3. Capt. A. G. HALL, B/210, will act as entraining officer in accordance with para 3 of attached order, and will be on duty from 6.45 p.m. 25th inst.

4. O.C. D/210 will detail two N.C.O.s as traffic controls in accordance with para 4 of attached order.

5. The following officers are detailed as O.C. Trains.

O.C. No 1 Train — Major R. Yates A/210
"   No 3   "   — Lt.Col. A. Birtwistle. C.M.G. H.Q. 210
"   No 5   "   — Major. N. Birtwistle. B/210
"   No 7   "   — Capt. H. H. Simon C/210
"   No 9   "   — Major. O. J. Mason. D/210

6. Marching Out States will be handed by each unit to Capt. A.G. Hall in accordance with para. 3 of attached order.

7. Reference para 9 of attached, each unit will detail one officer to collect the "clean camp" certificates from the Town Major. These certificates will be handed to the Adjutant on arrival at the destination.

Numbers of tents and trench shelters left on the ground will be notified to the Town Major prior to departure, and a copy sent to this office.

8. Motor lorries, mentioned in para 10 of attached order, are allotted as follows:- one to HQrs, and one to each of A.B.s.o. These units will send guides to collect.

9. All horses will be watered at BAPAUME before entraining. Horses will travel unharnessed and rugged up in the train. Harness will be put in sacks. 4' 9" should be used for breadths as mentioned in para 5 of attached.

10. Guns will be withdrawn from Ordnance BAPAUME on arrival of the unit at BAPAUME, an officer being detailed to supervise the withdrawal.

11. Instructions re rations and forage are contained in para 8. of attached

12. ACKNOWLEDGE.

C.G. Duff
Lieut. Adjt
210th Bde. R.FA

Issued by orderly at 4 p.m.

Copy No 1 ... 42nd D.A.
2 ... A/210
3 — B/210
4 ... C/210
5 ... D/210
6 ... 42 D.A.C.
7 ... 428 Coy. A.S.C.
8 ... Capt. A.G. HALL
9 ... War Diary
10 ... War Diary ✓
11 ... File

SECRET.   Copy No. 4.

210TH. B'DE. R.F.A. ORDER NO. 21.

Ref. Map Belgium
1/40,000 sheets 27 & 28.   27. 8. 17.

Hdqrs.
A 210
B 210
C 210
D 210

1. 210th. Bde. R.F.A. will relieve 40th Bde. R.F.A. on the nights 28/29th. & 29/30th. inst., under the following arrangements:-

2. 210th. Bde. R.F.A. in order of march as per margin, will proceed by march route via WATOU and switch roads to North of POPERINGHE to temporary wagon lines in the vicinity of H y C tomorrow 28th inst.

   Starting point on road by Bde. Hdqrs. facing east.

   Heads of column to pass starting point at 9 am.

3. One mounted officer per bty. will report to Lieut. S. WILSON at Bde. Hdqrs. at 7.30 am. tomorrow 28th inst.

   This party will report to 15th. Div. Arty. to be allotted camping ground and to meet and conduct units to selected sites.

4. One officer and two signallers mounted per bty. will report to Adjutant at Bde. Hdqrs. at 9 a.m. tomorrow, 28th inst.

This party will proceed and be attached to 70th Bde. R.F.A. at I.8.d.1.8. The kits of these officers will be sent up by batteries on arrival at the new wagon lines.

5. The following reliefs will take place on night 28/29th inst.

One section A/10 will relieve one section A/70 at I.3.d.45.75.

One section B/10 will relieve one section B/70 at I.3.d.45.80.

One section C/10 will relieve one section C/70 at I.2.a.5.1.

One section D/10 will relieve one section D/70 at I.3.d.8.4.

This relief will not take place until after midnight.

Remainder of A.B.@ & D/10 will relieve remainder of A.B.@ & D/70 on night 29/30th inst.

6. One officer per Bty. will report to Adjutant 210th Bde. R.F.A. at 70th Bde. H.Q. at I 8 d 1.8 during the afternoon of the 28th inst., to reconnoitre the approach to the battery position.

7. 210th Bde. R.F.A. will take its own guns into action.

8. Tents and trench shelters on present camping grounds will be left standing.

9. Instructions re rations and transport will be issued later.

10. ACKNOWLEDGE.

(Sd) C.G. Duff
Lt. & Adjt.
210th Bde. R.F.A.

Issued by orderly
at 10.30 pm.

Distribution.
Copy No. 1 — O.C. A 210.
2 — " B 210.
3 — " C 210.
4 — " D 210.
5 — R.S.M. Gillon T.
6 — 42nd. D.A.
7 — File.

CONFIDENTIAL

WAR DIARY
of
210th Bde R.F.A.

From 1-9-17
To 30-9-17.

Vol II.

Volume II

War Diary

of

210th Bde R.F.A.

From 1-9-17.
To 30-9-17.

Army Form C. 2118.

WAR DIARY
or
INTELLIGENCE SUMMARY.
(Erase heading not required.)

Ref Maps 1/20.000 20 S.E. } France and
28 N.E. } Belgium.

Place	Date	Hour	Summary of Events and Information	Remarks and references to Appendices
I 8 d 1·8	1/9		Composition and distribution of 210th Bde R.F.A. as follows:-	
			HQ I 8 d 1·8	
			A 210 I 3 d 45·95	
			B 210 I 3 d 45·80 } In Right Lus Group. 42nd Division	
			C 210 I 3 a 50·10	
			D 210 I 3 d 80·40	
			TOTAL STRENGTH Officers O.R. Horses	
			32 806 665	
			EFFECTIVE STRENGTH 32 495 665	
		12.15 a.m.	4·5" How gas concentration on old battery position at D 26 a 15·10.	
		2 am	4·5" How gas concentration on BORRY FARM, D 25 b 60·85	
		5.10 a.m.	S.O.S. sent up and barrage put down. No infantry action	
		10 p.m.	D 210 415210 Dr KENDALL. H. wounded (gas)	
		10 p.m.	C 210 Capt H.H. SIMON severely wounded	
			C 210 LTC HARTLEY killed in action	
		11 p.m.	Capt. A.G. HAM, B 210, temporarily attached to and assumed command of C 210.	C2/9

WAR DIARY
or
INTELLIGENCE SUMMARY

Army Form C. 2118.

Ref. Map 1:20,000
20.S.E.] France and
28 N.E.]
28 N.W.] Belgium.

Place	Date	Hour	Summary of Events and Information	Remarks and references to Appendices
I 8 d 1.8	2/9/17		Two guns of B.210 rendered unserviceable by shell fire and sent to I.O.M.	
			One gun B.210 returned from I.O.M.	Copy
			C.210 - 40562, O/B's SMITH, 9.H killed in action	
I 8 d 1.8	3/9/17	4am	Practice barrage carried out for forthcoming attack on GAPAPORT, IBERIAN, BECK HOUSE, and BORRY FARM.	
		4.50 p.m.	42nd D.A. carried out area shoot	
		6.15 p.m. to 6.30 p.m.	After enemy infantry had sent up many/grenade burst up into 2 red lights. Enemy artillery intensely bombarded our front line in D.19 a + c, D.25 a + c. During this enemy put up 9 golden rain rockets. Enemy fire slackened and his infantry put up more red lights, when heavy again came down heavily. During this second barrage were 9 other rain rockets were sent up. Two enemy aeroplanes at 2000 feet flew up and down our line howling and appeared to be correcting the enemy barrage.	Copy
		6.40p.m and 7.15p.m	D 210 engaged with 3 rds. gun fire two enemy batteries in response to N/F call from aeroplane.	

Capt. H.B. ECCLES, A.210, temporarily attached 42nd D.A. for Intelligence duties.

… WAR DIARY
or
INTELLIGENCE SUMMARY.

Army Form C. 2118.

Refer Map 1/20,000
20 S.E.
28 N.E. } France and
28 N.W. } Belgium

3

Place	Date	Hour	Summary of Events and Information	Remarks and references to Appendices
I8d.1.8	4/9 17	11:30 a.m.	Practice barrage carried out for fresh coming attack on GONNIPOR, IBERIAN, BECK HOUSE and BORRY FARM.	
		11 p.m.	50 rds. R.E.B.R fired into D26a 45.45.	
		11:45 p.m. to 1:45 p.m.	Ramparts and YPRES heavily shelled with "YELLOW CROSS" 9a shell.	
			B21a M01094 Gr. FITZHUGH. H.A. wounded, slight.	
I8d.1.8	5/9 17	4:30 a.m.	D210 fired 50 R.E.B.R. into BREMEN REDOUBT.	
		During morning to I.O.H.	A210 & B210 heavily shelled. One gun A210 damaged and sent	Wounded (9 am)
		4:30 p.m.	Practice barrage carried out for attack on IBERIAN, BECKHOUSE and BORRY FARM.	
			HQ M01048 Dr COWELL A.E.	
			M00366 Dr WATERHOUSE. N.	
			405440 Gr PRICHARD. D.	
			400473 Gr WILDING. S.	
			13488 2/AM CASSERLEY e (R.F.C)	
			598225 2/AM PIERSON T.H. (R.F.C.)	
			441925 Pioneer PINCHES H. (Sgn.)	
			Gr BENTHAM (attached 210)	

WAR DIARY or INTELLIGENCE SUMMARY

Army Form C. 2118.

Reference Maps 1/20,000
S.E. France
N.E. and
N.W. Belgium

Place	Date	Hour	Summary of Events and Information	Remarks and references to Appendices
I 8 d. I. 8	5/9/17		A210 400.156 Cpl. Lt. WALKER F. Slightly wounded 401.056 G. ROTHWELL H. 401.059 G. MERCER A.	
			B210 144706 G. MARSH G.F. slightly wounded	cgp
			C210 40025 a/B. WILTSHIRE A. severely wounded 40.5191 G. BIGGER O. slightly wounded	
			D210 415212 G. CLARK G. slightly wounded.	
I 8 d. I. 8	6/9/17	4.30 a.m.	125 Inf. Bde attacked IBERIAN, BECK HOUSE and BORRY FARM. IBERIAN and BECK HOUSE captured, but unable to capture BORRY FARM. Enemy counter attacks from BREMEN REDOUBT at 11.10 a.m. and 1 p.m. beaten off by our barrage. Counter attack in the afternoon forced our troops to retire from original line with the exception of a small post at D258 25.15 - 35.10. An enemy counter attack at 7.30 p.m. on our line on HILL 35 stopped by our barrage.	cgp
I 8 d. I. 8	9/9/17		A210 208568 D. NICE.T.G. wounded 415359 G. MAXWELL.J. killed in action D210 944301 G. BUOY.N.S. wounded 944627 Dr. PARDOE.J.H. wounded	cgp

WAR DIARY or INTELLIGENCE SUMMARY

Army Form C. 2118.

Ref e Map 1/20,000
20 S.E. } France
28 N.E. } and
28 N.W. } Belgium

Place	Date	Hour	Summary of Events and Information	Remarks and references to Appendices
I 8 d 1.8	8.9.17	9.54pm to 10.4pm	S.O.S. Gas alarm.	
			Hdqrs. Lt. J. WILSON } wounded gas.	
			2/Lt. A. AINSWORTH }	
			A 2.10 696.10 Gr. TILLARD. H. wounded slt.	
I 8 d 1.8	9.9.17	3pm	Lt Col. A. BIRTWISTLE. CMG. assumed command of Centre Sub- Group, command of 86", 210" and 211" Bdes. R.F.A.	e 89
		3.30pm to 5.30pm	D 210 and D 211 heavily shelled with 5.9s.	
			One gun A 210 and one how D 210 returned from I.O.M.	
I 8 d 1.8	10.9.17	4.55 am 6.58 pm	Grant fired on S.O.S. as counterpreparation to enemy barrage.	e 90
			A 210 401843 Sgt. PERKINS. G. } Hospital. Wounded gas.
			400144 Bdr. GANNON. T. }
			401377 Gr. COUPE. J. }
			400215 " HAWORTH E. }
			400288 " SELLERS. H. }

WAR DIARY
INTELLIGENCE SUMMARY

Army Form C. 2118.

Refer Maps: 1/20,000
20 SE } France &
22 NE } Belgium
22 NW }

Place	Date	Hour	Summary of Events and Information	Remarks and references to Appendices
78d.I.8 (continued)	10/7	C.2.10	400006 Pte LAYCOCK. A. 405724 Gt CRITCHLOW. J. 406293 " HORRISON. F. 405425 " FLETCHER. T. } Hospital wounded (gas)	6
	11/7		Two practice Barrages carried out during the day All gun positions heavily shelled with gas shell.	
		A.2.10	405434 Gt COXBURN. G.A. 400118 L/Sgt LEE. J. 400423 Sgt FITZPATRICK. D. 401345 Gt TURNER. J. } killed in action (gas) } wounded (gas)	
		B.2.10	184001 Gt EARL. A.L. killed in action (gas)	
		C.2.10	405247 Pte PYBUS. N. 95.1116 Pte WEBB. J.S. 406323 Gt COVERDALE. T. 405161 Cpl FURBER N } Wounded (gas)	

WAR DIARY or INTELLIGENCE SUMMARY

Army Form C. 2118.

Ref: Maps 1/20,000 { 20 SE } France and
                    { 28 NE } { 28 NW } Belgium

Place	Date	Hour	Summary of Events and Information	Remarks and references to Appendices
T8d1.8	12/9/17		Two practice barrages carried out during the day.	
		3 a.m.	Fired on S.O.S. line in retaliation to enemy shelling.	
			C/210 405268 Bdr. DIXON. E. ⎫	
			406304 Gr. ANSOR. W. ⎪	
			405296 Gr. DIXON. T.H. ⎬ wounded (gas)	C/210
			796108 Gr. NEATHER. H.S. A.D. ⎪	
			831132 a/Bdr. MARTIN. A. ⎭	
T8d1.8	13/9/17		Two practice barrages carried out during the day.	
			D/210 944585 Gr. MORGAN. G.N. wounded (gas)	D/210
T8d1.8	14/9/17	9 Noon	Personnel of A/210 pulled out to form basis for two days rest.	
		3 p.m.	Lt Col A. BIRTWISTLE. C.M.G. and Capt L. HIGHTON D/210 proceeded on 3 days sick leave to BOULOGNE.	
		5 p.m.	Lt Col BARTON. D.S.O. assumed temporary command of 210th & 211th Bde. R.F.A.	
			Area search carried out during the night.	

WAR DIARY or INTELLIGENCE SUMMARY

Army Form C. 2118.

Ref. Maps 1:40,000 France and Belgium
9w SE
28 NE
28 NW

Place	Date	Hour	Summary of Events and Information	Remarks and references to Appendices
(continued)	14.9.17		B.210 700115 Sgt RAYNOR J. 705622 Sgt CHARNE F. 701009 Cpl HENNEDY W. 700736 Gr. EDMONDSON J. 701010 Gr. MALLODY P. 700946 Gr. BIRCHENOUGH W. 705457 Gr. McGINNESS E. 786298 Gr. HALL H. 700255 Gr. AIREY J. 701013 Gr. JOHNSIN J. A.210 700428 Gr. WANNSHAM H. B.210 701158 " HILL A. 178336 Dr. HICKMAN F. C.210 700037 a/Sgt GEE C. 705225 " OWEN F. 705013 a/Br DOHERTY L.S.H. B. STONER	78660 Gr. AMBLER J. 788965 Gr. HUNT J. 701099 Gr. BULLOCK S. 701052 Gr. HADING J. 701049 Gr. HORSEFIELD T. 701072 Gr. FITZHUGH H. 700964 Gr. NUTTALL F. 700235 Gr. BOLTON W. 705369 Gr. REES G. C.210 LTA. BROOKS Sick to Hospital 705444 Gr. BRITCHKON J. Wounded 9a. C.210 706182 Gr. CARTWRIGHT A. 700032 Gr. RUTTER R. Arr Wounded (9a.)	} wounded (9a) C.228 C.L.
	15.9.17			
	16.9.17	10 am.	Practice barrage carried out.	
		11.15 am	4 + 5" How Concentration (9ao) on THAMES WOOD	

Army Form C. 2118.

WAR DIARY
or
~~INTELLIGENCE SUMMARY.~~
(Erase heading not required.)

Ref a Hat 1/20,000
20 SE } France +
28 NE
29 NW } Belgium

Place	Date	Hour	Summary of Events and Information	Remarks and references to Appendices
(continued)	16/9		B210 700428 C/	9
			B210 700163 Cpl HARRISON. C	
			700210 a/Cpl. STOTT	
			700476 B.d. HICKSON N.G	
			700119 G. EDWARDS. F. ⎫	
			700253 G. RYAN T ⎪	
			700360 G. GIBSON. W ⎪	
			700097 Bdr. BINGHAM ⎪	
			700224 Sgt Ftr KISHHAN ⎪	
			701064 G. BATTY. S ⎬ Wounded (Gas)	
			705568 G. PEAKE ⎪	
			701067 G. CROSS ⎪	
			705321 G. ROBERTS. J ⎪	
			700290 G. ATKINSON ⎪	
			706233 G. AMES L ⎪	
			700217 Ftr. McDERMOTT N ⎪	
			701150 G. HAWORTH. R ⎪	
			700286 G. PROCTOR. H ⎭	
				630

WAR DIARY or INTELLIGENCE SUMMARY

Army Form C. 2118.

Refer Maps 1/40,000
Dose } France and
26 N.E. } Belgium
28 N.W.

Place	Date	Hour	Summary of Events and Information	Remarks and references to Appendices
	19.9.17	9.30 a.m.	Practice Barrage carried out.	10

CASUALTIES (wounded gas)

A210
- Lieut. H.G. CLAPHAM
- 400278 Bdr. BEECH. T.
- 400106 " HARWOOD. P.
- 405006 Sgt. LODGE. P.
- 117534 Gr. SILCOCK
- 400450 " CRANSHAW. H.
- 400385 " BAIREY. J.
- 400194 " BALDWIN. R.
- 314872 " HOLDEN. P.
- 400294 " NIXON. H.
- 401989 " FARNWORTH. F.
- 401244 " CALVERT. T.
- 401063 " LONSDALE. T.
- 401161 " IVESON. G.
- 406161 " WEBB. J.
- 401299 " KNOWLES. J.
- 401174 " HEATON. T.
- 405305 " BINGHAM. A.
- 400999 " FRANKLIN. A.

- 400895 Gr. CONNOR. J.
- 400377 " KENTON. P.
- 401375 Dr. SMITH. J.

B210
- 405281 Bdr. MACHIN. W.
- 400936 a/Bdr. LANCASTER. L.

C210
- 405553 Sgt. COOPER
- 405217 Bdr. McARTHUR
- 405264 Gr. WILLIAMS
- 405419 " CHEETHAM
- 405290 " DANN
- 406309 " RYANCE
- 405538 Cpl. HENSHAW
- 406209 a/B. CONBOY
- 406332 Gr. BERRY. F.
- 405893 " ELLISON.
- 405649 " GARDENER

- 405542 Gr. HATHER
- 405364 " MIDDLEHURST
- 405450 " TYRER. R.
- 406186 " HUTTON.
- 405275 " MACHIER
- 405314 Dr. DOYLE. J.
- 405801 " RUDDICK

D210
- 415176 Cpl. BANKS. J.B.
- 944548 " GREENFIELD. D.R.E.
- 415221 Dr. HARKNESS. G.
- 944672 " HEASHAW. G.
- 713314 a/Bdr. HAISON. C.S.
- 415308 Gr. PICKERING. E.
- 889607 " SPINKS. B.
- 415160 " DAVIES. H.
- 400812 " DOYLE. E.
- 405123 Bdr. HESLOP. T.
- 406363 Gr. HARROP.

Army Form C. 2118.

WAR DIARY
or
INTELLIGENCE SUMMARY.
(Erase heading not required.)

Refer Map 1/20.000
28 S.E. } France and
28 N.E. } Belgium
28 N.W.

Place	Date	Hour	Summary of Events and Information	Remarks and references to Appendices
I8 d 1.8	18/11	6 am 6 pm	Practice barrage carried out. Lt Col A. BIRTWISTLE CMG and Capt L. HIGHTON, D.S.O. returned from 3 days rest in line at BOULOGNE.	C/80
		6 am	C/210 moved position from I.3.d.5.1. to I.10.d.35.75.	
			H.Q. 210th Bde R.F.A. moved to RAMPARTS, near MENIN GATE.	
I8 d 10.95	19/11	3 am	24 hour preliminary bombardment of enemy positions commenced. One gun C/210 sent to I.O.M. Military Medal awarded to 401843 Sgt G. PERKIN A/210, 405061 Sgt J. WEABY M/210.	C/80
			CASUALTIES (wounded gas) D/210 4/1637 G? LIDDELL C.R. 4/5340 " SIMPSON J. 4/15836 " SLATER F.	
I8 d 10.95	20/11		Major D.J. MASON returned from 14 days leave in U.K. One gun C/210 out of action, sent to I.B.H.	
		5.40 am	5th Corps attacked and captured enemy front line for a depth of 1000 yards. Positions consolidated and counter attack beaten off. 210 Bde R.F.A. co-operated in barrage. S.O.S. fired at 9.31 am, 10.50 am, 1.45 pm, 2.15 pm, 2.26 pm, 2.44 pm, 6.9 pm, 6.29 pm, 7.0 pm, 7.22 pm, 7.54 pm. Creeping barrage fired at 6 am, 8.30 pm, 10.15 pm, 11.55 pm.	

Army Form C. 2118.

WAR DIARY or **INTELLIGENCE SUMMARY.**
(Erase heading not required.)

Instructions regarding War Diaries and Intelligence Summaries are contained in F.S. Regs., Part II. and the Staff Manual respectively. Title pages will be prepared in manuscript.

Ref: Map { 20 S.E. 28 N.E. 28 N.W. } France and Belgium /12.

Place	Date	Hour	Summary of Events and Information	Remarks and references to Appendices
18d10.95	20/9/17		CASUALTIES B20. 400123 Gr WALSH. A. (wounded ga) A20. 400023 Cpl HINDLE. H. } wounded. 400389 Gr LOMAX. J.	C20
18d10.95	21/9/17		S.O.S. fired at 3.38am. 5.20pm. 5.32pm. 5.47pm. 7.10pm. 7.20pm. 7.45pm. 8.10pm. Creeping barrage fired at 2.25am. 4am. 5.20am. 12.30pm. 6.10pm. CASUALTIES D20 Lieut. A.S.E. RICHARDS. (wounded ga).	C20
18d10.95	22/9/17		S.O.S. fired at 3.38am. 6.20pm. 5.32pm. 5.47pm. 7.10pm. 7.20pm. 8.10pm. 4.49am 6.19pm Creeping barrage fired at 5.15am. During the night the move of D20 "B.O." RPM w/s to FREZENBERG RIDGE commenced. A20 moved to I.6.25.90 B20 " " I.6.21.6 One gun A20 sent to I.O.M. One gun C20 returned from I.O.M.	

WAR DIARY
INTELLIGENCE SUMMARY

Army Form C. 2118.

Ref a Map
20 S.E.
28 N.E. } France and
28 N.W. } Belgium

Place	Date	Hour	Summary of Events and Information	Remarks and references to Appendices
I8d10.95	22/7		**CASUALTIES**	
			A210	
			B210 405061 Sgt WELBY. J. wounded gas.	
			400184 Cpl. SHUTTLEWORTH. H. wounded gas	
			C210 405233 Gr BLACKWELL. H. Killed.	
			405335 Gr EARP. F.A. wounded gas.	
			446260 Cpl. BENNETT. C.H. } wounded Shell	
			405166 Gr WALNER. F. } and gas.	
			D210 415154 A/Cpl. FEE. H. wounded gas.	Cpl
I8d10.95	23/7	5.20 a.m.	S.O.S.	
			C210 moved to I 6 b 25.30	
			D210 moved to C 30 d 25.60	
			One gun A210 sent to I.O.M.	
			CASUALTIES	
			A210 91949 Dr HOWELL Wounded	
			B210 400338 Gr HAYES. T. Killed	
			C210 406220 Gr BOOTH. R. 405281 Gr WARD F. } Wounded	
			405498 " MOORE. J. 405220 " MATTHEWS. R. } gas	
			406423 " McKENNA. J.	
			HDQRS 999 Staff Sgt LAVERICK (A.O.C.) Wounded.	Cpl

WAR DIARY
or
INTELLIGENCE SUMMARY.

Army Form C. 2118.

Ref Maps
20 S.E.
28 N.E. } France and
28 N.W. } Belgium

Place	Date	Hour	Summary of Events and Information	Remarks and references to Appendices
I8d10g5.	24.9.17		The day spent in digging and work on new positions. CASUALTIES A210 400462 G.M.S. Whittaker. W. wounded. 400307 Dr Riding. K. wounded 400196 " Jowett. T. wounded B210 C210 221098 Gr Statham. W.M. wounded 9a.	C30
I8d10g5.	25.9.17	6pm	The day spent in work on new positions and registration. Practice barrage carried out by 18 pdr batteries. One gun A210 returned from I.O.M. One gun C210 sent to I.O.M. CASUALTIES H.Q. 415005 Staff Fr. Sgt. Akron wounded 9a. A210. 410445 Mr. Demaine. J. killed 400362 Dr Smith. A. wounded B210 400258 Cpl Burnock. R. 400638 Gr Pickup. E. ⎫ 400371 " Pate. W. 1698 " Price. J. ⎪ 405469 Bdr Ryan. T. 445934 Dr Watkins. T. ⎪ 1120 " Houlden. H. 400158 Bdr Bent. J.H. ⎬ wounded 405152 " Jones. R.D. 401176 " Ashworth. E. ⎪ 9a. 108426 Dr Jones A.S. 405236 Dr Holmes. T. ⎪ 400465 Gr Airey. T. 401103 Gr Slack. G. ⎪ 150820 " Smith. P.R. 401172 " Taylor. S. ⎭ 400019 Dr Hargreaves	

WAR DIARY or INTELLIGENCE SUMMARY

Army Form C. 2118.

Ref: Maps 20 S.E. } France
28 N.E. } and
28 N.W. } Belgium

15

Place	Date	Hour	Summary of Events and Information	Remarks and references to Appendices
I8d.10.95 25/9/17 (continued)			C.210 405462 Gr. PRATT. A. } 405515 Cpl. SIMPKINS. S. } Wounded gas. 405077 Gr. PHILLIPS } (gas) 406316 A/B Gr. GODDARD. F. } 405104 Gr. SENBY — Wounded D.210 416335 Gr. FISH. L. Killed. 416135 " WEIRDING. F. Wounded 415170 " SINTON E. do 415296 " BARWISE. N.H. do	C.90
I8d.10.95	26/9/17	3.50 a.m.	Preliminary bombardment commenced.	
		5.50 a.m.	V Corps attacked and captured enemy positions to a depth of 1000 yd. Line consolidated and counter attacks beaten off.	
			210 Bde RFA fired in support of 3rd Division.	
			Our attack on HILL 40 and ZONNEBEKE STATION was successful. S.O.S. fired at 2.6 p.m. 3.10 p.m. 3.55 p.m. 5.55 p.m. 6.30 p.m. 6.44 p.m. 6.58 p.m. 4.10 p.m. 4.40 p.m. 4.50 p.m.	
			CASUALTIES	
		6.30 p.m.	A.210 480101 Dr. INGHAM. W. Wounded	

WAR DIARY
or
INTELLIGENCE SUMMARY

Army Form C. 2118.

Ref e Maps 20 J/5, 28 N.E. } France and 28 S.W. } Belgium

16

Place	Date	Hour	Summary of Events and Information	Remarks and references to Appendices
T8d.10.95 (continued)	26.9.17		B.210 405465 Bdr BYRNE F. 400154 Gr TUDOR N. } Wounded gas. 188517 " HARGREAVE H. C.210 405656 a/Bdr GIKES G.W. 405018 Gr MACNAY N. } Wounded gas. 405369 Dr WILLIAMS A.W. D.210 50142 Gr WATSON G. } Warm Bed Lieut: R. HARTNEY. A.210 Wounded 2/Lt. N.F. ADENEY C.210 Wounded gas. Lieut H.S. SHANNON posted to D.210 from B.Bn Learning Barrage and gas concentration carried out during the night. Creeping Barrage carried out at 5am 8.40am 1.30pm 4.10pm 6.45pm	C.S.9
T8d.10.95	27.9.17	6.45pm 7.30pm	S.O.S. at 6.35pm 6.40pm 6.55pm 7.5pm Enemy counter attack beaten off. One gun A.210 sent to I.O.M.	C.S.9
T8d.10.95	28.9.17		Creeping barrage carried out by night and day. S.O.S. at 6.15pm and 6.35pm CASUALTIES B.210 400138 Gr JOBLING G.N. 400069 " RIMMER T. } Wounded gas. 405184 Dr WALMSLEY R.N.E.J.	C.S.9

WAR DIARY
or
INTELLIGENCE SUMMARY

Army Form C. 2118.

Ref. y Maps
20 S.E. ⎫ France and
28 N.E. ⎬
28 N.W. ⎭ Belgium

Place	Date	Hour	Summary of Events and Information	Remarks and references to Appendices

T Sd. 10.9.5	29/7	—	210 Bde RFA. Relieved by 3rd New Zealand Bde F.A. and returned to wagon lines. One gun handed over at front line. L/Col A. BIRTWISTNE. C.M.G. appointed a/CRA 42nd Division. Major D. J. MASON D.S.O. assumed temporary command of 210 Bde RFA.
			
			CASUALTIES
			D 210 715248 G. LAWSON. J. 715289 Dr MOORE. A.E. ⎫
			       944064 " BARRICAR. 715292 " HAGGANS. N ⎬ Wounded
			       715839 " WAIN. M. 715305 " TWEEDIE. J ⎭
			       715218 Dr FARISH. T.T. 715074 " WALTON. J. } bombs.
			       715426 " FLETCHER. T.E.
				C9.81

NORTHOUDT 30 P	30/7	9am	210th Bde R.F.A. proceeded by march route to NORTHOUDT and billetted the night.	C9.82

WAR DIARY
or
INTELLIGENCE SUMMARY

Army Form C. 2118.

Place	Date	Hour	Summary of Events and Information	Remarks and references to Appendices

	30/9/17		Composition and distribution of 210th Bde RFA as follows:
			
			Hq. 210 Bde RFA ⎫
			A. 210 ⎬ On the march to WORMHOUDT.
			B. 210 ⎪
			C. 210 ⎪
			D. 210 ⎭
			
			Drafts received during Harcourt. 1 Officer 13 O.R.
			
			                      O. O.R. Horses.
			TOTAL STRENGTH 26 607 658
			EFFECTIVE STRENGTH 25 597 648
			
			                             J. Mann
			                              Major
			                    Commanding 210 Bde RFA.
				18

SECRET

Copy No..........

No.2 SUB-GROUP ORDER NO.3.

1. No.2 Sub-Group will be relieved in accordance with Warning Order No.1 para.1.

2. Exchange of guns, sights and aiming posts will be carried out as follows :-

    (a) Units of 210th Bde R.F.A. will draw on 29th inst. from the relieving units of 1st N.Z.F.A.Bde from their wagon lines in vicinity of 210th Bde R.F.A. Wagon Line under arrangements to be made between B.Cs. concerned.

    (b) Units of 211th Bde R.F.A. will draw at 2 p.m. to-morrow 29th inst. from the wagon lines of the relieving Units of 3rd N.Z.F.A.Bde., Headquarters of which are at BUSSEBOOM - C.16.c.5.2.

    Guides to the various battery wagon lines can be obtained at the above position.

3. All area stores at Wagon lines will be handed over to relieving units in the case of 210th Bde R.F.A. and in the case of the 211th Bde R.F.A. by a representative of the 1st N.Z.F.A.Bde.
Receipt will be obtained.

4. Ammunition at Battery position will be handed over to relieving units at noon tomorrow 29th inst., Amounts handed over will be wired to reach this office by 1 p.m.

5. All echelons will travel full.

6. Headquarters 210th Brigade R.F.A. will move on relief to present Headquarters Wagon Lines.

7. Major D.J.MASON.,D.210., will assume temporary command of 210th Bde R.F.A. on completion of relief.

28-9-17.
O.C.211th Bde R.F.A.
O. i/c 210th Bde Wagon Lines.
A.B.C.D.210.
A.B.C.D.210.
FILE.

Captain., Adjutant.
No.2 Sub-Group.

S E C R E T.

3rd Div. Arty Order No. 18.

Reference GRAVENSTAFEL Map 1/10,000.

1. The 8th Infantry Brigade will attack WINDMILL HILL and THE STATION this evening at 6-30.pm.

2. Artillery Co-operation will be as follows:-

   (a) A Creeping Barrage (18-pdrs) will open on the BROWN LINE as shewn on attached maps.
   The first lift will be at Zero plus 5 minutes.

   Rate - 50 yards in 3 minutes.

   The barrage will halt and remain on the original BLUE dotted final protective barrage line.

   The barrage will be fired by Batteries of 2, 3 and 4 Groups in Group Zones.

   The Southern Boundary of the barrage should start in the Railway at D.21.d.60.45 (Railway exclusive) and lift along the Railway (Railway inclusive) after the first lift.

   The Northern Boundary will start at D.21.a.60.45 and move N.E. to D.15.d.3.0.

   Method of Fire.

   H.E. and Smoke. Every alternate Gun will open with 3 rounds of Smoke and during Creeping will fire 1 round of Smoke per minute.
   On reaching the Protective Line fire will slacken down to the rate of 2 rounds per Gun per minute for 10 minutes, afterwards 1 round per Gun per minute.

   (b) The 4.5" Howitzers will co-operate from Zero as follows:-

No. 1 Group.	2 Batteries gas.	DAISY WOOD D.23.a.8.2
No. 2 Group.	2 Batteries gas.	DARING Crossing.
No. 3 Group.	1 Battery gas.	THAMES S. of Railway and Railway at D.22.b.3.7.
No. 4 Group.	Search up Railway in D.22.c. & a. (H.E).	

   Rates of fire during Protective period 1 round per Gun per minute.

3. Watches will be synchronised at 5-0.pm.

4. ACKNOWLEDGE.

D N Graham
Major, R.A.
Brigade Major, 3rd Div. Arty.

Issued at 4.25 pm
26/9/17.

Copies to :- Nos. 1, 2, 3 and 4 Groups.
3rd Div. "G". R.A. V. Corps.
4th Aus. D.A. 59th D.A.
8th, 9th & 76th Inf. Bdes.

SECRET.

Addendum 1 to 3rd Div. Artillery Order No. 18.

1. Reference 3rd D.A. Order No. 18 Para. 6.

   The programme for intermittent fire from Zero plus 4 Hours 35' will be as follows:-

Time.	Rate of fire.
Zero plus 4 hrs 35' to Zero plus 4 hrs 40'	18-pdrs...2 R.P.G. per minute. 4.5" Hows..1 R.P.G. per minute.
Zero plus 4 hrs 55' to Zero plus 5 hrs 15'	18-pdrs....1 R.P.G. per minute. 4.5" Hows...1 R.P.G. per minute.
Zero plus 5 hrs 40' to Zero plus 5 hrs 45'	18-pdrs....2 R.P.G. per minute. 4.5" Hows...1 R.P.G. per minute.
Zero plus 6 hrs 2' to Zero plus 6 hrs 13'	18-pdrs....1 R.P.G. every 2 minutes. 4.5" Hows...1 R.P.G. every 2 minutes.
Zero plus 6 hrs 47' to Zero plus 6 hrs 55'	18-pdrs....1 R.P.G. per minute. 4.5" Hows...1 R.P.G. per minute.

2. At 2-30.pm. and again at 6-30.pm. the 18-pounder Guns of the Searching barrage and any 4.5" Howitzer Batteries not employed on the Gas Bombardment referred to in Para. 6 of 3rd D.A. Order No.18 will form a Creeping Barrage from the Protective Barrage Line forward for 500 yards, in Group Zones, Guns will be concentrated so as to pass over likely approaches or places of assembly; such as THAMES WOOD, along the Railway, ALMA, and will then return to the Protective Barrage line, lifts out and in will be 50 yards every 5 minutes.

   Rates of Fire

   | 18-pounders | 2 R.P.G. per minute. |
   | 4.5" Hows | 1 R.P.G. per minute. |

D.N.Graham

Major, R.A.

25/9/17. Brigade Major, 3rd Div. Arty.

Copies to Recipients 3rd D.A. Order No. 18.

SECRET.

~~No. 1 Group.~~
No. 2 Group.
~~No. 3 Group.~~
No. 4 Group.
~~3rd Div. "A".~~

M.G.42 is cancelled.

Zones for 4.5" Howitzers in Gas Barrage will be as follows:-

No. 1 Group. 1 Bty.	D.29.b.5.8
No. 1 Group. 1 Bty.) No. 2 Group. 1 Bty.)	DAISY WOOD.
No. 2 Group. 1 Bty.	TYNECOTT.
No. 3 Group. 1 Bty.	DARING Crossing and Area 200 yards South of it.
No. 4 Group. 1 Bty.	(Railway (D.22.b.3.7

Dupaha

Major, R.A.
Brigade Major, 3rd Div. Arty.

25/9/17.

S E C R E T.

~~No. 1 Group.~~
No. 2 Group.
~~No. 3 Group.~~
No. 4 Group.
~~3rd Div. "C"~~

Reference 3rd D.A. Order No. 18.

1. <u>Final Protective Barrage.</u>
   Between Zero plus 3 hours and Zero plus 4 hours 30 minutes Groups will arrange to search back 800 yards, three times at times to be selected by Group Commanders - with all 18-pounders in the Group.

2. <u>Rate.</u> - 100 yards in 2 minutes.

3. Lifts should be synchronised within Groups.

4. In the event of the S.O.S. Signal being received during one of the periods, the Line will be reformed on the Protective Barrage Line.

                                                  D.M.Faber
                                                  Major, R.A.

25/9/17.   Brigade Major, 3rd Div. Arty.

SECRET.

Addendum No. 2 to 3rd Div. Arty Order No. 18.

3rd Div. Arty Visual Communications.

1. No. 2 Group will man visual Station at DOUGLAS VILLA.

2. No. 3 Group will man NEWCOTT.

3. Messages will be taken by runner from NEWCOTT to HILLCOTT for transmission to RAMPARTS. HILLCOTT and RAMPARTS are manned by 3rd Div. Signal Coy.

4. The following points will be observed in messages transmitted by visual from F.O.Os.

   (a) No preamble will be sent.
   (b) 'Address to' in every case will be 'D.A'.
   (c) Text will follow.
   (d) Address from must contain :-
       Name ......F.O.O. & Bde Code Call thus (F.O.O.KILL).
       Place......Location of F.O.O. at the time of sending message.
       TIME.......This is most important.

5. Test messages will be sent from DOUGLAS VILLA to NEWCOTT thence by Runner to HILLCOTT and RAMPARTS to-day at 5-0.pm. and 7-0.pm. The text of these messages will contain the word PRACTICE only.

6. Visual Stations will be manned continuously from 8-0.pm. Y/Z Night.

7. PIGEONS.

Reference Para. 8 Arty Order No. 18.

Nos 1 and 3 Groups will arrange to draw from HILLCOTT at 5-0.pm. to-day each, two baskets of Pigeons. (Each basket contains two pigeons). Pigeon message forms and instructions for working will be handed over with the Pigeons.

8. ACKNOWLEDGE.

D. M. Graham
Major, R.A.
Brigade Major, 3rd Div. Arty.

Issued at 11am
25/9/17.
Copies to All Recipients 3rd D.A. Order No. 18.

S E C R E T.

TABLE "A".

Group.	0 to +5'	+5' to +11'	+11' to +35'	+35' to +47'	+47' to +59'	+59' to +100'	+100' to +144'	+144' onwards.
No.1	D.27.c.5.0 to D.27.c.1.8	Barrage creeps at rate of 50 yards in 2 minutes.	Barrage creeps at rate of 50 yards in 5 minutes.	Protective barrage D.27.d.4.8 to D.27.b.3045	Left half of barrage line swings to 2nd Protective line	Protective Barrage.	Barrage creeps at rate of 50 yards in 4 minutes.	Final protective barrage D.28.a.3.5 to D.22.c.5.2
No.2	D.27.c.1.8 to D.26.b.7025			D.27.b.3045 to D.21.c.8055				D.22.c.5.2 to D.22.c.0.9
No.3	D.26.b.7025 to D.20.d.5545			D.21.c.8055 to D.21.a.4015	Right half of barrage line creeps at rate of 50 yds in 5 minutes.			D.22.c.0.9 to D.21.b.4.8
No.4	D.20.d.5545 to D.20.d.1580			D.21.a.4015 to D.21.a.2.5				D.21.b.4.8 to D.15.d.2055

NOTE:- There will be no overlap with 4th Aus.Division.
There will be no overlap with 59th Division till protective barrage on the Red Line begins to move, whence the overlap 50 yards to the Final Protective Barrage Line will continue.

Ammunition. Shrapnel (where used) to give 40% on graze.

Rates of fire.
18-pounders during creeping 3 R.P.G. per minute.
During Protective barrage (first 10 minutes) 2 R.P.G. per minute, afterwards 1 R.P.G. per minute.

— sheet 4 —

13. **Synchronisation.**
 Watches will be synchronised at D.A. Headquarters (RAMPARTS) at 5-30.pm. and 7-30.pm. on Y day.

14. ACKNOWLEDGE.

Note. The Barrage will open on the line marked 5'. First lift at zero + 5 mins:

Issued at 10 pm.
24/9/17.

D.W.Graham
Major, R.A.
Brigade Major, 3rd Div. Arty.

Distribution:—
 Copies 1 – 9   No. 1 Group.
 ,, 10 – 20 No. 2 Group.
 ,, 21 – 31 No. 3 Group.
 ,, 32 – 36 No. 4 Group.
 ,, 37   D.A.C.
 ,, 38 – 39 3rd Div. "G".
 ,, 40   76th Inf. Bde.
 ,, 41   8th Inf. Bde.
 ,, 42   9th Inf. Bde.
 ,, 43   4th Aus. Div. Arty.
 ,, 44   59th Div. Arty.
 ,, 45   V Corps. R.A.
 ,, 46   V Corps. H.A.
 ,, 47   21st Sqdn. RFC.
 ,, 48   3rd Div. H.G.O.
 ,, 49   3rd D.A. Signals.
 ,, 50   S.C., 3rd D.A.
 ,, 51 – 52 No. 4 Group.

SECRET.   T.1278.

1. 9th D.A.O.O. No.153 is forwarded herewith.

2. Tasks are allotted as follows:-

Period. No.1.

(a) 18-pdrs A.211)   Sub Group.
          B.211)   Search and sweep zone as per attached trace.
          C.211)

4.5" Hows.
D.210.   Dugout D.26.c.65.60.
              Pits   D.26.d.0.5.
              POTSDAM.
D.211.   Trench from D.26.d.35.60. to D.26.d.20.90.
              Trench from D.26.d.85.90. to D.26.b.75.25.

RATE OF FIRE.
              18-pdr 20 rounds per gun per hour. A and AX.
              4.5" Hows. 10 rds per gun per hour BX.

(b)   ### Period No.2.
     Barrage lines as laid down for the actual attack in 210th
Bde R.F.A. Order no.26. up to Zero plus 45.

RATE OF FIRE.
              18-pdr 2 rds per gun per minute Shrapnel with
                     corrector to give 40% on graze.
              4.5" Hows. 1 rd per gun per minute BX.

Period No.3.
(c)   As laid down in attached.

Period No.4.
(d) 18-pdrs
     A.210)
     B.210) as for period No.1.
     C.210)
     4.5" Hows
     D.86.   Taking D.210 targets in period No.1
     D.211.   As for period No.1.

Period No.5.
(e) (1) As laid down in attached. 18-pdrs of 211th Bde only
        carrying out the searching and sweeping.
    (2) As laid down in attached.

Period No.6.
(f) 18-pdrs.
     A.210)
     B.210) As for para 1.
     C.210)

     4.5" Hows.
     D.86.) As laid down in attached.
     D.210)

Period No.7.
(g)   As for para 1.

-2-

3. F.O.O. at UHLAN FARM will report on Periods 2, 3, & 5.

4. ACKNOWLEDGE.

                                                  Adjutant.
                                                No.2 Sub-Group.

18-9-17.

Copies to :-
- 9th D.A.
- S.African Inf. Bde.
- A.B.C.D. 210.
- A.B.C.D. 211.
- D.86.
- File.

Special attention is directed to attached amendments.

SECRET

Copy No....11....

No. 2 SUB-GROUP ORDER NO.2.

Ref. CRAVENSTAFEL Map 1/10,000.   25-9-17.

Ref. attached 3rd D.A. Order No. 18. :-

1. The attack will be proceeded by a two hours bombardment as under:-

   (a) <u>18-pdrs.</u>   Zero -90 minutes.

   From the blue line lifting 100 yards every 2 minutes to a line
   500 yards N.E. of above, then dropping 100 yards every 2 minutes
   to the line D.27.c.45.90. - D.27.a.0.8., when fire will cease.
   Battery zones as per attached map. B.210 will not co-operate in
   this preliminary bombardment.

   RATE OF FIRE. 2 rds. per gun per minute SHRAPNEL (40% graze)

   (b) ~~4.5" Ho.   Zero -90 minutes.~~   vide CBS 35, 35/2

   ~~As for 18-pdrs in para. (a) above. D.210 will cover the Right
   half, D.211 the left half, of the Sub-Group Zone.~~   attached

   ~~RATE OF FIRE. 1 rd. per how. per minute. H.E.~~

   ~~From completion of above barrage to Zero 4.5" Hows will engage the
   following strong points :-~~

   ~~D.210. Dug-outs. D.27.a.3.3., D.27.a.1.4., D.27.a.10.45., D.27.c.17.40.
          HUT D.27.a.4.4.~~

   ~~D.211. Dug-outs. D.27.a.35.55., D.27.a.15.70., D.27.a.20.80.,
          D.27.a.27.83., D.27.a.6.8. and Trench D.21.d.0.3.~~

   ~~RATE OF FIRE. 15 rds. per how. per hour.~~

2. (a) <u>18-pdrs.</u>.

   From Zero onwards all 18-pdr. batteries with the exception of
   B.210. will carry out a creeping barrage as laid down in attached
   map. The times shown against each line on attached map is the time
   at which batteries will lift from that line.

   (b) The barrage will start at Zero on the plus 5 line, the plus 3
   line having been cancelled.

   (c) When a portion of the creeping barrage arrives on a lift just
   short of a strong point, the guns in front of it and just overlapping
   it will dwell on this line for a period of two lifts instead of one,
   and rejoin the barrage by lifting 100 yards in one lift. The 18-pdrs
   that dwell will fire alternate rounds of smoke during the time they
   dwell on this line.
       The following will be considered strong points for purposes of
   above :-
       Concrete emplacements D.27.a.1.4. and D.27.a.95.40.
       ST. JOSEPH's INSTITUTE.

   (d) B.210 will carry out a searching barrage, 3 guns starting 100 yds,
   and 3 guns starting 200 yds beyond creeping barrage. Each half of
   battery will lift 50 yds. whenever the creeping barrage lifts and will
   sweep the whole front of the Sub-Group Zone between each lift.

-2-

(e) RATE OF FIRE for 18-pdrs.

Creeping Barrage. During advance of the Infantry - 3 rds per gun per minute. H.E. & Smoke. The creeping barrage will open with 3 rounds of smoke fired in rapid succession from alternate guns. When creeping, every alternate gun will fire 1 round of smoke per minute.

PROTECTIVE BARRAGE. First 10 minutes, 2 rounds per gun per minute, 50% H.E. & 50% Shrapnel,(to give 40% on graze). No smoke will be fired.
When the creeping barrage re-opens after a protective period it will do so with "3 rds rapid" smoke from alternate guns as a signal to the Infantry.

SEARCHING BARRAGE. (B.210) As for creeping barrage except that shrapnel only, to give 40% graze, will be used.

(f) Zero plus 185.

Creeping barrage by all 18-pdr. batteries from final protective barrage line, lifting 100 yds every 2 minutes to a line 800 yds. N.E. of above.
The above to be repeated at Zero plus 220 and Zero plus 240.

RATE OF FIRE. 2 rds. per gun per minute. 50% H.E., 50% Shrapnel.

In the event of the S.O.S. being received during above, the line will be reformed on the final protective barrage line.

(g) 18-pdr. batteries will carry out intermittent fire on their final protective barrage line as under :-

Zero plus 4 hrs.35')
    to   ) 2 rds. per gun per minute. 50% A., 50% AX.
Zero plus 4 hrs.40')

Zero plus 4 hrs.55')
    to   ) 1 rd. per gun per minute. 50% A., 50% AX.
Zero plus 5 hrs.15')

Zero plus 5 hrs.40')
    to   ) 2 rds. per gun per minute. 50% A., 50% AX.
Zero plus 5 hrs.45')

Zero plus 6 hrs.2')
    to   ) 1 rd. per gun every 2 minutes.
Zero plus 6 hrs.13')   50% A., 50% AX.

Zero plus 6 hrs 47')
    to   ) 1 rd. per gun per minute. 50% A., 50% AX.
Zero plus 6 hrs.55')

(h) At 2.30 p.m. and 6.30 p.m. all 18-pdr. batteries will carry out a Creeping Barrage from the final protective Barrage line, lifting 50 yds. every 3 minutes to a line 500 yds N.E. of above, then dropping 50 yds every 3 minutes to the final protective barrage line.

RATE OF FIRE. 2 rds. per gun per minute. 50% A., 50% AX.

-3-

3. (a) <u>4.5" Hows.</u>

<u>Zero to Zero plus 5.</u>

D.210.) Concrete emplacements D.27.a.10.45. and D.27.a.20.40.
D.211.)

<u>Zero plus 5 to Zero plus 11.</u>

D.210. Dug-outs D.27.a.4.4.
D.211. Dug-outs D.27.a.2.8.

<u>Zero plus 11 to Zero plus 14.</u>

D.210. ST. JOSEPH's INSTITUTE.
D.211. HUT D.27.a.55.72.

<u>Zero plus 14 to Zero plus 23.</u>

D.210. Dug-outs D.27.a.95.40.
D.211. Railway from D.27.a.70.85. to D.27.a.85.93.

<u>Zero plus 23 to Zero plus 35.</u>

D.210. HUTS D.27.b.35.52.
D.211. Railway from D.21.d.0.0. to D.21.d.25.13.

<u>Zero plus 35 to Zero plus 100.</u>

D.210. Buildings D.28.a.05.90.
      " D.21.d.85.05.
D.211. Buildings and trench D.21.d.65.25.
Buildings D.21.d.5.4.

<u>Zero plus 100 to Zero plus 112.</u>

D.210. 2 Hows. Road from D.28.a.1.9. to D.22.c.3.0.
2 Hows. Building. D.22.c.0 8.12.
2 Hows. Building. D.22.c.0.2.
D.211. Railway D.21.d.80.50. to D.21.d.95.60.

<u>Zero plus 112 to Zero plus 120.</u>

D.210. 2 Hows. Road from D.22.c.3.0. to D.22.c.50.12.
2 Hows. HUTS (D.22.c.20.15.
        (D.22.c.25.20.
2 Hows. D.22.c.12.35.
D.211. Railway D.21.d.95.60. to D.22.c.10.65.

<u>Zero plus 120 to Zero plus 136.</u>

D.210. D.22.c.67.17. to D.22.c.40.55.
D.211. D.22.c.40.55. to D.22.c.20.95.

(b) <u>RATE OF FIRE.</u> During the advance of the Infantry 2 rds. per gun per minute H.E.
During protective barrages 1 rd. per gun per minute H.E.

(c) <u>Zero plus 136 to Zero plus 211.</u>

D.210. TYNECOTT.
D.211. DAISY WOOD D.23.a.8.3.

3. (c) Contd.

   RATE OF FIRE.   R.P.G. per minute.   GAS, with occassional salvoes of H.E.

   The above Gas bombardment will be repeated from 2.15 p.m. to 3.30 p.m. and from 6 p.m. to 7.15 p.m.

4. LIAISON & F.O.Os.

   Capt. H.B. ECCLES   as F.O.O. at DOUGLAS VILLA.
      42nd D.A.
   Lieut. R.A. SMITH.   as F.O.O. at FREZENBERG RIDGE, South of
      D.210.   DOUGLAS VILLA.
   LIEUT. F.J.G. JACKSON.   as F.I.O. following up the Infantry along
      C.211.   the line of the Railway, finally taking up
                   his station at CHARING.

   All above officers will be provided with daylight signalling lamps, together with telephone and necessary telephonists.
   Special instructions will be given to the officers concerned.

5. Zero Day and Hour will be notified later.

6. An officer from each battery will meet an officer from this H.Q. at BAVARIA HOUSE at 9.15 p.m. to-day 25th inst.

7. ACKNOWLEDGE.

Issued by Orderly.
At............
Copies to:-
   No. 1 - 3rd D.A.
      2 - A.210.
      3 - B.210.
      4 - C.210.
      5 - D.210.
      6 - A.211.
      7 - B.211.
      8 - C.211.
      9 - D.211.
    10 - War Diary.
    11 - War Diary.
    12 - FILE.

Captain., Adjutant.
No.2 Sub-Group.

S E C R E T.

3rd DIVISION
ARTILLERY ORDER No. 18.

September 24th. 1917.

Ref:- GRAVENSTAFEL Map 1/10,000.

1. The V Corps will resume the offensive on a date to be notified. The Objective will be the Blue Line, which includes the BRICK KILN, ZONNEBEKE Church and Station, WINDMILL HILL, concrete dugouts about JACOBS HOUSE, DOCHY FARM, OTTO FARM and TORONTO FARM.

   The 3rd Division will attack on the Right and the 59th on the Left, each on a front of 2 Brigades. The dividing line is a line from WATEREND HOUSE to South End of VAN ISACKERE FARM, the latter inclusive to 59th Division.

   The 4th Australian Division, I ANZAC Corps will attack on the Right of the 3rd Division.

   Divisional Boundaries are shown on attached Map. The 76th Inf.Bde will attack on the Right, the 8th Inf.Bde on the Left; the dividing line being the YPRES - ROULERS Railway (inclusive to 76th Infantry Brigade).

2. The attack of the 3rd Division will be supported by the following Artillery:-

No. 1 Group.	40th & 42nd Bdes.	(3rd D.A.)
No. 2 Group.	210th & 211th Bdes.	(42nd D.A.)
No. 3 Group.	50th & 51st Bdes.	(9th D.A.)
No. 4 Group.	64th Brigade. 465) Batteries. 466)	(18-pdrs).

3. Divisional Artillery barrages supporting the attack will be (a) Creeping, (b) Searching.

   (a) The Creeping Barrage will be composed of all 18-pounders less 2 Sections per Brigade.
   H.E. and Smoke (see Para.5) will be fired.
   Times of lifts are shown on barrage maps attached.
   Special Tasks for 465th and 466th Batteries (firing 50% H.E. and Shrapnel). 1 Battery will creep 500 yards ahead of the Creeping barrage along the YPRES - ROULERS Railway.
   1 Battery will creep 500 yards ahead of the Creeping Barrage along the Northern half of No. 3 Group Zone.

   (b) The Searching Barrage will be composed of 2 Sections per Brigade. 1 Section will start 100 yards beyond the Creeping Barrage and the 2nd Sections 200 yards in advance of that. Each Section will lift 50 yards whenever the Creeping Barrage lifts, and will swweep the whole front of its Brigade Lane between each Lift, to deal with the open country between strong points.
   Strong Points will be dealt with by Howitzers.
   Shrapnel will be fired by "Searching" barrage Guns.

/(c) 4.5" Hows.

- Sheet 2 -

(c) 4.5" Howitzers will search back in their Group Lanes. The normal procedure will be for half the Howitzer Battery to start 200 yards, and the remaining half to start 400 yards, beyond the Creeping Barrage. Each half will then lift back conforming with lifts of the Creeping Barrage and sweeping the whole Brigade Front. 4.5" Howitzers should collect on strong points in their Group and zones dwell on them before lifting but should never be less than 100 yards beyond the Creeping Barrage.

Rates of Fire for Howitzers:-

During the advance of the Infantry 2 R.P.G. per minute.

During Protective Barrages 1 R.P.G. per minute.

4. Special treatment of Strong Points.
When a portion of the Creeping Barrage arrives on a lift just short of a Strong Point, the Guns in front of it and just overlapping it will dwell on this line for a period of two lifts instead of one, and rejoin the barrage by lifting 100 yards in one lift.
The 18-pounders that dwell will fire alternate rounds of Smoke during the time they dwell on this line.

5. Nature of Ammunition.
   (a) Smoke Shell.
   The Creeping barrage will open with 5 rounds of Smoke fired in rapid succession from alternate Guns.
   When creeping every alternate Gun will fire 1 round of Smoke per minute.
   During Protective periods no Smoke will be fired.
   When the Creeping Barrage reopens after a Protective period it will do so with "5 rounds rapid" Smoke from alternate Guns as a Signal to the Infantry.

   (b) During Protective periods H.E. and Shrapnel (50% of each) will be fired.

   (c) Shrapnel will be used within 150 yards of the Divisional Boundaries.

6. Final Protective Barrage. Fire will be continued at a steady rate for 2 hours after which intermittent fire will be carried out - a programme for which will be issued.
After the capture of the Final Objectives the Infantry will push forward strong patrols along the ZONNEBEKE - BROODSCUIDE Road and to occupy the line ALMA - JUDAH HOUSE.
Orders will be issued by this office if and when the Protective Barrage should be lifted.
On arrival on Final Protective Barrage, a Gas barrage for a period of 1¼ hours will be put down by 4.5" Howitzers on likely assembly points, provided the wind is safe.
Area to be dealt with D.29.b.5.8 - D.23.a.8.3 - DARING Crossing - TYNECOTT.
Salvoes of H.E. will be occasionally interspersed with the Gas.
This barrage will be repeated from 2-15.pm. to 3-30.pm., and from 6-0.pm. to 7-15.pm.
Groups will engage Area in their lanes, but not without orders from this office.

/Para.7.

-sheet 3-

7. **Preliminary bombardment.**
(1) The attack will be preceded by a 2 hours bombardment which will consist of (a) at zero less 1 hour 30 minutes a Chinese Barrage
  18-pounders and 4.5" Hows opening on the BLUE LINE and searching forward 500 yards by lifts of 100 yards every 2 minutes, and dropping back 100 yards every 2 minutes till a line through D.27.c.5.0 - D.27.a.0.4 - BOSTIN FARM - D.20.b.4.0 is reached when fire will cease.
(b) For the remainder of the 2 hours 4.5" Howitzers will deal with Strong Points inside a line through HUHLE - ST JOSEPHS Institute - WINDMILL - LEVI Cottages - VAN ISACKERE FARM, (all exclusive). These points and Zone outside them are being dealt with by Corps Heavy Artillery.
(2) Except for desultory rounds 18-pounder bombardment will stop at Zero less 5 minutes.
The bombardment will not be intense so that the enemy may suppose it is the beginning of a 24 hours bombardment.

Rates of Fire will be 18-pounders - 2 R.P.G. per minute.
               4.5" Hows   - 1 R.P.G. per 2 minutes.

Shrapnel will be fired during the Preliminary Bombardment.

8. **F.O.Os.** - No.1 Group will detail a F.O.O. and party to follow the progress of the attack of the 76th Infantry Brigade and No.3 Group one to follow the attack of the 8th Infantry Brigade. These parties will take daylight lamps, flags, Very lights and Pistols, flappers and pigeons.
Pigeons will be issued to Groups concerned under arrangements made by 3rd D.A. Signal Officer.
Each Group will man an Intermediate Observing Station and will arrange for one Visual Station through which messages can be transmitted. The visual station at the RAMPARTS will be manned by 3rd Div.Signals, and messages transmitted from there.

9. Table "A" attached shows rates of fire and boundaries between Groups on the various lines.

10. **Tanks.** 4 Tanks will operate on the 76th Infantry Brigade front and 8 Tanks on the 8th Infantry Brigade front.

11. **Contact Aeroplanes.**
(a) A Contact machine will be over the objective at about:-
  Z plus 1 hour.
  Z plus 1¾ hours.
  Z plus 2¼ hours, at which time the Infantry will notify their position when called for by the Aeroplane by lighting RED FLARES.
(b) A Counter attack patrol machine will also be continually in the air from Zero plus 1 hour till dusk. When indications appear of a Hostile Counter Attack the Aeroplane will sound one long blast on the Klaxon Horn and will discharge a Smoke Bomb.

12. **Liaison.**
At 8-0.pm on Y/Z Night the G.O.Cs 76th and 8th Infantry Brigades assume Command of their respective Sectors. From that hour No.1 Group will find a Senior Liaison Officer with the 76th Infantry Brigade and No. 3 Group with the 8th Infantry Brigade.
Battle Headquarters are as follows :-

  76th Infantry Brigade KIT & KAT (J.1.d.3.6.)
  8th Infantry Brigade Square Farm (C.30.b.8.8).

SECRET.   Copy No......12.

No.2. Sub-Group Order No.1.

Reference Map: 1/10,000 FREZENBERG   18-9-17.

Re attached 9th D.A.O.O. No. 152.

1. (a) 18-pdr will barrage in accordance with attached map, due attention being paid by the batteries concerned to para 6 of above order, the strong point being Gunpits D.26.c.35.80.

    Re para, 6 (b) the barrage up the railway will be carried out by A.210 and B.210, in accordance with the instructions contained therein.

    Re para, 3 (b) 2 sections of C.210 will carry out the sweeping barrage mentioned, within the Sub-Group boundaries as shown on attached map. This sweeping barrage will be carried out 200 yards in advance of the creeping barrage, on the 211th Bde. zone only, the right of the zone being the railway, until reaching the YELLOW LINE, and then sweeping the whole Sub-Group front.
    The remaining section C.210 from Zero plus 3 will lift to the YELLOW LINE from D.26.d.05.25 to D.26.c.8580, sweeping to cover this front and firing 1 round T.S. and 2 rounds SMOKE per gun per minute, until Zero plus 29 when this section will fire on the line marked on attached map.

(b) 4.5" Hows
    D.211.   D.211 will fire on the railway from Zero onwards keeping 100 yards in front of the 18-pdr barrage and lifting with it.
    D.86   D.86 will fire on the railway from Zero onwards keeping 200 yards in front of the 18-pdr barrage and lifting with it. On reaching the protective barrage lines this unit will open out as laid down in para, 5 (c) of attached.
             This unit will also comply with para, 5 (e) and gas programme attached.

    D.210.   Zero to Zero plus 9.
             3 Hows - Gunpits D.26.c.35.80.
             3 Hows - Gunpits D.26.a.15.10.

    D.210   Zero plus 9 to Zero plus 17.
             3 Hows - POTSDAM.
             3 Hows - Trench D.26.c.8.9.

    D.210   Zero plus 17 to Zero plus 1 hour 28.
             3 Hows - Pits D.26.d.05.55.
             3 Hows - Dug-outs D.26.b.25.00.

    D.210   Zero plus 1 hour 28 to Zero plus 1 hour 36.
             3 Hows - Trench D.26.d.45.70.
             3 Hows - Dug-outs B.26.b.25.00.

    D.210   Zero plus 1 hour 36 to Zero plus 1 hour 44.
             3 Hows - Trench D.26.b.28.35 to D.26.b.5.2.
             3 Hows - Dug-outs D.26.b.55.18.

-2-

Zero plus 1 hour 44 to Zero plus 2 hours.

D.210. 2 Hows - Trench from D.26.d.9.9. - D.26.b.85.15.
       2 Hows - Trench from d.26.b.85.15. - D.26.d.80.25.
       2 Hows - M.G. at D.26.b.75.40.

Zero plus 2 hours to Zero plus 2 hours 4.

D.210 3 Hows - Trench D.27.c.15.95. 9 D.27.a.00.15.
      3 Hows - Dug-outs D.26.b.9.3.

Zero plus 2 hours 4 to Zero plus 5 hours 17.

D.210. 2 Hows - Hut D.27.a.2.0.
       2 Hows - Hut D.27.a.38.18.
       2 Hows - Dug-out D.27.a.3.3.

2. Re para.7. This liaison Officer will be detailed later.

3. Re para.8. This F.O.O. will be detailed later.

4. Re para.9. 211th Bde.R.F.A. will man UHLAN FARM, 210th Bde. R.F.A. will man GREY RUIN.

5. Orders re synchronization will be notified later.

6. "Z" Day and Zero Hour will be notified later.

7. ACKNOWLEDGE.

                              Captain., Adjt.
                              No.2.Sub-Group.

Issued by Orderly.
At..10.pm..........

Copy No. 1. 9th Div.Arty.
      2. S.African Inf.Bde.
      3. A.210
      4. B.210
      5. C.210
      6. D.210
      7. A.211
      8. B.211
      9. C.211
     10. D.211
     11. War Diary
     12. War Diary.
     13. File.

9th Divisional Artillery　　　　　　　Copy No. 11
Operation Order
No. 152.
==*=*=*=*=*=*=*=*=*=*=*=*=*

September 17th 1917.

1. The 9th Division is attacking on a front from J.2.c.6.7. to D.19.d.1.6. on "Z" Day at Zero hour.
The 2nd Australian Division is attacking on the Right of the 9th Division and the 55th Division on the left.
The 9th Division is attacking with two Infantry Brigades in the line; the 27th Infantry Brigade on the Right and the S. African Infantry Brigade on the left. Divisional boundaries and boundary between Infantry Brigades are shewn on Map "A" attached.

2. The 9th Division attack will be supported by the following Field Artillery:-

No. 1 Group. { 295th Brigade.
              { 296th Brigade.

No. 2 Group. { 210th Brigade, R.F.A.
              { 211th Brigade, R.F.A.
              { D/86th Battery, R.F.A.

No. 3 Group. { 50th Brigade, R.F.A.
              { 51st Brigade, R.F.A.

No. 4 Group.   64th Brigade, R.F.A.

3. The 18-pdr. barrages will be

   (a) A <u>creeping barrage</u> composed of all 18-pdr. guns less 2 Sections per Brigade.
   Group Zones, times of lifts, nature of ammunition etc. is given in Table "A" attached and shown on Map "A" attached.

   (b) A <u>Searching barrage</u> composed of 2 Sections per Brigade. These sections will search and sweep in their Brigade lanes from 100 yards to 500 yards in advance of the creeping barrage; these sections will deal with the open country between strong points. Strong Points will be dealt with by Howitzers.
   The Sections of the Searching Barrage will fire at the same rates as 18-pdrs. in the creeping barrage, but will fire salvoes as far as possible.
   <u>AMMUNITION</u>. SHRAPNEL.

4. <u>SMOKE SHELL</u>.

   (a) If the wind is in the West all 18-pdrs. in the creeping barrage will open with a round of smoke.
   Every alternate gun in the creeping barrage will fire one round of smoke per minute during the time the Infantry are advancing.

/(b)

(2)

(b) If the wind is not in the West, one gun in the centre section of each battery will fire one round of smoke just before lifting on each lift to mark the line of the barrage and denote the lift.
Whether the procedure (a) or (b) will be employed will be notified by 9th Divisional Artillery.

In all cases

When a protective barrage is reached every alternate gun will fire two rounds of smoke in quick succession to note that this line is reached.

5. (a) The 4.5" Howitzers will fire on strong points in their Brigade Zones, such as BECK HOUSE, BORRY FARM, Gun Pits West of POTSDAM, the railway, D.26.c.6.1. HANEBEEK WOOD, VAMPIR, BIT WORK and BREMEM REDOUBT.
(b) D/86 will reinforce the battery on the railway so that there will be 2 4.5" Howitzer Batteries on the railway whilst the infantry are advancing.
(c) D/86 will fire at 100 yards longer range than the other 4.5" Howitzer Battery and immediately on reaching the protective barrage lines, will open out to 20 yards interval with the left gun on the railway.
(d) 4.5" Howitzers will on no account fire within a less distance than 100 yards of the 18-pdr. creeping barrage.
(e) D/86 is placed at the disposal of the 5th Corps Heavy Artillery for the purpose of carrying out a gas bombardment from Zero + 3 hours 17 minutes to Zero + 5 hours 17 minutes. Programme will be issued later.
(f) No. 1 Group will detail one 4.5" Howitzer to fire from J.2.a.9.4. to J.2.b.1.1. from Zero till Zero + 11 minutes; at Zero + 11 minutes this battery will lift to its protective barrage.
(g) Rate of fire.
During the advance of the infantry.
2 rounds per gun per minute.

During protective barrages
for first 10 minutes
3 rounds per gun every 2 minutes.

For remainder of periods
1 round per gun per minute.

6. Special treatment of strong points.

When a portion of the creeping barrage arrives on the lift closest in front of a strong point such as those enumerated in para. 5, the guns in front of and overlaping in breadth to the extent of 20 yards on either side will dwell on this line for a period of two 50 yard lifts instead of one, and then rejoin the barrage by lifting 100 yards in one lift.
The 18-pdrs. that dwell will fire one round of smoke per gun per minute during the time they dwell on this line.

(a) POTSDAM. In the case of the gun pits at D.26.c.35.80. the dwell will last 2 minutes, after which the guns will ~~rejoin the barrage in one lift of 200 yards.~~ lift 150 yards and wait until overtaken by the rest of the Barrage.

/(b)

(3)

(b) D.26.c.1.3. After firing for 3 minutes on the barrage line through D.26.c.1.3. the guns firing for 250 yards to Right (South East) of the Railway will lift 50 yards and concentrate on to the actual line of the railway which must be accurately registered beforehand, and continue to lift up the railway conforming to the lifts of the creeping barrage; thus leaving a gap of 250 yards to the Right (South East) of Railway line; on reaching the protective barrage guns will open out again to their normal intervals.

(c) HANEBEEK WOOD. The No. 1 Group will detail one section of 18-pdrs. to fire Shrapnel and one round smoke shell per gun per minute on J.2.a.85.35. and J.2.a.85.30 from Zero till the creeping barrage reaches the first protective barrage, when these guns will resume their normal task.

7. LIAISON.

No. 2 Group will detail an officer not below the rank of Captain as Liaison Officer with the 27th Infantry Brigade.

The 51st Brigade will detail an officer not below the rank of Captain as Liaison Officer with the South African Infantry Brigade.

8. F.O.Os.

No. 2 Group will detail a F.O.O. and party to follow the progress of the attack of the 27th Infantry Brigade.
50th Brigade will detail a F.O.O. and party to follow the progress of the attack of the South African Infantry Brigade.
F.O.O. parties will be provided with Daylight Lamps, flags, Very Lights, pistol, flappers and pigeons.
F.O.Os. will not as a rule move forward till Battalion Headquarters advance; their chief duty is to send back information as to the position of the Infantry.

9. Each Brigade will man one intermediate observing station. These officers will watch and report on barrages, they will also report if our infantry are being heavily shelled and call for a smoke barrage to screen them.

10. After the capture of the final objective, till further orders, the S.O.S. barrage will be that detailed for the final protective barrage.
When the S.O.S. is received all guns and Howitzers will open fire at 3 rounds per gun per minute for 5 minutes, and continue at one round per gun for 10 minutes. They will then cease fire unless the signal is repeated.
The S.O.S. Signal is a rifle grenade breaking into two red and two green lights.

11. There is no intention to move batteries forward till the objectives have been consolidated and counter attacks driven off, but Brigades will reconnoitre positions with a view to a further advance.
Positions reconnoitred will be sent into 9th Divisional Artillery Headquarters.

/12.

(4)

12. 4.5" Howitzer Batteries will fire 50% Gas Shell in repelling counter-attacks if the wind is favourable.

13. There will be a continuous bombardment for 24 hours before Zero.
To avoid any semblance of a lull one gun per battery will fire at the rate of one round per minute from Zero - 30 minutes till Zero and work on to its Zero line by Zero, so as to quicken up and join the barrage.

14. Orders re synchronization of watches will be issued later.

15. "Z" Day and Zero hour will be notified later.

A C K N O W L E D G E.

Major R.F.A.
Brigade Major,
R.A., 9th Division.

Copies Nos 1 to 9 to No. 1 Group.
" Nos 10 to 20 to No. 2 Group.
" Nos. 21 to 31 to No. 3 Group.
" Nos. 32 to 36 to No. 4 Group.
" No. 37 to 9th D.A.C.
" No. 38 and 39 to 9th Division.
" No. 40 to 26th Inf. Brigade.
" No. 41 to 27th Infantry Brigade.
" No. 42 to S.African Inf. Brigade.
" No. 43 to 2nd Australian Divisional Artillery.
" No. 44 to 55th Divisional Artillery.
" No. 45 to 42nd Divisional Artillery.
" No. 46 to V Corps R.A.
" No. 47 to V Corps Heavy Artillery.
" No. 48 to 21st Squadron, R.F.C.
" No. 49 to 9th Divisional Machine Gun Officer.
" No. 50 to 9th D.A.Signal Officer.

TABLE "B".

Programme of intermittent fire from Zero + 5 hours 17 minutes
to Zero + 8 hours.

1. (a) All 18-pdrs. of the creeping barrage will fire on their
   final barrage at the rates and times as stated below.

   (b) The 18-pdrs. of the searching barrage will search and sweep
   in their Brigade Zones beyond the final barrage at the rates
   and times as stated below.

   (c) 4.5" Howitzers will search and sweep in their Brigade Zones,
   beyond the final barrage, paying particular attention to
   strong points, at the rates and times as stated below.

   (d) Times and rates of intermittent fire.

   Zero + 5 hours 40 minutes) 18-pdrs. 2 rds. per gun per minute.
   to
   Zero + 5 hours 45 minutes.) 4.5"Hows 1 rd. per gun per minute.

   Zero + 6 hours   ) 18-pdrs. 1 rd. per gun per minute.
   to
   Zero + 6 hours 20 minutes.) 4.5"How. 1 rd. per gun per minute.

   Zero + 6 hours 45 minutes) 18-pdrs. 2 rds. per gun per minute.
   to
   Zero + 6 hours 50 minutes.) 4.5"How. 1 rd. per gun per minute.

   Zero + 7 hours 52 minutes) 18-pdrs. 1 rd. per gun per minute.
   to
   Zero + 8 hours.   ) 4.5" How.1 rd. per gun per minute.

<u>SECRET</u> Copy no 5

<u>210th Bde R.F.A. Order No 24</u>

Ref: Map 118   5-9-17
1/10,000

Re THB 1-9-17.

1.   126 Inf. Bde. will attack &
capture the strong points in the
neighbourhood of BORRY FARM,
BECK HOUSE and IBERIAN on
"Z" day
    The 61st Division is attacking
GINCHPORT on the same day and
at the same time.

2.   The Bde Arty will co-operate
as follows:—
(a) <u>18 pdrs</u> Commencing at zero, a
    creeping barrage from the line
    A210 D25 b 05 30 – D25 b 04 55
    B210 D25 b 04 55 – D25 b 06 74
    C210 D25 b 06 74 – D19 d 05 05
                 77
    Lifting at + 100 yds every 5 minutes
    to the line

    A210 D26 a 12 88 – D20 c 10 15
    B210 D20 c 10 15 – D20 c 10 37
    C210 D20 c 10 37 – D20 c 10 65

...while a protective barrage will be formed until ZERO + 1 hour 30 minutes. (Vide attached map).

RATES of FIRE
ZERO to ZERO + 10 - 4 rds per gun per minute
  A (60% on graze)
ZERO + 10 to ZERO + 20 - 3 rds per gun per minute
  A (60% on graze)
ZERO + 20 to ZERO + 30 - 2 rds per gun per minute
  A (60% on graze)
ZERO + 30 to ZERO + 1 hr 30 mins - 2 rds per gun
  per minute
  50% A with long corrector
  50% A+

(b) 4.5 How.
  ZERO to ZERO + 20

D 210 3 hows. Dugout D 25 b 97.75
       2 hows.   "   D 25 b 95.63

RATE of FIRE
  ZERO to ZERO + 20 - 2 rds per how per
                        minute DX

9. ZERO day and hour will be notified later.

4. Any necessary registration will be carried out at once.

5. From ZERO to ZERO + 1 hour 30 minutes, any S.O.S. signals sent up WILL BE DISREGARDED. From ~~ZERO~~ ZERO + 1 hour 30 minutes until further orders, S.O.S. Line will be as follows:-

<u>18 bde.</u> PROTECTIVE BARRAGE Line (vide attached map)

<u>4.5" Hows.</u>
D 210   3 hows Trench running thro'
                O in ZEVENNOTE.
        2 hows X roads D20 a 5.45

6. ACKNOWLEDGE.

Issued by order, C. J. Duff Capt. Adjt
at
                    210th Bde. R.F.A.

Copy No. 1 - A210
        2 - B210
        3 - C210
        4 - D210
        5 - War Diary ✓
        6 - War Diary
        7 - File

Secret.

210th Bde R.F.A.
Order No 25

Ref.ce Map 1/10,000 Frezenberg.   11-9-17

1. 126th Infty Bde will attack and capture strong point at D26c 12·30, and capture and consolidate the line running S.E.-N.W. from D26c 25·15 to D26c 00·40.

2. This Group will co-operate as follows:-
   On three green Very lights being fired from Sexton House, B210 will open fire on :-
   Battery Position D26a 20·00 to D26a 10·15

3. Rate of Fire   Battery Fire 10 seconds for 4 minutes, when fire will cease, Shrapnel to be used.

4. B210 will remain on its S.O.S. lines until the signal is sent up, and will switch back as soon as the shoot is completed.

5. The N.O.P. officer will keep a sharp look-out for the signal passing same at once to B210.

6. Zero hour will be notified later.

7. ACKNOWLEDGE.

Issued by orderly
at ....
Copies to
No 1 - OC Rt Sub Group.
   2 - " B 210.
   3 - War Diary.
   4 - F do -
   5 - File

Capt.
Adjut 210th Bde R.F.A.

210th BDE RFA ORDER No 26

Ref⁴ Maps 1/40.000, BELGIUM and FRANCE.

29-9-17.

1. Copy of 42nd D.A. Order No 38 is attached herewith.

2. 210th Bde R.F.A. in order of march as per margin, will proceed by march route to WORMHOUDT tomorrow 30th inst via Switch road North of POPERINGHE - PROVEN ROAD - FORK road, L 4 9 2 - St JAN -TER-BIEZEN - Cross roads E 30 c 4.5 - HOUTKERQUE - HERZEELE - WORMHOUDT.

Margin:
Hd 210 Bde RFA
A 210
B 210
C 210
D 210

3. Starting point will be x roads G 5 d 1.2. Head of column will pass starting point at 8 a.m.

4. Distances will be maintained as laid down in para 5 of attached order.

5. Caps will be worn, the steel helmet being worn on the left shoulder strap.

6. Units will hand to Adjutant at starting point a return showing amount of ammunition in the limbers, and registered numbers of guns in their possession.

7. One motor lorry per Hdqrs and battery will be available for the march. These lorries are already in the possession of units.

8. Rations and forage will be drawn in accordance with para 11 of attached order.

9. A billeting party composed of 1 officer or sergeant per Hdqrs and battery will report to Commandant Staging area, WORMHOUDT at 9 am as laid down

in para 12 of attached order.

10. The billetting party of Lt Cooper, and 1 N.C.O. and 3 O.R. per H.Qrs. and battery proceeding to 66 Division will assemble at A 210 lines at 7.30 am. A 210 will place their cooks cart at the disposal of this party to carry kits to POPERINGHE CHURCH.

11. B.Cs will see that their camp is left in a clean and sanitary condition. 3 men per unit (on bicycles) will be left behind as rear party.

12. ACKNOWLEDGE on attached form.

Issued by orderly at 11 p.m.
Copies to A. B. C. D 210
War Diary
War Diary
File

Copy No

210th Bde RFA Order No 27

Ref: Map 1/40,000. Sheets 27 and 19, Belgium and France.

30-9-17

1. Copy of 42nd D.A.O.O. No 39 attached herewith

H.Q. 210
B+RFA
C 210
D 210
B 210
A 210

2. 210th Bde RFA in order of march as per margin, will proceed by march route to TETEGHEM tomorrow 1st Oct via WYLDER - MAISON BLANCHE - Cross roads O.17.d.5.3.

3. Starting point will be Cross roads C.17.a.5.8 (N.E. end of SQUARE in WORMHOUDT). Head of column will pass starting point at 10.45 am.

4. Distance will be maintained as laid down in para 6 of attached order

5. Rations and forage will be delivered to units in TETEGHEM by Divisional Train on conclusion of days march. Each unit will send guides to offices of Area Commandant to guide supply wagons to billets.

6. A billeting party composed of LT. HT. R. MOORE, and one NCO and one man per battery will report to Area Commandant TETEGHEM at 9 am. It is most important that this party arrives in time, it is suggested that this party proceeds by motor lorry of Battery.

7. B.Cs will see that their billets and camps are left in a clean and sanitary condition and that billeting certificates are rendered in accordance with the usual procedure

8. Mechanical transport will proceed independently under orders of units.

9. ACKNOWLEDGE by lantern receipt form in his possession.

G. Duff (Capt & Adjt)
for O.C. 13 Bn, 12 FA.

Issued by
orderly at
11 p.m.

Copy No 1 - A Coy
       2 - B Coy
       3 - C Coy
       4 - D Coy
       5 - War Diary
       6 - War Diary
       7 - File

Copy Nº

210th Bde R.F.A. ORDER Nº 28

Ref: Map 100.000
DUNKERQUE   1-10-17

H Qs
A 210
B 210
C 210
D 210

1. 210th Bde RFA, in order of march as per margin, will proceed by march route to 42nd Divisional Area, near COXYDE tomorrow 2 inst and will relieve the 330 Bde RFA on nights 2/3rd and 3/4th inst.

2. Starting point - Road junction 600x North of C in LEFFRIN-KHOUCKE. Head of column to pass starting point at 9.15 a.m.

3. The CO, Adjutant, Signal Officer, and 1 officer per battery will assemble at starting point at 7.30 a.m. The battery officers will proceed to wagon lines and will then return to ADINKERKE on roads to act as guides to units.

4. Batteries will relieve their opposite numbers. One section

per battery will be taken up by 60th D.A. teams tomorrow night 2/3rd inst.

B.C.s will arrange to have one officer at the battery position in charge of this section.

Remainder of batteries will relieve on night 3/4th inst.

5. OC C 210 will arrange for one officer to accompany the party mentioned in para 3, to relieve Lt R L C LOWCOCK.

6. Supplies will be delivered to units on the conclusion of the days march.

7. On the conclusion of the march tomorrow, all motor lorries will be returned to 42nd A.S.P at PETITE SYNTHE. The attached sketch shows the route which they should take.

8. Careful attention is directed to paras 4. 5. 6. 9. 10. 11. & 12 of attached 42nd D.A. OO No 40

Volume II

War Diary

of

210th Bde R.F.A.

From 1-10-17
To   31-10-17

WAR DIARY
or
INTELLIGENCE SUMMARY

Army Form C. 2113.

Ref a Maps 1/40.000 Sheet 27. Belgium and Annex
Sheet 19
Sheets 11 & 12 OOST-DUNKERKE 1.

(Erase heading not required.)

Place	Date	Hour	Summary of Events and Information	Remarks and references to Appendices
NORMHOUDST	1/10/17		Sheet 1. Composition and distribution of 210th Bde R.F.A. as follows:-	
			Headquarters A.210 B.210 } at WORMHOUDT, en route for NIEUPORT BAINS Sector C.210 D.210 } to relieve 66th Division	
		10.45 p.m.	210th Bde R.F.A. proceeded by march route to HERRINKHOUCKE and billetted the night.	C.19
R30c 05.15	2/10/17	9 a.m.	210th Bde R.F.A. proceeded by march route to NIEUPORT BAINS Sector and relieved units of 66th D.A. as under:- One section A.210 relieved one section A.330 at H.30.c.6.3 " " B.210 went into position at R.36.a.3.1 " " C.210 relieved one section B.330 at H.30.c.18.50 " " D.210 " " " D.330 at M.19.d.3.5	
			Following officers posted from 42nd D.A.C. Lieut. T.H. WALMESLEY } to A.210 2/Lt. G.A. BICK Lieut. T.A. STUTTARD to C.210 2/Lt. H. WARD to D.210	C.19

2449 Wt. W14957/M90 750,000 1/16 J.B.C. & A. Forms/C.2118/12.

Army Form C. 2118.

WAR DIARY
or
INTELLIGENCE SUMMARY
(Erase heading not required.)

Ref Map 1/40,000 Sheet 11 and 12 OOST-DUNKERNE

Sheet 2

Instructions regarding War Diaries and Intelligence Summaries are contained in F. S. Regs., Part II. and the Staff Manual respectively. Title Pages will be prepared in manuscript.

Place	Date	Hour	Summary of Events and Information	Remarks and references to Appendices
R.30 c 05.15	3/6/17		2nd Lt E.G. HOWKER posted to B210 from 42nd D.A.C. Remainder of battery relieved Remainder of 330 Bde R.F.A.	C.29
R.30 c 05.15	4/6/17	5 am	H.Q. 210th Bde R.F.A. assumed command of "C" Coy, 42nd Division relieving H.Q. 330 Bde R.F.A.	C.30
			Registration carried out during the day.	
		3.30 pm to 5.30 pm	D210 shelled with 5.9, no damage to equipment.	
			Following officers posted from 42nd D.A.C. T/Lieut. L. BUCK to B210 2/Lt C.E. HUMPHREY to A210.	
R.30 c 05.15	5/6/17		Various gun cell dealt with during the day.	C.31
		6 pm to 7 am	B210, C210 and D210 carried out four neutralizing burst on enemy battery at M5d.6.7.	
			Following postings from 42nd D.A.C. B210 — 5 O.R. C210 — 6 O.R.	

Army Form C. 2113.

WAR DIARY
or
INTELLIGENCE SUMMARY
(Erase heading not required.)

Ref. Maps 1/40,000
Sheets 11 and 12.
OOST-DONGRUE
Sheet 3

Place	Date	Hour	Summary of Events and Information	Remarks and references to Appendices
R30c05.15	6/10/17		Various zone call shoots during the day. Our gun C210 pulled out to wagon line for calibration. Our gun D210 pulled out to wagon line for sending to O.M./r instead.	SD
R30c05.15	7/10/17		Orders received for relief of 42nd D.A. by 41st D.A. and for relief of 33rd D.A. by 42nd D.A. Our gun B210 pulled out to wagon lines for calibration.	SD2
R30c05.15	8/10/17		Our gun A210 pulled out to wagon lines for returning to I.O.M. s/n instead.	SD3
R30c05.15	9/10/17	9am to 10am	Various zone call shoots with shelling the day. B210 position shelled by 5.9" about one round every four minutes.	SD4
			CASUALTIES B210 110296 GUNDAMS. J. killed in action. 1182 A/B'MNDREWS. H. wounded 80686 G. DEMAINE. J. wounded	

WAR DIARY or INTELLIGENCE SUMMARY

Army Form C. 2118.

Ref. Maps 1/40,000 Sheets 11 and 12
60ST - DUNKERQUE

Sheet 4

Place	Date	Hour	Summary of Events and Information	Remarks and references to Appendices
R30c05.15	9/10/17	—	Military Medals awarded to following N.C.O.s and men, for gallantry during the battle at YPRES of 20th Sept and 26th Sept 1917. 400025 — Sgt. BENTLEY H 405376 — Sgt. BUTTERWORTH A } A210 405696 — Sgt. NKR ARMESA N 405108 — Cpl. W.S. FLETCHER E. } C210 405274 — Dr. HUGHES A 415145 — Sgt. CARRUTHERS R } D210	C59
R30c05.15	10/10/17		One officer and 2 signallers for battery attached to 168 Bde R.F.A. Various gun calls answered during the day Lt. H.T.P. MOORE proceeded to 168 Bde H.Q. One officer and 2 signallers for battery returned from attachment to 168 Bde R.F.A.	C60
R30c05.15	11/10/17	HQ WH	Various gun calls answered during the day One officer and two signallers for battery of 190th Bde attached to D210 Bde R.F.A. C210 bombarded with gas shell. Headquarters wagon lines moved to new front in at A14a29 2nd Lt. E.G. WALKER. C210 proceeded on ten days leave to U.K.	C61

WAR DIARY
or
INTELLIGENCE SUMMARY

Army Form C. 2118.

Ref @ Maps 1/40,000
Sheets 11 and 12
OOST-DUNKERKE

Sheet 5

Place	Date	Hour	Summary of Events and Information	Remarks and references to Appendices
R30c05.15	11/10/17	12:20 am to 1:30 am	B.10 position bombarded with 7.7 cm gas shell.	CR2
R30c05.15	12/10/17		2/Lt C.C. REES. A 210 proceeded on 10 days leave to U.K. Having your call direct with during the day. C210 main position shelled with 75 cm. One gun slightly damaged and two pits driven in.	CR4
R30c05.15	13/10/17	2pm to 3pm	Having your calls and shell stores direct with during the day.	
		6 pm	210 Trd Bde R.F.A. pulled out to wagon lines for 10 days rest. 2/Lt T.H. WARMSLEY A 210 and one N.C.O. for battery proceeded to G14 y.VELDE on 5 days gas course.	CR30
X14a2.9	14/10/17		Following 10 days spent in construction of gun position, overhauling and calibration of gun, overhauling of equip., must and training of gun layers.	CR30
X14a2.9	16/10/17		Draft of 39 O.R. arrived	CR30

WAR DIARY or INTELLIGENCE SUMMARY

Army Form C. 2118.

Ref & Hq/40,000 FURNESS

Sheet 6

Place	Date	Hour	Summary of Events and Information	Remarks and references to Appendices
X14a2.9	17/10/17		Lieut. A.E. HIGHAM posted to C/210 from Base.	CRA
X14a2.9	18/10/17		Draft of 18 OR arrived. Capt. T.A. HIGHAM, B/210 and one N.C.O. per battery proceeded on 5 days gas course to GHYVELDE. LIEUT WALMESLEY and 40/RW returned from gas course. 2/Lieut. G.W. HORRIS posted to D/210 from 42© D.A.C.	CRA
X14a2.9	19/10/17		Capt. R.A. SMITH, D/210 Lt B.H. HORNER, A/210 } proceeded on 10 days leave to U.K.	CRA
X14a2.9	21/10/17		2/Lieut. G.W. HORRIS, D/210 proceeded on Signalling Course. Draft of 210th Bde RFA retained details of 2 N.Z. Army F.A. 90? as follows:— One section A/210 retained one section 2nd Bty at M26a 05.05. " " " B/210 " " " 5th " " M26c 69.80 " " " C/210 " " " 9th Bty " M20c 05.25 " " " D/210 " " " 6th Bty " M20c 05.90	CRA
X14a2.9	23/10/17		Lt. L. BUCK, B/210 proceeded on 10 days leave to U.K. Capt. T.A. HIGHAM - B/210 and Lt Neg., returned from gas course.	CRA

WAR DIARY
or
INTELLIGENCE SUMMARY

(Erase heading not required.)

Army Form C. 2118.

Ref. Map 1/40000 FURNES
1/20,000 - KOMBARTZYDE

Sheet 7

Place	Date	Hour	Summary of Events and Information	Remarks and references to Appendices
R30 a 85.85	24/7/17	During the night	H.Q. 210th Bde R.F.A. relieved H.Q. 2nd N.Z. Bde Army F.A. at R30 a 85.85. Remainder of 210th Bde R.F.A relieved remainder of 2nd N.Z. Army F.A. Bde. 210th Bde R.F.A. becomes "F" for 42nd Divisional Artillery. 2/Lieut. H. WARD D210 aged 1 N.Z. for battery personnel on 5 days gas course to GHYVELDE.	Copy egg
R30a 85.85	25/7/17	8am	2/Lt E.G. WALKER returned from 10 days leave in U.K.	
R30a 85.85	26/7/17	2pm to 6pm	G.O.C. and (?)CRA inspected battery position. Forward position A210 heavily shelled with 5.9s mostly S.2. About 250 rounds fired - but in their gas. No casualties. A personnel gun number 53411 A210 slightly damaged and sent to ordnance. Lce R.REES A210 returned from 10 days leave in U.K. G.O.C. 42nd Divison presented medal ribbon to N.C.O.s and men of the Brigade.	Copy egg
R30a 85.85	27/7/17	2.15 pm	A210 H00350 Dr BRADFORD F.W. killed by shellfire.	Copy egg

WAR DIARY or INTELLIGENCE SUMMARY

Army Form C. 2118.

Ref. Map 1/40,000 – FURNES
1/20,000 – LOMBARTZYDE

Sheet 8

Place	Date	Hour	Summary of Events and Information	Remarks and references to Appendices
R30 a 85.85	28/10/17	12 noon to 1.30 pm	D210 position at M26a 40.25 shelled with 15cm. no damage done.	egy
"	30/10/17		Neutralization and retaliation carried out during the day. 2/Lt H.WARD D210 and 4 N.C.O.s returned from Divisional Gas Course.	egy
"	31/10/17	11am to 12 noon	Various neutralizations carried out during the day. C210 subjected to two bursts of fire from H.D? D210 exchanged how rounds 21/3 for how rounds 17/0 with D190. 2/Lt P.L. COLLINSON attached to 210th Bde H.A. from H.Q. = D.W. Signal by an infantry officer.	C 22
			CASUALTIES	
			C 210 — 911527 Gr. SMITH, J.A. Killed in action. Shellfire
			405389 Bdr. TIPPETTS, A.
			405209 " CONBOY, J. } Severely wounded. Shellfire
			405168 Bdr. SMITH, W.
			234376 Gr. CUTHBERT, A }
			411041 Gr. WALMSLEY, F. } Slightly wounded. Shellfire

Army Form C. 2118.

WAR DIARY
or
INTELLIGENCE SUMMARY
(Erase heading not required.)

Ref. Map 1/10.000 — FURNES.
1/20.000 — LOMBARTZYDE.

Sheet 9.

Place	Date	Hour	Summary of Events and Information	Remarks and references to Appendices
R30a 85.85	31/10/17		Composition and distribution of 210th Bde R.F.A. as follows:	
			H.Q. R30a 85.85	
			A210 (3) M26a 05.05	
			(3) M26a 40.25	
			B210 (3) M32a 6.9	
			(3) M26c 69.80	
			C210 (3) M20d 00.55	
			(1) M20c 05.25	
			D210 (2) M20c 30.85	
			(2) M20c 05.90	
			(2) M20a 25.15	
			"F" GROUP } 2nd D.A.	
			O. OR. Horses.	
			TOTAL STRENGTH 30 441 669	
			EFFECTIVE STRENGTH 32 440 680	
			DRAFTS 8 officers and 54 other ranks joined during the month.	

Volume II ~~Vol 10~~

War Diary

of

210th Bde

R.F.A

From   1-11-17
To   30-11-17

WAR DIARY
or
INTELLIGENCE SUMMARY

Army Form C. 2118.

Reference Maps 1/40,000. FURNES and LEPPINGHE

Place	Date	Hour	Summary of Events and Information	Remarks and references to Appendices
R30a85.85	1/7/7		Composition and distribution of 210th Bde R.F.A. as follows:—	1
			H.Q. R30a85.85	
			A210 ① M26a05.05	
			② M26a40.25	
			B210 ① M32a6.9	
			② M26c69.80	
			C210 ① M20c05.25	
			② M20d00.55	
			D210 ① M20c30.85	
			② M20c05.90	
			③ M20a25.15	
			⎫ "F" GROUP — 42ⁿᵈ D.A. ⎬	
			Various neutralization and retaliation carried out during the day.	
		3.25pm–3.55pm 4.10pm–4.55pm	A210 shelled by 5.9's. No damage done	
		7pm	One section B210 moved to S4 21.8 and came under tactical command of "E" Group.	
		9pm to 9.20pm	H.Q. & D210 subjected to burst of gas shell and H.E.	

Army Form C. 2118.

WAR DIARY
or
INTELLIGENCE SUMMARY
(Erase heading not required.)

Reference Maps
1/40,000. FURNES
and LEFFINGHE.

Instructions regarding War Diaries and Intelligence Summaries are contained in F.S. Regs., Part II. and the Staff Manual respectively. Title Pages will be prepared in manuscript.

Place	Date	Hour	Summary of Events and Information	Remarks and references to Appendices
R30 a 85.85	2/4/7	4.55 pm – 7 pm	D210 carried out retaliatory shoot. Remainder of B210 moved to S4 21.8 and came under tactical command of "E" Group. During the evening salvage work carried out on unoccupied battery position. Capt. T.A. HIGHAM, B210 Lieut. A.E. HIGHAM, C210 } proceeded on artillery course to VAUX-en-AMIENOIS. One N.C.O. per battery Lt. H.T.P. MOORE, H.Q. proceeded on wireless course to ABBEVILLE.	C.R.A.
R30 a 85.85	3/4/7	12 noon 3.10 pm – 4.50 pm	C.R.A. inspected battery position. A210 shelled with 5.9's. No damage done. Various neutralization and retaliation carried out during the day. During the night salvage work carried out in unoccupied battery positions.	C.R.A.
R30a 85.85	4/4/7		Capt. R.A. SMITH, D210 Lt. B.H. HORNER, A210 } returned from 10 days leave in U.K. Salvage work carried out during the night. CASUALTIES Capt. L. HIGHTON D210, died to hospital	C.R.A.

2449 Wt. W14957/M90 750,000 1/16 J.B.C. & A. Forms/C.2118/12.

WAR DIARY or INTELLIGENCE SUMMARY

Army Form C. 2118.

Reference Maps 40.000 FURNES and LEFFINGHE

3

Place	Date	Hour	Summary of Events and Information	Remarks and references to Appendices
R30a 85.85	5/1/17		Lt.Col. A. BIRTWISTLE, C.M.G. proceeded on one months leave to U.K. Various neutralization and retaliation carried out during the day. Salvage work carried out during the night. Capt. J. CHURCHLEY. R.F.A. (Captain Instructor of Gunnery) attached to A210. Capt. A.G. HALL assumed the temporary rank of Major, with effect from 5-9-17, while in command of C210. CASUALTIES 4/5835 GR. OVENDEN. D210. Killed while mounting	SD
R30 a 85.85	6/1/17		Salvage work carried out during the night. 2/Lt. F.G. WALKER and 1950 gr. battery returned from gas course at GHYVELDE. CASUALTIES 172694 G. LINSEY. M. H.A. Slightly wounded. Major H. BIRTWISTLE, B210 proceeded to U.K. to Overseas School, with 14 days leave on conclusion of course.	SD
R30a 85.85	7/1/17	11.50 a.m. 12.15 p.m. 12.56 p.m. 2 p.m - 8 p.m	Lt. T.H. WALMSLEY. A210 proceeded on 14 days leave to U.K. C 210 shelled with 5.9". No damage done	

Army Form C. 2118.

Ref "H.Q." /40.000
FURNES & LAMPERNISSE

WAR DIARY
or
INTELLIGENCE SUMMARY

(Erase heading not required.)

Instructions regarding War Diaries and Intelligence Summaries are contained in F. S. Regs., Part II. and the Staff Manual respectively. Title Pages will be prepared in manuscript.

Place	Date	Hour	Summary of Events and Information	Remarks and references to Appendices
R30a 85.85	8/7/17		H.A. and D210 shelled intermittently during the day. No damage done. Salvage work continued during the night. CASUALTIES 156698 Q/13th GRIMWOOD, W.J. D210. slight shell wound	C.99
R30a 85.85	9/7/17	12.45pm to 1pm / 5pm	A210 and H.A. shelled with 5.9's. One gun A210 slightly damaged and sent to ordnance. Salvage work continued during the night. CASUALTIES 405198 Cpl. Wm. FLETCHER, E. C210. slight shell wound.	C.90
R30a 85.85	10/7/17	2.15pm to 5pm / 2.45am	C210 and D210 shelled intermittently with H.E. 2". No material damage done. Punishment fire carried out in retaliation to hostile shelling of NIEUPORT. CASUALTIES 415113 Cpl. KENDALL, T. / 415834 G' ORMROD, P. / 944595 " FURNISS, A. / 944033 " ROBERTS, C.A.L. } D210. Wounded by shellfire.	C.90

2449 Wt. W14957/M90 750,000 1/16 J.B.C. & A. Forms/C.2118/12.

WAR DIARY or INTELLIGENCE SUMMARY

Army Form C. 2118.

Ref. Maps 1/40,000 FURNES & LEFFINGHE 5

Place	Date	Hour	Summary of Events and Information	Remarks and references to Appendices
R30a.85.85	11/7/17		Capt. G.O. CONNER, R.A.M.C. left the Brigade on special duty. 1st Lieut. F.C. HOWARD, U.S.A.M.C. attached 210th Bde R.F.A.	C.B.R.
		9.15 p.m.	Punishment fire carried out on retaliation to enemy shelling of NIEUPORT. CASUALTIES 4/15203 Gr HAMILTON. D-210. Slight shell wound	C.B.R.
R30a.85.85	12/7/17		2/Lt. R.L. COLLINSON, R.E. attached to 125 Inf. Bde.	C.B.R.
R30a.85.85	15/7/17	11am to 3 p.m.	H.A. shelled by 15 cm. how. Several direct hits obtained but no damage done. CASUALTIES 40/340 Dr CAREY V.C. - D210. Slight shell wound	C.B.R.
R30a.85.85	16/7/17	6 p.m.	Capt. L. HIGHTON - D210 returned from hospital. French Cmdt. H.A. Staff of 355 Regiment d'artillerie arrived at 210th Bde H.A.	C.B.R.
R30a.85.85	18/7/17	10 am 3/0 3pm 2.45.	D210 shelled intermittently with 15 cm how. Capt. J. CHURCHEY, R.F.A. attached to A210, proceeds to XV Corps H.A. Punishment fire carried out. CASUALTIES LT H.S. SHALLMAN. - D210 Slight shell wound 4/15837 Gr SNOWDEN. J-210 " "	C.B.R.

WAR DIARY or INTELLIGENCE SUMMARY

Ref & Maps 1/40,000 FURNES & LEFFINGHE
1/100,000 - HAZEBROUCK

Army Form C. 2118.

Place	Date	Hour	Summary of Events and Information	Remarks and references to Appendices
R30a 85.85	19/7	11 am & 2pm	C210 and D210 shelled with 5.9's. No damage done.	
		During the morning	3 guns for battery of which out to wagon lines. 2/Lt. G.W. Morris returned to D210 from Signalling course.	C89
R30a 85.85	20/7	During the morning	H.Q. and sub sections of battery of which out to wagon lines. Being shown relieved by 55th Regiment d'Artillerie.	C89
GHYVELDE	21/7		Major R. Yates, A210 } Proceeded to U.K. on month's course at Capt. L. Highton, D210 } Gunnery School, with 14 days leave on conclusion.	C90
		4.30 pm	210th Bde R.F.A. proceeded by march route to GHYVELDE.	C91
NORHHOUDT	23/7	8.45 am	210th Bde R.F.A. proceeded by march route to WORHHOUDT.	C91
WEMAERS - CAPPEL	24/7	9.20 am	210th Bde R.F.A. proceeded by march route to WEMAERS-CAPPEL.	C92
HONDEGHEN	25/7	9.25 am	210th Bde R.F.A. proceeded by march route to HONDEGHEN.	C91
WITTERNESSE	26/7	9.25 am	210th Bde R.F.A. proceeded by march route to WITTERNESSE. Lt T.H. Walmesley, A210 returned from 14 days leave in U.K.	C93

Army Form C. 2118.

WAR DIARY
or
INTELLIGENCE SUMMARY

(Erase heading not required.)

Ref. Map 1/100,000
HAZEBROUCK.

Place	Date	Hour	Summary of Events and Information	Remarks and references to Appendices
WITTERNESSE	28/7	10.15 a.m.	Lt.Col. A. BARTNISTLE. C.M.G. promoted temporary Brigadier-General struck off the strength of the Brigade. Capt. C. A. HILTON (Chaplain C. of E.) to hospital.	CgS.
ROBECQ	30th		210th Bde. R.F.A. proceeded by road route to ROBECQ.	
		6.30 pm	One section four battery proceeded to GIVENCHY sector to relieve following sections of 25 Dn in the line :—	
			One section A 210 relieved one section B 110	
			" " B 210 " " C 110	
			" " C 210 " " B 112	
			" " D 210 " " D 110	
			Remainder of Brigade billetted thro'out at ROBECQ.	

SECRET   COPY No 4
210th BDE R.F.A. ORDER No 31

Reference Map 1/100,000
DUNKERQUE & HAZEBROUCK

                    22.11.17

    1 Copy of 122nd D.A. Order
       No. 52 is attached hereto

HO   2. 210th Bde R.A. in order of
B210   march as per margin will
C 210 march to WORMHOUDT (A)
D 210 tomorrow 23rd. inst.
A 210
    3 Starting point will be
    road junction opposite GHYVELDE
    CHURCH.
       Head of column will pass
    starting point at 8.45 am
    4 Distances as for march
    to GHYVELDE.
    5 Battery transport will
    march in rear of each Battery
    and will be treated as a
    section for distances.

& Halts by Batteries independently 10 minutes every clock hour. No halt will be made at 9 a.m. An officer from each unit will meet the Adjutant at the starting point at 8.40 a.m. to synchronize watches.

7 Billeting parties under charge of an officer from each battery will meet LIEUT. G.H. COOPER at Area Commandant's office WORMHOUDT at 9 a.m.

Billeting parties of C 210 & D 210 will proceed in the motor lorries of B 210 & A 210 respectively. Lorries will leave GHYVELDE CHURCH at 7 a.m.

8 Extra transport allotted today to C 210 & D 210 will be rationed & foraged by those units from 26th inst inclusive.

9. Particular attention is directed to paras 3, 4, & 5 of attached order.
Receipts must be obtained for the following tents
```
   HQ    4
   A 210  7
   B 210  11
   C 210  17
   D 210  24
```
A 210 will collect from HQ and hand in 4 tents.

10. Reports during march to head of column.

11. Camps will be left clean.

12. ACKNOWLEDGE on envelope.

J. Dill Capt Adj
200th Bde R.F.A.

Issued by orderly
at 8.15 P.M.

Copy No. 1   A 210
        2   B 210
        3   C 210
        4   D 210
        5   R.S.M. BURTON
        6 } WAR DIARY
        7
        8   FILE

Army Form C. 2118.

WAR DIARY
or
INTELLIGENCE SUMMARY

(Erase heading not required.)

Ref e Map 1/40,000 BETHUNE

Army Form C. 2118 — No. 8

Instructions regarding War Diaries and Intelligence Summaries are contained in F. S. Regs., Part II. and the Staff Manual respectively. Title Pages will be prepared in manuscript.

Place	Date	Hour	Summary of Events and Information	Remarks and references to Appendices
ROBECQ	30/11/15		Composition and distribution of 210th Bde R.F.A. as follows:—	
			H.Q. Billets at ROBECQ	
			A/210 2 Sections Billets at ROBECQ	
			1 Section in the Line at GIVENCHY Section	
			B/210 2 Sections Billets at ROBECQ	
			1 Section in the Line at GIVENCHY Section	
			C/210 2 Sections Billets at ROBECQ	
			1 Section in the Line at GIVENCHY Section	
			D/210 2 Sections Billets at ROBECQ	
			1 Section in the Line at GIVENCHY Section	
			Officers O.R. Horses	
			TOTAL STRENGTH 31 741 657	
			EFFECTIVE STRENGTH 30 732 657	
			DRAFTS RECEIVED during NOVEMBER	
			3 Officers 14 O.R.	

S. Vincent
Major R.F.A.
Comdg 210 Bde R.F.A.

Secret   Copy No. 6

210th Bde. R.F.A. WARNING ORDER No 1.

Reference Map.
1/40000 FURNES   November 14th 1917.

1 This Brigade will be relieved by the Artillery of the 133rd French Division on or about the nights 19/20th and 20/21st inst. After relief the 42nd D.A. will concentrate at GHYVELDE and will march from there to WORMHOUDT on 23rd inst. Detailed orders will be issued later.

2 The gun dumps at Batteries will be reduced to the following amounts by the night 18/19th inst

  18 pdrs   252 rounds per gun
  4.5 Hows   156 rounds per how.

As the amounts surplus do not appear to justify the use of the Light Railway, units will arrange to return a certain amount each night to HULL DUMP by wagons, the reduction to the above amounts being completed by the night 18/19th inst.

3 The final removal of ammunition from the gun positions will be carried out as follows:

On the nights 19/20th and 20/21st the gun dumps of guns withdrawn that night will be returned to HULL DUMP. Six ammunition wagons per battery will be available from the D.A.C. to assist in this.

The loads of battery ammunition wagons required for this work will be deposited in the wagon lines.

After returning to HULL DUMP the gun dumps of the guns withdrawn on night 20/21st battery wagons will be reloaded with their original ammunition deposited at the Wagon Line.

4. Units will notify this office not later than noon tomorrow 15th inst how many of the 6 D.A.C. ammunition wagons which are available for each battery will be required by them on the nights 19/20th and 20/21st inst. Instructions will then be given as to when and where these wagons should be collected.

C. G. Duff
Capt & Adjt
210th Bde R.F.A.

Issued by orderly at 1 p.m.

Copy No 1 — A 210
2 — C 210
3 — D 210
4 — B 210
5 — Lieut G.H. Cooper } (for information)
6 — War Diary
7 — War Diary
8 — File

SECRET   T 1627

With reference to para 3 of attached 42nd D.A. Order No 51, two limbered G.S. wagons will be supplied by Brigade H.Q. to be at Area Commandants' office GHYVELDE at 10 am 21st inst to carry tents.

Bde H.Q. and Batteries will each have 6 cyclists at above place and at above time. These men will be in addition to the Billeting party and will be used to erect tents before the Brigade arrives.

                     Capt. Adjt

20-10-17   210th Bde RFA

SECRET   Copy No 11

210TH BDE ORDER No 30

Refce Map 1/40.000   November 20th 1917
FURNES.

H.Q.   1.   210th Bde R.F.A. (less D210) in
A 210   order of march as per margin, will proceed
B 210   by march route to GHYVELDE on 21st inst.
C 210

        2.   Starting point will be ~~_____~~ Road
x 19 d.7.4 ← junction ~~_____~~. Head of column will
              ~~pass~~ starting point at 4.30 p.m.

        3.   D 210 will proceed to GHYVELDE direct
              from wagon lines in accordance with 42nd
              D.A. Order No ~~=~~ 51.

        4.   The following distances will be
              maintained on the march.
                    Between Batteries - 200 yards.
                       "   Sections - 50 " .
              The leading battery will keep 50
              yards distant on the march from H.Q.

        5.   Halts by units independently
              10 minutes every clock hour. NO halt
              will be made at 5 p.m., ~~but an extra~~
              ~~halt for 10 minutes will be made at~~
              ~~5.20 p.m.~~
              One officer from each unit will
              meet the Adjutant at Starting point
              at 4.25 p.m. to synchronize watches.

        6.   In addition to the one G.S. wagon
              already in possession, the following
              transport (complete turn out) has been
              allotted to units:—

              H.Q. - 2 G.S. wagons   from D.A.C.
              A 210 - 2   "   "   "   "
                       1   "   "   "   A.S.C
                       1 limbered G.S.   "   D.A.C
              B 210   2 G.S. wagons   "   "
                       1   "   "   "   A.S.C
                       1 limbered G.S.   "   D.A.C

6. (continued)

    <u>C 210</u> - 3 G.S. Wagons - From D.A.C.
               1 Limbered G.S. -   "   "

    <u>D 210</u> - 3 G.S. Wagons - From No 1 Sec. D.A.C.
           - 1 Limbered G.S. -   "   " 3 "   "

(D210 will collect these direct on the morning of 21st inst. under mutual arrangement with O.C. No 1 & No 3 Section D.A.C.)

    O.C. A, B, & C 210 will send guides to be at H.Q. Wagon Line office at 9.45 a.m. 21st inst. to collect above transport.

    All Batteries will ration and forage the transport allotted to them from 23rd inst. inclusive.

    The above transport will march in rear of the unit to which it has been allotted.

7.   One officer and one other rank per battery will meet Lt. G.H. Cooper at Area Commandant's office, GHYVELDE at 10 a.m. 21st inst. for billeting purposes.

    Lt. Cooper will report for instructions to S.C.R.A. at the same time and place.

8.   Detailed instructions re arrangements for rations and forage on the march will be issued in due course. Refilling point on 22nd inst. will be GHYVELDE CHURCH.

9.   The attention of units is directed to Administrative instructions issued by 42nd D.A. on 16th inst.

10.   Brigade H.Q. will close at R 30 a 85.85 at 7.30 p.m. 20th inst. and reopen at same hour at H.Q. Wagon Line Office - COXYDE.

11.   Reports during march to head of column.

12.   210th Bde. R.F.A. will march from GHYVELDE to WORMHOUDT on 23rd inst.

13.   ACKNOWLEDGE.

Issued by orderly at 2 p.m.

                          Capt. Adjt.
                          210th Bde R.F.A.

SECRET   Copy No. 6

210th Bde R.F.A. Order No. 32

Refce Map 1/100000
   HAZEBROUCK   23-11-17

        1 Copy of 42nd D.A. Order No 53 is attached hereto.

H.Q.
C/210
D/210
A/210
B/210

        2 210th Bde R.F.A. in order of march as per margin, will march to WORMHOUDT (B) Area tomorrow 24th inst.

        3 Starting point will be X roads 500 yards South of O in WORMHOUDT. Head of column will pass starting point at 9.20 a.m.

        4 Distances as for march today.

        5 Halts by batteries independently 10 minutes every clock hour.

        One officer from each unit will meet the Adjutant at starting point at 9.15 am to synchronize watches.

        6 Billeting parties will report to Lieut G.H. Cooper at WORMHOUDT CHURCH at 8. am. The party will be mounted on cycles and all cycles of the Brigade will be utilized, as their presence is not desired in the column on the march. If possible, billeting officers should be provided with maps.

        7 A/210 and B/210 will each draw 30 gallons of petrol at refilling point tomorrow 24th inst.

        8 Camps will be left clean.

        9 Correct distances will be maintained. In many cases today distances were two or three times greater than those laid down

10 Reports during march to head of column
11 ACKNOWLEDGE on envelope.

C.R.Dill
Capt & Adjt
210th Bde R.F.A

Issued by orderly
at 10.30 pm
Copy No 1. - A 2w
       2 - B 2w
       3 - C 2w
       4 - D 2w
       5   R. Sm. Bourbon
       6 } War Diary
       7 }
       8   File

SECRET   Copy No 6

210th Bde R.F.A. Order No 33.

Refce Map. 1/100000
HAZEBROUCK.   24. 11. 17.

<u>1</u> Copy of 42nd D.A. Order No 54 is attached hereto

HQ
A 210
B 210
C 210
D 210

<u>2</u> 210th Bde R.F.A. in order of march as per margin will march to STAPLE Area tomorrow 25th inst.

<u>3</u> Starting point will be road and track junction 1100 yards S.S.W. of WAEMARS-CAPPEL. Head of column will pass starting point at 9.25 am

<u>4</u> Distances as for march today.

<u>5</u> First halt will be for 10 minutes at 10.30 am after that for 10 minutes every clock hour. One officer from each unit will meet adjutant at starting point at 9.20am to synchronize watches

<u>6</u> Usual billeting parties will report to Lieut G.H. Cooper at Area Commandant's office STAPLE at 9 am. These parties should travel by lorry, if possible, and will be accompanied by all cyclists of the Brigade

<u>7</u> Camps will be left clean

<u>8</u> Reports during march to head of column

<u>9</u> ACKNOWLEDGE in envelope

Issued by orderly at
10 pm

Copy No 1 — A 210
     2 — B 210
     3 — C 210
     4 — D 210
     5 — RSM Burton
     6 } War Diary
     7 }
     8 — File

Capt & adjt
210th Bde R.F.A.

SECRET.   Copy No. 6

210th Bde R.F.A. Orders No 34

Refce Map. 1/100000
HAZEBROUCK.   25. 11. 17.

HQ
A 210
B 210
C 210
D 210

1. Copy of 42nd D.A. Order No. 55 is attached thereto

2. 210th Bde R.F.A. in order of march as per margin, will march to AIRE area tomorrow 26th inst.

3. Starting point will be X roads LONGUE CROIX. Head of column will pass starting point at 9.25 am

4. Halts as laid down in para 2 of attached order.

5. Usual billeting parties will report to Lieut G.H. Cooper at office of Area Commandant LAMBRES at 10 am. All cyclists of the Brigade will also be sent on in advance of the column.

6. Camps will be left clean.

7. Particular attention will be paid to the fitting of breeching. Units will also ensure that drivers stirrup leathers are not too long.

8. Reports during march to head of column.

9. Haversack rations should be taken

10. ACKNOWLEDGE on envelope.

Issued by orderly
at 8.15 pm.

Copy No 1.   A 210
     2   B 210
     3   C 210
     4   D 210
     5   R.S.M. Burton
     6 } War Diaries
     7
     8   File

Capt & Adjt
210th Bde R.F.A

Secret   Copy No. 6

210th Bde R.F.A. Order No. 35

Refce Map 1/40000
Sheet 36 a.   29th Nov 1917

HQ
D Bw
a Bw
B Bw
C Bw

1. Copy of HRA DA Order No. 54 is attached hereto

2. 210th Bde R.F.A. in order of march as per margin will march to ROBECQ area tomorrow 30th inst

3. Starting point will be road junction N 15 c 5.4. Head of column will pass starting point at 9.40 a.m.

4. Distances on the march :-
   Between batteries   500 yards
   — Sections   50 yards
   Leading Battery will keep 50 x distant from H.Q.

5. Halts by batteries independently 10 minutes every clock hour. Watches should be synchronized at Bde H.Q. prior to 9.15 a.m.

6. Usual billeting parties will report to Lieut G.H. COOPER at Area Commandants Office ROBECQ at 9.30. Cyclists of the Brigade will accompany the billeting party

7. Lieut C.C. REES A Bw will report to OC B Bw at 8 a.m. tomorrow morning 30th inst, and will be attached to B Bw until the relief of the 25th DA is completed

8. Billets will be left clean and usual billeting certificates rendered to the Mayor

9 Reports during march to head of column
10 ACKNOWLEDGE on envelope

[signature] Capt & Adjt
20th Bde RFA

Issued by orderly
at 10 pm
   Copy No 1. - A 2io
   —   2 - B 2io
   —   3 - C 2io
   —   4 - D 2io
   —   5 - R S M Burton
   —   6 } War Diary
   —   7 }
   —   8   File

Secret   Copy No 6

210th Brigade Order No 36

Ref:ce Map. 1/40000
Sheet 36a BETHUNE   1st Dec 1917

HQ
C/210
B/210
D/210
A/210

1. 210th Bde R.F.A, in order of march as per margin, will march to wagon lines already notified and relieve units of 25th D.A. in the line today 1st inst.

2. Starting point will be road and canal crossing P.36.a 8.7. Head of column will pass starting point at 1.40 pm

3. Distances as in march yesterday

4. One halt of 10 minutes will be made when the head of the column reaches VENDIN-lez-BETHUNE.

5. As ordered in march table issued by 42nd DA yesterday, B.Cs will arrange with the units they are relieving to have guides at BEUVRY (or in the case of C/210 (GORRE)) to conduct them to the Battery positions.

6. Reference 42nd D.A. Order No 57, para 3, 25th D.A. will withdraw all 4.5 Hows which will be relieved in action by the 4.5 Hows of the 42nd D.A.

7. Units will report amount of ammunition taken over, and also amount in wagon lines, by 9 am tomorrow, 2nd inst.

8. Motor lorry at present with C/210 will, after making journey in the morning, return to Bde HR where a guide from D/210 will collect it. D/210 will carry in this lorry as much surplus H/Q kit as possible and will call at Bde HR for that purpose.

Issued by order,
at 10 am

Copy No 1 - A/210
        2 - B/210
        3 - C/210
        4 - D/210
        5 - R.Sh. Burton
        6)
        7) War Diary
        8 - Bde

                                    (Sgd)
                                    Capt. Adjt
                                    210th Bde R.F.A

Confidential

VOLUME II

WAR DIARY

210th BDE R.F.A.

From 1-12-17
To 31-12-17

Army Form C. 2118.

Reference Map 1/10.000
BETHUNE COMBINED SHEET
BEUVRY 2
LA BASSÉE

WAR DIARY
or
INTELLIGENCE SUMMARY. 1/10.000

(Erase heading not required.)

Instructions regarding War Diaries and Intelligence Summaries are contained in F. S. Regs., Part II. and the Staff Manual respectively. Title pages will be prepared in manuscript.

Place	Date	Hour	Summary of Events and Information	Remarks and references to Appendices
Rue Fiolet	1/7/17		Composition and distribution of 210th Bde R.F.A. as follows:—	
			H.Q. F.10 b 6.2	
			A210 4 guns F.24 a. 36.84 ⎫	
			2 " G.7 b 82.23 ⎬ Canal Group — 42nd D.A.	
			B210 4 " F.17 a. 1.2 ⎬	
			2 " F.18 a. 2.1 ⎭	
			D210 3 hows A20 c 32.71	
			C210 4 guns F.11 d 25.45 ⎫ attached to Givenchy Group	
			2 guns A.7 d 7.1 ⎭ 42nd D.A.	
			Capt. J. CHURCHLEY. R.F.A. attached to D210 from 110 Bde. R.F.A.	
			B210 exchanged two guns with 110th Bde. R.F.A.	
			210th Bde R.F.A. relieved remainder of 110 Bde R.F.A. in positions mentioned above.	

WAR DIARY
or
INTELLIGENCE SUMMARY

Army Form C. 2118.

Reference Map 1/40.000 BETHUNE Combined chart.
1/10.000 BEUVRY & LA BASSEE

Place	Date	Hour	Summary of Events and Information	Remarks and references to Appendices
F10 b 5.2	3 12/7		Lt A.E. HIGHAM C210 and 1 N.C.O. from each battery returned from Artillery Course at VAUX. 2/Lt E.G. WALKER C210 transferred to VII Corps. Following officers posted from 4 2nd D.A.C. 2/Lt G. FRASER to D210 D.H. HEWITT " B210	
F10 b 5.2	4 12/7		Military Medals awarded to :— 4/15288 a/Bdr EDWARDS. J. D210 ⎫ 4/15043 Sgt. McKENZIE. H. " ⎬ For gallantry in extinguishing burning charge at the battery position in the NIEUPORT sector 4/5122 Cpl RYAN. R. " ⎪ 4/15260 a/Bdr DENWOOD T. " ⎭	
F10 b 5.2	9 12/7		2/Lt C.E. HUMPHREY A210 proceeded for course to First Army Artillery School, AIRE. Lt G.H. COOPER C210 posted to Brigade H.Q., vice him the Lieut establish- went of the post of orderly officer.	

WAR DIARY or INTELLIGENCE SUMMARY

Army Form C. 2118.

Reference Maps /40,000
BETHUNE COMBINED Sheet
/10,000 BEUVRY D
LA BASSÉE

3

Place	Date	Hour	Summary of Events and Information	Remarks and references to Appendices
F10 b 5.2	14/9/17	—	Following Officers, N.CO's and men mentioned in dispatches:— Lt Col. A. BIRTWISTLE, C.M.G. Major D.J. MASON Capt. A.G. HALL 2/W. N.F. ADENEY 400025 Sgt. BENTLEY H. A210 405553 " COOPER F. C210 400206 Cpl. CATLOW, J.B. H.Q. 400257 " GARDNER. A.D. B210 400383 Gnr. HUTCHINSON. P. B210 Lt H.S. SHANAHAN, D210 awarded the Military Cross.	C30
F10 b 5.2	16/9/17		Following postings took place:— Lt T.H. WALMSLEY, A210 to H.Q. D.A.C. 2/Lt. E.W. JAMES H.Q. D.A.C. to D210 " H.L. PENN " " C210	C30
F10 b 5.2	19/9/17		Lieut. L. BUCK, B210 posted to D211.	C30
F10 b 5.2	21/9/17		Lieut. H. FINCH, C210 proceeded on fourteen days leave to U.K.	C30

Army Form C. 2118.

WAR DIARY *Reference Maps 1/40,000 BETHUNE.*
Combined Sheet BETHUNE
INTELLIGENCE SUMMARY. *1/10,000 BEUVRY 2*
LA BASSÉE.

(Erase heading not required.)

Place	Date	Hour	Summary of Events and Information	Remarks and references to Appendices
F10 b.5.2	22/7/17		Batteries reported by B.G.R.A. I Corps. Detached Section of A20 moved a following: 1 gun to main posn at F.24 a 36.84 1 " " F.24 c 78.39	A CBJ
F10 b.5.2	24/7/17	9.30 pm to 9.30 pm	Gas projected on enemy trenches between GIVENCHY and the LA BASSÉE CANAL. Supported by artillery bombardment	CBJ
F10 b.5.2	26/7/17		Following postings from Base:— Capt. A.J. HIGGS to C20 2/Lt W.H. BRADFIELD " B20 2/Lt W. BOYD " A20 " H. CAWTHORNE " A20. 1 gun D20 moved to F.23 23.6	CBJ
F10 b.5.2	27/7/17		1 gun D20 moved to F.23 23.6	CBJ
F10 b.5.2	28/7/17		Major W. BIRTWISTLE B20 Returned from Overseas School and leave in U.K.	CBJ

WAR DIARY
or
INTELLIGENCE SUMMARY.

(Erase heading not required.)

Army Form C. 2118.

Reference Maps 1/40,000 BETHUNE.
Contoured Sheet. 1/10,000 BEUVRY 2
& BOUTE

Place	Date	Hour	Summary of Events and Information	Remarks and references to Appendices
F10b5.2	30/7		G.O.C. 2nd Division presented medal ribbons to N.C.O.s and men of the Brigade.	C30
F10b5.2	31/7		"X" "Z" & 3 guns of "V" T.M. Batteries placed under tactical command of 210th Bde R.F.A. H.Q.	C31
			GENERAL	
			Work carried out during the month consisted of :-	
			(a) Improvements to O.P.'s	
			(b) Construction of shell proof command posts and telephone exchanges.	
			(c) Wiring of Battery positions	
			(d) Construction of dummy positions	
			(e) Improvements to wagon lines.	
			With regard to above (a) (c) (d) have been completed. (e) work is proceeding. (b) has been started but work is held up owing to first shifting the wiring of cement.	
			No enemy aircraft bombing firing has been carried out daily, with short bursts on selected spots at night.	

WAR DIARY or INTELLIGENCE SUMMARY

Rye Hats. 1/10,000. BEUVRY & LA BASSÉE

Army Form C. 2118.

Remarks and references to Appendices: 6

Composition and distribution of 210th Bn R.E. in June 1

H.Q. FIOb.6.2

A 210   5 gun   F 24 a 36.84
         1 gun   F 24 c 78.39   } CANAL GROUP 42ND D.A

B 210   4 gun   F 19 a 1.2
         2 gun   F 18 a 2.1.

D 210   4 how   A 20 c 37.71
         2 how   F 23 2 85.60   } attached to GIVENCHY GROUP 42ND D.A

C 210   4 gun   F 11 d 25.45
         2 gun   A 7 d 7.1

DRAFTS received during the month
8 officers 27 OR. 3 hours.
TOTAL STRENGTH
36 off. 960 or 664 horses
EFFECTIVE STRENGTH
35 off. 951 OR. 664 horses.

D. Marin
Major
Comm dg 210th Bn R.E.

Confidential

VOLUME III

WAR DIARY

OF

210TH BDE., R.F.A.

From 1-1-18.
To ... 31-1-18. } 7 p.p.

WAR DIARY
or
INTELLIGENCE SUMMARY

Army Form C. 2118.

Reference Map 1/40000 BEUVRY and LA BASSÉE.

Remarks and references to Appendices: 1

Place	Date	Hour	Summary of Events and Information
F10 b 5.2	1/8		Composition and distribution of 210th Bde R.F.A. as follows:—
			H.Q. F10 b 5.2
			A 210 5 guns F24 a 36.84, F24 c 78.39 ⎫
			B 210 4 " F19 a 1.2, F18 a 2.1 ⎬ CANAL GROUP. 42nd D.A.
			2 "
			D 210 4 hows. A20 c 32.71, F23 b 35.60 ⎭
			2 "
			C 210 4 guns F11 d 25.45, A4 d 4.1 } attached to GIVENCHY GROUP 42nd
			2 "
			Major A.G. HALL, C 210. Proceeded on one month's course to U.K. with 14 days leave to follow.
			Capt. J. CHURCHLEY (Instructor of Gunnery) attached D 210, posted to command C 210.

WAR DIARY or INTELLIGENCE SUMMARY

Army Form C. 2118.

Reference Maps /10,000 BEUVRY + LA BASSEE

Place	Date	Hour	Summary of Events and Information	Remarks and references to Appendices
F10 b.5.2	2/1/18		Major D.J. MASON promoted a/Lt. Colonel Capt. L. HIGHTON. D.10 " a/Major Lt. G.W. GREENWOOD. B.10 " a/Captain	GPd
F10 b.5.2	3/1/18		I Corps Conv'n order and B.G.R.A. I Corps instructed Matthieu of CANAL GROUP. Brig. Gen. A. BIRTWISTLE. C.M.G. (late D.10 Bde RFA) Lt.Col. D.J. MASON } awarded D.S.O.	GPd
F10 b.5.2	4/1/18		Lieut. C. MACKRELL. B.10 proceeded for attachment to No.2 Squadron R.F.C. An officer of No.2 Squadron R.F.C. attached to B.10	GPd
F10 b.5.2	6/1/18	2.50 p.m.	Lt.Col. C.C. REES. A.10 proceeded to AIRE on one month's artillery course. 2/Lt. C.E. HUMPHREY. A.10 returned from one month's artillery course at AIRE. Enemy put up a simple screen from behind the N.E. BRICKSTACK at A.22.a.80.95. which opened to the CANAL. Simultaneously enemy T.M.'s commenced a heavy bombardment of A.21, CANAL GROUP replied with fire on enemy support line in A.16 c and A.22 c. and at 3.15 p.m. put a 10 minute Concentration onto enemy support line between the LA BASSEE- BETHUNE road and the CANAL. at about 3.30 p.m. enemy activity died down, but recommenced at 4 p.m. and lasted until 5 p.m. Further commentary	

WAR DIARY
or
~~INTELLIGENCE SUMMARY~~
(Erase heading not required.)

Army Form C. 2118.

Reference Map. 1/10,000 BEUVRY & LA BASSÉE

Place	Date	Hour	Summary of Events and Information	Remarks and references to Appendices
(continued)	6/8		were carried out by CORAR Group on enemy H.B. A22 d.6.6. & A23.a.5.0, also on various enemy T.M. emplacements. At the commencement of the enemy bombardment a few gas shells were put into KINGSCLERE O.P. at A15.c.6.3. Sgt. GRIFFITHS, R.A.B. (Pte M20) Dawes, M. (B20) Ph. S. TOWCESTER. (D20) } awarded D.C.M.	C.R.A.
	4/8	5.25am to 6.25am	About 100 H.T.M.s fell in A21. No artillery action. Capt. J. CHURCHER (Gunnery Instructor) attached to C210. Lieut. C. MATHEW. B210. Returned from attachment to No.2 Squadron R.F.C. Officer from No.2 Squadron R.F.C. attached B210, returned to R.F.C.	C.B.D.
	8/8		Lt. G.H. COOPER. H.Q. posted to C210. 2/Lt. D.H. HEWITT. B210. " " " " Lt. H. FINCH. C210 returned from 14 days leave in U.K. H.Q. as orderly officer.	C.B.D.
	10/8		Major R. YATES. A210 returned from course and leave in U.K. 2/Major L. HIGHTON. D210 " " " " " " posted forward and D21.	C.B.D.

WAR DIARY
INTELLIGENCE SUMMARY.
(Erase heading not required.)

Army Form C. 2118.

Refce Maps
/10,000. BEUVRY
and LA BASSEE

Instructions regarding War Diaries and Intelligence Summaries are contained in F.S. Regs., Part II. and the Staff Manual respectively. Title pages will be prepared in manuscript.

Place	Date	Hour	Summary of Events and Information	Remarks and references to Appendices
F10 b 52	11/8		Lt G.H. COOPER C210 and M. GOURDON forwarded to WITTERNESSE to investigate declarations.	See
	12/8	12.55pm to 2.35pm	Forward section of B210 at F18 a.2.1. shelled with 15 cm (about 200 rounds) No damage either to personnel or material.	See
	13/8		Lt G.H. COOPER C210 returned from WITTERNESSE and posted to H2 R.D.A.C.	See
			2/Lt H.A. HAMILTON H2 R° D.A.C. posted to C 210.	
	14/8		C.R.A and two American Officers visited battery positions and O.P.S Capt. G.W. GREENWOOD (B210) forwarded on 14 days leave to U.K. Lt T.A. STUTTARD (C210)	See
	16/8		Capt H.B. ECCLES A210 to hospital (Pneumonia)	See
	17/8		O/L CE. HUMPHREY A210 to Divisional Signalling School on one month Course. Major General TOWNSEND, American Army, visited Group H.Q.	See
	18/8		2/Lt H.T.R. MOORE (Offr Sig.) proceeded on 14 days leave to U.K.	See

WAR DIARY
or
INTELLIGENCE SUMMARY.
(Erase heading not required.)

Army Form C. 2118.

Ref^{ce} Map. BEUVRY
1/10,000 and LA BASSEE.

5.

Place	Date	Hour	Summary of Events and Information	Remarks and references to Appendices
F 10 b. 52	20/1/18	1.30 pm	C.Os and B.Cs. reconnoitred positions for reinforcing batteries. Group fired a concentration on enemy trenches in S.W. corner of A17b. as punishment for enemy shelling of "KINGSCLERE" and GUINCHY CHURCH.	Nil
F 10 b. 52	21/1/8		2/Lt T.W. MORRISS D/210 posted to 42 D.A.C.	Nil
F 10 b. 52	22/1/8	3 pm	LT A.E. HIGHAM C/210 proceeded for 3 days attachment to No 2 Squadron R.F.C. An officer from No 2 Squadron R.F.C. joined C/210 for three days attachment.	Nil
F 10 b. 52	23/1/8	2.0 pm	Capt. H.B. ECCLES A/210 returned from Hospital	Nil
		2.30 pm	LT H.B. BARCLAY reported for duty from U.K. & joined (temporarily) to 210 Bde H.Qrs	Nil
F 10 b. 52	24/1/18		Capt C.G. DUFF - H.Q. 210 } Proceeded on 14 days leave to U.K. LT G.P. HARTLEY - B/210 } Capt. H.B. ECCLES - A/210 proceeded on 5 days leave to PARIS	Nil
		4.0 pm	C/210 came under orders of Canal Group from Guinchy Group	
F 10 b. 52	25/1/18	2.30 pm	LT A.E. HIGHAM returned from 3 days attachment to No 2 SQUADRON R.F.C.	Nil
F 10 b. 52	26/1/18	3.0 pm	Two American Artillery Officers attached to Batteries for 1 day.	Nil
F 10 b. 52	27/1/18	3.30 pm	The two American Officers returned to 42 Div. Arty H.Qs.	Nil

Army Form C. 2118.

WAR DIARY
or
INTELLIGENCE SUMMARY.
(Erase heading not required.)

Reference Map.
1/10.000. BEUVRY and LA BASSEE.

Instructions regarding War Diaries and Intelligence Summaries are contained in F.S. Regs., Part II. and the Staff Manual respectively. Title pages will be prepared in manuscript.

Place	Date	Hour	Summary of Events and Information	Remarks and references to Appendices
F10 d.5.2.	28/8	2:30/h	CANAL GROUP fired on LES BRIQUES (A28.b.) a concentration of the Brigade field guns Howitzers — as punishment for enemy shelling of Road near. Rt. BTN. H.Q. (A21.C.)	Nil
F10 d.5.2	31/8	—	LT. T.A. STUTTARD C210 returned from 14 days leave to U.K.	Nil
			GENERAL	
			Work carried out during the Month consisted of:-	
			(a) Construction of well-built Command Posts telephone Exchanges	
			(b) Wiring of Battery Positions	
			(c) Improvements to Wagon Lines.	
			(d) Selection + making of Reinforcing Positions.	
			(e) Improvements + repairs to Battery Positions	
			(f) Construction of Rifle Ranges at Battery Positions	
			With regard to Move (f) is completed. The remainder are still in progress.	
			Routine firing has been carried out daily by night firing from has been taken place.	

A5834 Wt.W4973/M687 750,000 8/16 D. D. & L. Ltd. Forms/C.2118/13

Army Form C. 2118.

Reference Map 1/40,000
BETHUNE

7

WAR DIARY
or
INTELLIGENCE SUMMARY.
(Erase heading not required.)

Place	Date	Hour	Summary of Events and Information	Remarks and references to Appendices
F10.b.5.2	31/1/18		Composition & distribution of 210th Bde, R.F.A. as follows.	
			H.Q. F10.b.5.2.	
			A210. In action 5 guns F24a.36.84	
			1 gun F24c.78.39	
			B210. " " 4 guns F17a.1.2.	
			2 guns F18.a.2.1.	CANAL GROUP
			C210. " " 4 guns F11.d.25.45.	
			2 guns A7d.7.1	42nd D.A.
			D210. " " 2 Hows. A20.c.32.71	
			4 Hows F23.b.35.60	
			DRAFTS received during the month	
			1 Officer. 33 OR. — Horses.	
			TOTAL STRENGTH	
			35 Officers. 76 OR, 618 Horses.	
			EFFECTIVE STRENGTH.	
			31 Officers 736 OR 618 Horses	Swinton Lt Col. Commdg 210th Bde R.F.A.

WO 13

CONFIDENTIAL.

WAR. DIARY.

OF.

210ᵈ. BRIGADE. R.F.A.

From. 1-2-18.   To. 28-2-18

Vol. III

Army Form C. 2118.

WAR DIARY
or
INTELLIGENCE SUMMARY.
(Erase heading not required.)

Ref. Map.
1/40.000 Combined Sheet 1
BETHUNE

Place	Date	Hour	Summary of Events and Information	Remarks and references to Appendices
F10 b 5.2	3/7/18		Lt H.T.P. MOORE (O/C Sigs) returned from 14 days leave in U.K.	C30
			Capt. C.R. BROWN posted to A 210	C30
			Lieut A.E. HIGHAM C210 proceeded to A 210 on Artillery Course	
F10 b 5.2	6/7/18		13 O.R. (Reinforcements) Received.	C30
F10 b 5.2	8/7/18		Capt. C.G. DUFF (HQ) Lieut G.P. HARTLEY (B 210) } Returned from 14 days leave in U.K.	C30
			Lieut R. HARTLEY arrived from Base and posted to B 210	
F10 b 5.2	13/7/18		Lieut C. MAURICE B 210 proceeded on 14 days leave to U.K. Advance party from 276 Bde R.F.A arrived for attachment to Battery.	C38
F10 b 5.2	14/7/18		Capt. R.A. SMITH D 210 proceeded to U.K. on Overseas Course with 14 days leave to follow.	C30
		12 noon to 4.10 pm	HH.un 9 gm. bombardment of support lines and HARLEY STREET from CANAL to BRADDEL CASTLE (approx)	
		12.30 pm to 12.25 pm	210 "B" de R.F.A fired on enemy trenches in retaliation.	

WAR DIARY or INTELLIGENCE SUMMARY

Army Form C. 2118.

Refer Maps. 1/40000 Cruikshank Sht 2 BETHUNE

Place	Date	Hour	Summary of Events and Information	Remarks and references to Appendices
F10 b 6.2	15/3/18		Advance party from Brigade HQ and the Batteries proceeded to FOUQUIERES and HERDIGNEUL to the allotted Billets.	
		3pm to 4pm	2/Lt D.H. HEWITT (H.Q.) proceeded to R.F.C. on an necks aeroplane photograph course. Maj J Battery of 276 Bde R.F.A. relieved R25J Battery of the Brigade in the Line.	C.R.S.
		During the night	Hostile artillery fired short bursts on various parts of the front. Our artillery retaliated.	
F10 b 6.2	16/3/18		Remainder of Brigade relieved in the line by 276 Bde R.F.A. 210 m Bde proceeded into rest billets as under:-	C.R.S.
			H.Q. FOUQUIERES E 21 a 40.35 A 210 HERDIGNEUL D 30 d 6.0 B 210 FOUQUIERES E 21 a 85.35 C 210 HERDIGNEUL E 25 d 4.4 D 210 HERDIGNEUL E 25 c 0.4 210 m Bde Signal Subsection joined 42 Div. Signal Coy. for special training. Lt.Col. D. J. MASON, D.S.O. appointed a/CRA 42 m Division Major N. BIRTWHISTLE, B 210 a/C.O. 210 m Bde R.F.A. 2 Lieut. D 210 exchanged for 2 Lieut of D 276.	

Army Form C. 2118.

Ref. Map 1/40,000
Containing Aire-BETHUNE
and 1/20,000 36 c, N.E.

WAR DIARY
or
INTELLIGENCE SUMMARY.
(Erase heading not required.)

Place	Date	Hour	Summary of Events and Information	Remarks and references to Appendices
FOUQUEREUIL	17/8		Major N.F. HIGHER. M.C. arrived from Base and posted to command D.A.C.	C98
do	18/8		2/Lt G.F. BICK A.D.C. proceeded to HOUCHIN on 14 days Miniature Dugout Course.	C99
			One gun sent from A.B. x C.A.C. sent to D.A.C. A.13. x D.A.C. sent to Arboraining for overhaul.	
do	21/8		Major A.G. HART M.C. C.R.O. returned from Arras School and 14 days leave in U.K.	C91
			2/Lt D.H. HEWITT (H.A.) returned from Aeroplane Photograph Course.	
do	22/8		Capt. F.L. STAPLES (S.F.) attached 210 "732" R.F.A. B.G.R.A. I Corps visited batteries.	C92
do	23/8		Lieut R.L. LONGER C.D.O.} proceeded on 14 days leave to U.K. Lieut. R. COOKE. D.A.C.}	
			One How. D.A.C. sent to 11" D.A. Artillery School HOUCHIN.	
do	25/8		G. Oc. and C.R.A. inspected batteries. Lt B.H. HORNER proceeded on 2 days leave to PIONIER.	C93
do	26/8		1 How D.A.C. sent to N°13 B.M.N. (higher) for Gunnery fathom.	C94

A 5834 Wt. W4973/M687 750,000 8/16 D. D. & L. Ltd. Forms/C.2118/13

WAR DIARY
or
INTELLIGENCE SUMMARY.
(Erase heading not required.)

Army Form C. 2118.

Rg⁰ H.q⁴⁰⁄₂₀,₀₀₀
Communick Chief
BETHUNE and ⁄₂₀,₀₀₀
3ᵉ C.V.S.

Place	Date	Hour	Summary of Events and Information	Remarks and references to Appendices
FOUQUIÈRES	28/2/18	—	L:B.H. HORNER A210 Returned from two days leave to STOHER.	4
			From the 14th to 28th inclusive, three men devoted to training, and Reconnaissance of the I Corps area.	
			DISTRIBUTION	
			H.Q. — FOUQUIÈRES — E 21 a 40.35	
			A210 — HERDIGNEUL — D 30 d 6.0	
			B210 — FOUQUIÈRES — E 21 a 85.35	
			C210 — HERDIGNEUL — E 25 d 4.4	
			D210 — HERDIGNEUL — E 25 c 0.4	
			DRAFTS RECEIVED during FEBRUARY	
			24 O.R.	
			TOTAL STRENGTH 37 Officers M.M.I. O.R. 623 Horses	
			EFFECTIVE STRENGTH 36 " 766 " 621 "	
				N.H.Witt
Commdg 210th B.L.R.M. Major

210TH BRIGADE RFA   ORDER. No 37.

Copy No. 8

Reference BETHUNE
Combined Sheet
40.000.

12.2.18

1. 210TH Bde. R.F.A. will be relieved by the 276th Bde R.F.A. in the line on the nights 15/16th and 16/17th insts as under.
15/16th inst. Relief of one section per battery in the main position and one gun of each detached section (In the case of A/210 relief of single gun)
16/17th inst. Completion of relief
Batteries will be relieved by their opposite numbers
All reliefs to be complete by 8 p.m. 16th inst.
Relieving units will not arrive at battery positions before 5 p.m. on each night.

2. There will be **NO** interchange of equipment

3. The half battery relieved on each night will march, complete with ammunition wagons, direct to new wagon lines, particulars of which are given in para 7.

4. Aeroplane photographs, log books, map boards, etc. and those maps mentioned in this office TH071 d/ 9.2.18 will be handed over.

5. Ammunition at battery positions will be handed over at 10 am 16th inst.
Units will move out with full echelons, 18 pdr. batteries having 50% A 50% Ax. Units will ensure that this ammunition is serviceable and does not include any proscribed marks or makes. 18 pdr batteries will at once adjust the amounts in their echelons to the proportion laid down.

6. All trench and area stores will be handed over to incoming units at 10 AM 16th inst.

(1.)

7. New Wagon Lines of units will be as follows:-
HQ & D210   FOUQUIERES (F.21)
B.A.C. & ?   HESDIGNEUL (F.25)

Advance parties under charge of one officer per battery, will report mounted to 2/Lt. D.H. Hewitt at A/210 wagon lines at 10am 15th inst. These parties will remain at the new wagon lines until the arrival of the Brigade.

8. O.C. D.A.C. will despatch sufficient transport to arrive at HQ and Battery wagon lines on the morning of the 14th inst to complete units to the following:-
HQ   4 G.S. wagons ⎫
A210   4 G.S. wagons ⎬
B210   2 G.S. wagons ⎬ Complete with drivers and teams
C210   4 G.S. wagons ⎬
D210   2 G.S. wagons ⎭

The following G.S. Wagons belonging to HQ 42nd D.A.C. will be replaced by DAC on the morning of the 14th inst.

9. Attached A 210 Wagon N°E 63201
             B 210   "   . E 47955
             C 210   "   . E 63209
             D 210   "   . E 48070

Units will arrange for these wagons to be in camp.
Units will return to O.C. S.A.A. Section on morning of 14th inst. the limbered G.S. Wagons at present attached to them.

D.A.C. personnel and horses will arrive rationed up to 16th inst. inclusive. Units will arrange to include them on their ration strength (on the scale of 6 horse teams per vehicle) for consumption 14th inst, on which date they will rejoin the D.A.C.

Two motor lorries will report at A 210 wagon lines at 8 a.m. on the mornings of the 15th & 16th insts. These are allotted to B210 & D 210 who will send guides each morning to collect.

RETURNS   Following returns etc are required by this Office:-
Due by 11 a.m. 16th inst
Return of ammunition handed over (by wire) on
including S.A.A. in gun pits.
Return of ammunition being removed to new wagon
lines in echelons (by wire)
Receipts of trench and area stores handed over,
signed by an officer of the relieving unit. (Due by HQ
morning orderly.)

10. Particular attention is directed to the instructions
contained in H 2 D.A. Administrative instructions, a
copy of which is attached hereto.

11. Completion of each night's relief will be wired to this
office by code word "MAP".

12. Command of CANAL GROUP will be handed over to
O.C, 275th Brigade R.F.A. on completion of relief.

13.   ACKNOWLEDGE.

Issued by orderly
at 7 pm 12/2/18
Copy No 1 - A 210
       2 - B 210
       3 - C 210
       4 - D 210
       5 - 125th Inf. Bde ⎫
       6 - 275th Bde R.F.A ⎬ For information
       7 - R.S.M. Buxton
       8 - ⎫
       9 - ⎬ War diary
      10 - ⎭ File.

J. Duff
Capt Adj
210th Bde. R.F.A.

SECRET

AMENDMENTS TO 210th BDE R.F.A.
ORDER No 37.

1. Para 3 is cancelled and the following substituted:-

No portion of batteries will move from their present wagon lines till 16th inst.

The batteries of 55th Division are only bringing up guns have said with other transport so is absolutely necessary on the 15th inst and batteries of this Brigade will make arrangements to accommodate at their wagon lines for the night those cases three detachments observers either to but the few men and gun teams of relieving batteries.

If so desired baggage may be sent in advance and dumped on the 15th inst.

On 16th inst batteries will move under orders of the O.C. concerned subject to the following distances being maintained:-

Between batteries — 300 yards.

2. Para 9 is amended as follows:-

   HQ 183 Bde — FOUQUIERES
   A C 122W — MESCINEUL

14/2/18

Capt May
2ich Bde R.F.A

Copies to all recipients of 2 183
Bde R.F.A Order No 37.

42nd Divisional Artillery.

210th BRIGADE

ROYAL FIELD ARTILLERY

MARCH 1 9 1 8

Confidential.

YA 14

WAR DIARY
OF
210th BRIGADE. R.F.A.

From 1/3/18   To 3/3/18

Vol. III

WAR DIARY
or
INTELLIGENCE SUMMARY.
(Erase heading not required.)

Army Form C. 2118.

REFERENCE MAP.
1/40.000 Combined Sheet.
BETHUNE

Place	Date	Hour	Summary of Events and Information	Remarks and references to Appendices
FOUQUIERES	1 3/18		2/Lt L.G. LEWIS B/210 proceeded on GAS COURSE at CHOCQUES. Lt. C. MACKRELL B/210 returned from 14 days leave in U.K.	R.H.
"	2 3/18		Billeting Parties proceeded to HAM-EN-ARTOIS. G.O.C. 42d Division gave address to Officers + N.C.O's of the Brigade at CHURCH ARMY HUT. FOUQUIERES.	R.H.
HAM-EN-ARTOIS.	3 3/18		2/Lt T. NICHOLSON B/210 proceeded on 14 days leave to U.K. 210² Bde R.F.A proceeded to HAM-EN-ARTOIS via CHOCQUES and LILLERS. Units located in HAM-EN-ARTOIS.	R.H.
"	6 3/18		2/Lt G.F. BICK A/210 returned from 1 Month August Course	R.H.
"	7 3/18		LIEUT A.E. HIGHAM C/210 returned from one months Artillery Course at AIRE.	R.H.
"	8 3/18		2/Lt G.F. BICK A/210 proceeded on 14 days leave to U.K.	R.H.
"	9 3/18		2/Lt L.G. LEWIS returned from GAS COURSE	R.H.
"	11 3/18		LT. COL. D.J. MASON. D.S.O. proceeded on leave + leave Officers Course to U.K.	R.H.

WAR DIARY or INTELLIGENCE SUMMARY

Army Form C. 2118.

Ref. M.F. 1/40 000 Combined Sheet 2. BETHUNE.

Place	Date	Hour	Summary of Events and Information	Remarks and references to Appendices
HAM-EN-ARTOIS.	12/3/18		G.O.C & B.G.R.A 42nd Division visited Batteries.	A.H.
"	14/3/18		Maj. HIGHET. M.C. proceeded on B.C's Course in U.K.	A.H.
"	16/3/18		Capt. F. HOWARD. M.O.R.C. U.S.A. proceeded on 14 days leave to PARIS. 10 reinforcements (Gunners & Drivers) arrived from BASE.	A.H.
"	17/3/18		2/Lt. HUMPHERY (A/210) returned from Signals Course. Capt. C.G. DUFF (HQ) to Hospital. 2/Lt. L.G. LEWIS "B"/210 proceeded on 2 days Camouflage Course.	A.H.
"	18/3/18		Lt. HIGHAM & Lt. C. MACKRELL proceeded to LOCON to reconnoitre their bounds at reinforcing Battery Positions in rear of Portuguese troops. 3 reinforcements (Signallers) arrived from Div. Sig. School.	A.H.
"	19/3/18		2/Lt. L.G. LEWIS "B"/210 returned from Camouflage Course. During the Brigade's stay in HAM-EN-ARTOIS the time was spent on training, particularly in gun drill. Gas drill was	A.H.

WAR DIARY or INTELLIGENCE SUMMARY

Army Form C. 2118.

Reference Maps: Continued Sheet 1/40000 BETHUNE.
1/100000 LENS 11 & 57 D. N.3.

Place	Date	Hour	Summary of Events and Information	Remarks and references to Appendices
GAUCHIN LEGAL	23/3/18		210th Bde R.F.A moved by road to GAUCHIN LEGAL area. Batteries located as follows:— H.Q. — GAUCHIN LEGAL. A/210 } C/210 } CAUCOURT. B/210 } D/210 } HERMIN.	Nil
ADINFER	24/3/18		210th Bde R.F.A. received orders to proceed to BAVINCOURT. This was cancelled during the march & the Brigade proceeded to the N.W. side of ADINFER WOOD & bivouaced there.	Nil
ABLAINZEVELLE	25/3/18	2.0 am	Orders received to be in action before dawn before morning N.E. from ABLAINZEVELLE – COURCELLES le COMTE. Brigade Commander & staff reconnoitred whole position before dawn. Batteries were located as follows:— H.Q. F.23.d.7.7. A/210 F.24.c.1.9. B/210 F.24.a.5.0 C/210 F.24.c.20.95. D/210 F.23.a.5.4.	Nil

WAR DIARY or INTELLIGENCE SUMMARY

(Erase heading not required.)

Army Form C. 2118.

Ref. Maps. LENS 11 + 20040 57D. N.E.

Place	Date	Hour	Summary of Events and Information	Remarks and references to Appendices
ABLAINZEVELLE	25/3/18	(cont)	Batteries fired all day on various targets in the direction of ERVILLERS & southward thereof.	N/1
" "		11.pm	210? Brigade retired to positions in valley S.W. of ABLAINZEVELLE but did not fire. It was found necessary to again retire at dawn the following day. (2 O.Rs. wounded)	
ESSARTS	26/3/18	5.0 am	210? Brigade retired to positions near ESSARTS-LES-BUCQUOY. Locations of Batteries as follows:- HQ F19.c.0.0.9. A/210 F19.c.h. B/210 F19.c. C/210 F19.c. D/210 E24.b. Batteries fired large amounts of ammunition. 2/210 was shelled & suffered 9 casualties (LT. R.L.C. LOWCOCK wounded 7 O.Rs wounded + 1 OR killed).	N/1
" "	27/3/18		Battery positions shelled during the day. The enemy were reported to be filling back again behind ABLAINZEVELLE. Batteries fired on enemy formations	3/1

WAR DIARY
or
INTELLIGENCE SUMMARY.

Army Form C. 2118.

Ref. Map. LENS II 1/10000
1/20,000 57 D. N.E.

5

Instructions regarding War Diaries and Intelligence Summaries are contained in F. S. Regs., Part II. and the Staff Manual respectively. Title pages will be prepared in manuscript.

(Erase heading not required.)

Place	Date	Hour	Summary of Events and Information	Remarks and references to Appendices
ESSARTS	27 3/18 (continued)		LOGEAST WOOD harassed two S.O.S. Calls from Infantry. 4 O.R. wounded.	AW.
-"-	28 3/18		Batteries fired on various targets commenced digging in. Enemy quieter than the previous two days. 1 O.R. killed 1 O.R. wounded.	AW.
-"-	29 3/18		Batteries fired 250 rounds on LOGEAST WOOD turning the day kept up bursts of fire on F30a. L.6. L.12. & L.18 little shelling all day and a quiet night. Prisoners report that barrage fired by us on 28" at 1.0 am on LOGEAST WOOD, killed a complete Battalion less 40 men. Amm. Expended 950 rounds. Casualties - 1 O.R. wounded. LT COL MASON D.S.O. rejoined from Senior Officers Course in U.K.	AW.

WAR DIARY or INTELLIGENCE SUMMARY

Army Form C. 2118.

Ref. Map. LENS 1/100000 Army Form C. 2118.
& 57 D.N.E. 1/20000

Place	Date	Hour	Summary of Events and Information	Remarks and references to Appendices
ESSARTS	30/3/18		Enemy very quiet all day. We suffered no casualties.	
		7.10 p.m	All batteries concentrated their fire on PUISIEUX.	
		8.50 p.m	Batteries maintained throughout day harassing fire on Roads, Woods &c. Lines relieved by 41st Div. 42nd Div. Inf. relieved by 41st Div. Right group covering Rt. of Bde. remnants of 210 Bde R.F.A. 211 Bde R.F.A. & 293 Bde A.F.A. 59th Divisional on our left. 62nd Div. on own right.	
- " -	31/3/18		Enemy fairly quiet. Shelled our front line in the morning between 6-0 am & 8-0 am. We shelled L5d. L12a. L11c in bursts of fire during the day. C/210 moved to position next to D/210. G.O.C. 42nd Div. called whether batteries (210 & 211) for their good work.	

WAR DIARY
or
INTELLIGENCE SUMMARY.
(Erase heading not required.)

Army Form C. 2118.

Reference Maps. LENS 11 1/10,000
57D N.E. 1/20,000

Place	Date	Hour	Summary of Events and Information	Remarks and references to Appendices
ESSARTS			Composition + distribution of 210th Bde. R.F.A as follows:-	
			H.Q. F.19.c.09.	
			A/210 E.18.b.6.5.	
			B/210 F.19.c.1.2. } Half of Right Group	
			C/210 E.24.b.0.0. 4.2" D.A.	
			D/210 E.24.b.2.5.	
			WAGON LINES (Bde). Bienvillers-au-Bois.	
			Drafts received during the month.	
			Offrs. — OR's 34 Horses 40	
			__Casualties__	
			Killed — 2 OR's.	
			Wounded — 1 Officer	
			115 OR's.	
			Total strength	
			Offrs 39 OR's 778 Horses 657.	
			Effective strength	
			Offrs 37 OR's 770 Horses 657.	
			S. Macall	
			Lt Col.	
			Commanding 210th Bde R.F.A.	

Copy No 7

F.87

SECRET.

210th BRIGADE ORDER NO. 36.   2nd March 1918.

cf. Map BETHUNE combined sheet 1/40000 - Sheet 36a 1/40000.

Copy of 42nd D. A. Order No. 60 is enclosed herewith.

210th Brigade R.F.A. in order of march as per margin will march to HAM-EN-ARTOIS tomorrow 3rd instant.

H.Q.
B/210
C/210
D/210
A/210

Starting Point Road Junction E.21.c.10.95. Units will pass starting points at the following times :-
```
H. Q.    ...   7.45 a.m.
B/210    ...   7.50 a.m.
C/210    ...   8.0  a.m.
D/210    ...   8.10 a.m.
A/210    ...   8.20 a.m.
```

Distances on the march will be :-
- Between H.Q. and leading Battery ... 25 yds.
- " Batteries ... ... 500 yds.
- " Sections ... ... 25 yds.
- " Battery and Transport ... 25 yds.

The transport of each battery will march in rear of the Battery.

Unless held up (in which case Units will ensure that all cross-roads, railway crossings &c. are clear of vehicles) NO HALT will be made until the head of the column reaches cross-roads BAS-RIEUX at U.24.b.2.6.

Billeting parties under charge of an Officer per Battery will report mounted at this Office at 9.0 a.m. today (2nd inst) Parties may return as soon as billeting is completed if Units so desire.

A.S.C. Baggage Wagons have been ordered to report to Units this afternoon. Teams from D.A.C. to horse the two O.S. Wagons in possession of each Battery have been instructed to report to Batteries early today. NO ADDITIONAL TRANSPORT is available.

Units will march F.S.M.O. as laid down in C.R.A's instructions enclosed herewith.

- Billets will be left clean and usual billeting certificates rendered prior to departure.

- Attention is drawn to para. 10 of attached D.A. Order No.60

- One Officer per Unit will synchronise watches with the Adjt. at 9.0 p.m. today 2nd instant.

- O.C. B/210 & C/210 will each detail one Officer to remain behind three hours after the column has left, at FOUQUIERES and HINDIGNEUL respectively to receive any 'reclamations' for their respective areas and to obtain clean certificates from the TOWN MAJOR for all Units of this Brigade in the respective above mentioned villages.

2.

12. Reports during March to head of column.

13. ACKNOWLEDGE.

							[signature]
							CAPT. & ADJT.
						210th BRIGADE R.F.A.

Issued by Orderly
at 1:20 a.m.
2nd March 1918.

COPY No. 1.   A/210
"   2.   B/210
"   3.   C/210
"   4.   D/210
"   5.   R.S.M.Burton.
"   6. } War Diary
"   7. }
"   8.   File.

42nd Div.
IV.Corps.

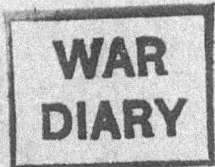

Headquarters,

210th BRIGADE, R.F.A.

A P R I L

1 9 1 8

Confidential

VOL III

210th BRIGADE R.F.A

WAR DIARY

From 1-4-18
To 30-4-18.

Army Form C. 2118.

WAR DIARY
or
INTELLIGENCE SUMMARY.

4 57D continued 40000 1

(Erase heading not required.)

Place	Date	Hour	Summary of Events and Information	Remarks and references to Appendices
ESSARTS - BUCQUOY	1/4/18		Enemy shelling very active on all battery positions. 1 gun of B/210 } damaged by shell fire. 1 " " C/210 } During night we fired 250 rounds per battery on roads, tracks in our zone & put down a practice barrage on S.O.S. lines from 4.43 am to 5.15 am. Casualties:- 1 O.R. wounded B/210 + 1 O.R. wounded Bde H.Qrs. A/210 moved their position to 300 yds in the rear (E.14.b)	At. DH.
ESSARTS	2/4/18	3p	Enemy put a shell storm on ESSARTS for half an hour then kept up continuous fire from 12 noon to 6 pm on the village.	
		11-30p	We fired a concentration on the huts in L.11.d. thinking the enemy fired 200 rounds per battery on areas in our zone. Major HIGHET D/210 refd from leave in U.K. 2 O.R.s " "	At DH

WAR DIARY
or
INTELLIGENCE SUMMARY.

Army Form C. 2118.

Place	Date	Hour	Summary of Events and Information	Remarks and references to Appendices
ESSARTS	3/4/18		Hostile shelling not so intense as on the previous day. ESSARTS again received particular attention all afternoon through the night.	
		8.0 pm	We fired a concentration on BUCQUOY - ACHIET LE PETIT ROAD the usual harassing fire on our gone during day tonight. A/210 new position is E.18.b.6.5. tonight they are placing a sniping gun at E.19.d.5.9. Orders to regate points on the front on our night to cooperate in a proposed minor operation	
-"-	4/4/18	9.0 pm	Enemy deluged the country from the front line to HANNESCAMPS with gas & HE until 10 am 5th. 2/Lt. E. N. JAMES D/210 to Hospital (sick)	
-"-	5/4/18	9.0 am	Enemy pushed in our line at BUCQUOY. All	

WAR DIARY
or
INTELLIGENCE SUMMARY. Lens 11 and 57d contd.

Army Form C. 2118.
3

Place	Date	Hour	Summary of Events and Information	Remarks and references to Appendices
ESSARTS	5/4/18		communication was broken down owing to the gas it was impossible to see the S.O.S. Rockets. A/210 however kept up a slow rate of fire on their own. 3 - 18pr guns damaged. D/210 attempted a smoke barrage to assist Div on our right but could only keep 1 How going. Our line this evening through X roads of BUCQUOY at L3 b to along main road No. 5. 2/LT JAMES D/210. 1.O.R killed. 8. O.R. wounded.	AN
-ll-	6/4/18		A very quiet day & night. visibility impossible. We kept up continuous fire on roads running into BUCQUOY on L4 & L10 by day & night. 1 O.R. wounded.	A
-ll-	7/4/18		2/Lt. HUMPHERY to Hospital (gassed) 3 O.R. wounded.	

WAR DIARY or **INTELLIGENCE SUMMARY**

Army Form C. 2118.

57d continued. 4

Place	Date	Hour	Summary of Events and Information	Remarks and references to Appendices
ESSARTS	7/7/18	6 am.	Enemy reported moving EAST of BUCQUOY. We opened out at a slow rate on our S.O.S lines which run from L3d.9.7 - F28.d.3.1. The S.O.S went up at 8.15 am. Infantry at 10-0 am ask for fire to be kept up on L3d. & L10.	A.
"	9/7/18		Location of 210° Bde as follows:- HQ. E24 d.6.9. A/210 E.18 & 6.5. B/210 F.13 a. 10.55. } RIGHT GROUP C/210 E24.b. 3.1. D/210. E12. & 8.3. Enemy Division being relieved opposite our front. Our howitzers fire 20 arranged to be fired simultaneously with relief. Enemy fire NIL. C.R.A 42 D.A handed over command to C.R.A 62 D.A. 62= D.A took over LEFT-GROUP from 59° D.A. 6. O.R. wounded	A.

//
WAR DIARY or INTELLIGENCE SUMMARY

Army Form C. 2118.

LENS & 57 d contoured

Place	Date	Hour	Summary of Events and Information	Remarks and references to Appendices
ESSARTS	10/4/18		C/210 took over position just vacated by D/210. (E24.b.30.25) Right group Akeleny Shineon with 185 Inf Bde at PIGEON WOOD. Enemy night we fired a "Counter Preparation Barrage" at 5.0 am to 5.15 am. 2/Lt L.G. LEWIS to Hospital (gassed). 6 O.R. wounded.	M
"	11/4/18		Lt. Col. A.J. MASON. D.S.O. takes over command of Rt Group from Lt. Col. INCHES. D.S.O. the H.Q. moved to E 23.c.6.7. 211th Bde staff press to his command whilst 210th Bde H.Q. remains in before. Another quiet day except for usual road strafing near ESSARTS.	M
E23.c.6.7	14/4/18		210's HQ moved to PIGEON WOOD & joined 211th HQ at E23.c.6.7. A, B + C/210 also moved to E 22. b. 4. & had orders to be silent batteries. 6. O.R. wounded	M

WAR DIARY or INTELLIGENCE SUMMARY

Army Form C. 2118.

Reference Maps LENS 11
57d combined 1/10000

Place	Date	Hour	Summary of Events and Information	Remarks and references to Appendices
E.23.c.6.7.	15/4/18		Warning order received that the group would reform the 42nd Div. in the line, & would consequently have to take over positions now occupied by 310 + 187 Brigades. The group will now become the LEFT GROUP of the CENTRE DIVISION at present commanded by LT. COL. CARDEN whose HQ's are at E.28.d.8.3. locations from tomorrow will be :— 210" Bde H.Q. E.10.d.8.8. A/210 E.15.c.9.2. B/210 E.17.b.0.3. C/210 E.17.d.5.5. D/210 E.18.c.75.70. } LEFT GROUP. LT. L. COOPER DAC to C/210. 2/Lt BREMNER " A/210. 2/Lt CHAPMAN " D/210. Batteries of 210 Bde exchanged personnel with 310 Bde guns handed over in situ. Batteries came under the command of LT. COL. CARDEN. D.S.O. until noon 18th inst. A/210 silent battery. 3. O.R. wounded	N.
E.10.d.8.8.	16/4/18			
E.10.d.8.8.	17/4/18			N.

WAR DIARY or INTELLIGENCE SUMMARY.

(Erase heading not required.)

Reference Maps. LENS II 1/10000 & 57d combined 1/40000

Place	Date	Hour	Summary of Events and Information	Remarks and references to Appendices
E.10.d.8.8.	18/9/18		210 Bde HQ changed over with HQ. 310 Bde at E.11.a.2.2. The Brigade now covering 125 Inf. Bde. which is left Brigade, of Centre Division IV Corps. 190, 210 & 211 Bdes R.F.A. from the Left Group covering 125 & 126 Ind. Bdes. Capt. R.A.Smith rejoins from Canal in U.K. & posted to A/210. Capt. H.B.Eccles appts Apj. vice Capt. C.G.Duff on from 25/3/18 (Auth. IV Corps)	A1
E.11.a.2.2.	19/9/18	9.0 p.m.	210 & 211 assisted 125 Inf. Bde. to Raid K.12. The raid failed owing to M.G. fire & grenades – no prisoners taken Enemy had trench. 4. O.R. wounded.	A1
"	20/9/18		Have orders to select "PURPLE LINE" positions, but impossible on ground so already full of batteries. Group HQ. (190 Bde) moved to CHATEAU-de-la-HAIE.	A1
"	22/9/18		1 O.R. killed	A1

INTELLIGENCE SUMMARY

(Erase heading not required.)

Reference Maps. LENS 11
57B 15000 1/40,000

Place	Date	Hour	Summary of Events and Information	Remarks and references to Appendices
E11.a.2.2.	24/4/18		42nd Div. now only 2 Brigades in the line (125+126 Inf Bdes) we form part of Left Group covering Left Division. Lt Bde. Group under Col. Curleu D.S.O. consists	
			190 Bde R.F.A. (37th Div.)	
			210 " " (42 Div.)	
			211 " "	AA
			We shall cover the same front unperimpose over the other Brigades. All batteries now man a day O.P the N.O.P by turn. A/210 put a section out at E.22.b.1.5 & B/210 a forward section at E.29.a.4.1. Major A.G. Hall c/210 killed in action and buried at MILITARY CEMETRY - BIENVILLERS. LtH FINCH c/210 to hospital	
"	25/4/18		D/210 now firing gas on K.18.d.7.5, every night when conditions are favourable, about 70 rounds each night from line held by 126 Inf Bde in K.12.d.30.85 - K.12.b.25.70. K.12.d.4.8 - L.7.a.4.1 - L.7.c.8.0. - L.7.d.3.8 - L.8.a.0.2 - L.8.a.2.3. L.2.c.9.2. 1. O.R. killed. 1. O.R. wounded.	AA

INTELLIGENCE SUMMARY.

Reference Maps: LENS 11 & 57d Combined 1/10,000

Place	Date	Hour	Summary of Events and Information	Remarks and references to Appendices
E.11.a.2.2.	26/4/18		B/210 forward Section engaged hostile battery at L.25.a.2.7. Men observed to run from position. 2/Lt. F.C. Cawthorn detailed to be D.A. Gas Officer in addition to his ordinary duties. 1. O.R. wounded. forward Section of B/210 engaged (see above).	A.1.
"	27/4/18		C/210 moved to E.22.b.15. still cover the same front.	A.1.
"	28/4/18		B/210 have orders to move to E.21.c. but this was cancelled owing to the bad state of position to be taken over. Div. Commander visited all batteries with C.R.A.	A.1.
"	29/4/18		B/210 moved to E.21.c.1.7. with 4 guns leaving their forward section at "LITTLE Z". Minimum ammunition allotment: - 800 18 pr per brigade. 6000 empties returned by tramway by B/210.	A.1.

INTELLIGENCE SUMMARY.

Corrected Sheet 4/5000 57o.
Lens II.

Place	Date	Hour	Summary of Events and Information	Remarks and references to Appendices
E.11.a.2.2.	30/4/18		187 Bde under Lt Col. LYON relieves the 190 Bde R.F.A in the Line Group commanded by Lt Col. LYON. Lt Col. INCHES D.S.O. to command 210 & 211 Brigades & Lt Col. D.J. MASON D.S.O. to be in charge of combined Wagon Lines. Ammunition allotment changed. Maximum expenditure 600 rounds per Brigade. Batteries located as follows. A/210 6 E.15.c.6.2. B/210 4. E.21.c.1.7. 2. "LITTLE Z" C/210 6. E.22.x.1.5. D/210. 6 E.18.c.75.70. Bde. H.Q E.11.a.22. Drafts received during April:- 3 Officers 54 OR. 28 horses. Total Strength:- O 35 OR 781 Horses 843. Effective Strength:- 35 728 619. D. Mason Lt Col Cmdg 210° R.F.A	AM Nil

Confidential

Vol 16

VOL III

WAR DIARY

210ᵀᴴ BRIGADE R.F.A.

From 1-5-18
To — 31-5-18   } 6 pp.

WAR DIARY or INTELLIGENCE SUMMARY.

Army Form C. 2118.

Reference Map LENS 11 1/100,000
57D 1/40,000

Place	Date	Hour	Summary of Events and Information	Remarks and references to Appendices
HANNESCAMPS	1/5/18		Hostile Artillery very quiet. Harassing fire carried out by batteries on zone allotted. Capt. Hastings (C/210) assumed duties of Adjutant 210 Bde R.F.A. vice Major H. Beecles posted to C/210 to command.	AH
-do-	2/5/18		Hostile Artillery very quiet. Usual harassing fire carried out by Batteries.	AH
-do-	3/5/18		Enemy Artillery active. Frequent bursts on ESSARTS-HANNESCAMPS ROAD. Two minute barrage on our front line about K.12.a at 8-30 a.m. to 9.18 a.m.	AH

WAR DIARY
or
INTELLIGENCE SUMMARY.

Army Form C. 2118.

Reference Maps LENS 11 1/20000
57d 1/20000

2

Place	Date	Hour	Summary of Events and Information	Remarks and references to Appendices
HANNESCAMPS.	4/5/18		D/210 heavily shelled at frequent intervals during day. Casualties during this bombardment amounted to 1 Sgt. 3 gunners 2 R.A.M.C. O.R. + 1 R.A.F wireless operator. The guns were not damaged were withdrawn to W.L. at night. Minor operation on K11c50 - K17a50 dummy which B+C/210 put down an Enfilade Barrage at 8.50pm to 30 minutes.	A/A
-"-	5/5/18		Hostile Artillery quiet. D/210 took up position on Battery: - 4 Hours at E21c.5.6 + 2 Hours at E29.c.7.9. 210 2 Bde Wagon Lines moved from SOUASTRE to SOUASTRE-COIGNEUX VALLEY on account of hostile shelling of village.	A/A
-"-	6/5/18		We put up continuous fire on trenches on E13b + L14a 41 SA D/A took over command at 9.0pm	A/A

WAR DIARY
INTELLIGENCE SUMMARY

Army Form C. 2118.

Reference Map LENS. 11 1/10,000
57 b 1/40,000

Place	Date	Hour	Summary of Events and Information	Remarks and references to Appendices
HANNESCAMPS	7 5/18		Concentrations harassing fire on BOX WOOD, FORK WOOD & K12.8. 37.37 to K12.d. 47.22. New S.O.S. lines 9-0 pm from L7.c.25.30 to L7.d. 60.20. to A8+c/20 D/20 K12.d.15+5.k K12.d 75.95	AW
" "	10 5/R		1 Gunner accidentally wounded. Usual harassing fire during night	AW
" "	11 5/18		Lt. C. MACKRELL proceeded to Rest Camp - ST. VALERY. Enemy heavy gun shells FONQUEVILLERS. Estimated 10,000 rounds of all calibres were used. No retaliation of D/210 own batteries were not affected 4.5 stores field gun at several targets during night in retaliation	AW
" "	14 5/18	4-0 am 4-45	Target in counter-preparation was engaged by all batteries.	AW

WAR DIARY or INTELLIGENCE SUMMARY.

Army Form C. 2118.

Reference Maps.
LENS 11 1/40000
57d Continued 1/10000

4

Place	Date	Hour	Summary of Events and Information	Remarks and references to Appendices
HANNESCAMPS	16/5/18		1 O.R. wounded (gas) C/210 had one gun damaged by still fire.	AH
BIENVILLERS	17/5/18		HQ 210" Bde moved to new HQ in splinter proof shelters at E.8.C.7.2. 2 O.R's wounded	AH
-"-	18/5/18		Capt F.S.G. JACKSON, M.C. from 211 Bde to C/210.	AH
-"-	19/5/18		Capt. C.R. BROWN from B/210 to 211 Bde. Capt. C.I. SCOWCROFT from 211 to B/210. 2 gunners wounded - gas.	
-"-	20/5/18		LT COL D.J. MATON. D.S.O took over command of LEFT ARTY GROUP in the line from LT. COL. E.J. INCHES (211) at noon. Much harassing fire during the day.	AH
-"-	21/5/18	4.00	Batteries fired a concentration on front line in retaliation for shelling BIEZ WOOD.	AH

WAR DIARY or INTELLIGENCE SUMMARY

Army Form C. 2118.

Reference Map Lens 11 1/40000 & 570 1/10000

Place	Date	Hour	Summary of Events and Information	Remarks and references to Appendices
BIENVILLERS.	23/5/18	—	Batteries fired their normal harassing fire during the night. Enemy's shelling of back areas slightly above normal. One O.R. wounded.	AH
-"-	24/5/18		A/210 position shelled. Three gun were moved to E.21.a.80.00. 2/Lt A.H. BREMNER A/210 to Hospital.	AH
-"-	25/5/18		The remaining 3 guns of A/210 moved to E.21.a.80.00. Lt C. MACKRELL returned from Rest Camp. Majors HIGHET & YATES visited Battery Positions.	AH.
-"-	26/5/18		Slight gas shelling of A/210 Battery position. FONQUEVILLERS again received some particular attention from the enemy's gas shells. 1 gun of B/210 damaged by premature.	AH
-"-	27/5/18		2 O.R. killed. 1 wounded. All guns oriented. Right group in daylight and changed. K12.b.15.15 — K12.a.95.15. 2/Lt R.W. BOWLES from D.A.C. to C/210. MAJOR W. BIRTWISTLE was Bty Position from aeroplane.	AJ.

Army Form C. 2118.

WAR DIARY
or
INTELLIGENCE SUMMARY.
(Erase heading not required.)

Ref. Maps
LENS 11 1/100000
57d 1/40000

Place	Date	Hour	Summary of Events and Information	Remarks and references to Appendices
BIENVILLERS.	28/5/18		One Sgt. + one Gunner Killed, 3 gunners wounded during 'strafe' on B/210 forward section.	SA
-"-	30/5/18		One O.R. killed + one O.R. wounded accidentally by machine gun bullets during operations carried out by '18. L.F's. near C/210 Wagon Lines.	SA
			Batteries located as follows:-	
			H.Q. E.8.c.7.2	
			A/210 (6) E.21.a. 8.0.	
			B/210 (3) E.23.c. 3.1 (4) E.21.c.10.85.	
			C/210 (2) E.22.c. 9.3. (4) E.26.A. 02.91	
			D/210 (2) E.29.c. 7.9. (4) E.21.c.65.62.	
			Offrs O.R. Horses	
			Total Strength 40. 802. 660	
			Effective " 35 778. 648.	
			Reinforcements received during month 116	

J Murray
Lt Col
Cmdg 210 Bde R.F.A.

- CONFIDENTIAL -

WAR DIARY

OF

210TH BRIGADE R.F.A.

FOR THE MONTH OF JUNE 1918.

VOLUME IV

WAR DIARY or INTELLIGENCE SUMMARY

Army Form C. 2118.

Reference Map:
LENS 11 1/10,000
57d combined 1/40,000

Place	Date	Hour	Summary of Events and Information	Remarks and references to Appendices
BIENVILLERS	2/6/18	—	B/210 forward section heavily shelled. Both guns were damaged. 2 O.R. wounded.	AM
"	"	10.0 p	All batteries co-operated in bombardment of L.7.c. to assist 170" bty. The raid was cancelled before completion.	AM
-"-	4/6/18	4.0 a	The raid ordered for the night of 2/3 June was carried out, all batteries co-operating. 2 O.R. wounded.	AM
-"-	6/6/18	—	2 O.R. wounded	AM
-"-	8/6/18	10.0 a	Batteries fired THERMIT on ROSSIGNOL WOOD in an endeavour to set it on fire. Lt. E.M.James D/210 arrived from Base & posted to C/210.	AM

Lt. E.M.James D/210 arrived from Base & posted to C/210.

Army Form C. 2118.

WAR DIARY
or
INTELLIGENCE SUMMARY.
(Erase heading not required.)

Reference Maps
LENS 11
57 d. contoured

Place	Date	Hour	Summary of Events and Information	Remarks and references to Appendices
BIENVILLERS	9/9/18		Lt Col. D.J. MASON D.S.O. handed over Left Artillery Group to Lt Col. E.J. INCHES 211th Bde, itself command of Left Group. Wagon line.	AM.
"	11/9/18		Lt Col. D.J. MASON D.S.O. again took command of Left Artillery Group to relieve Lt Col. E.J. INCHES (sick). 4 guns of C/210 + 4 guns of D/210 transferred from Left Artillery Group to Right Artillery Group.	AM
"	12/9/18		Lt. A.E. HIGHAM, C/210 posted A/210.	AM
"	14/9/18		Lt. Statham returned from Vet. bonne ABBEVILLE. Lt. Beck proceeded to 3rd Army Army School.	AM
"	19/9/18		Lt Cooper Lt Hewitt proceeded on leave to England	AM
"	20/9/18		All batteries co-operated in bombardment of K.11c ed to assist 171 INF Bde raid.	AM

WAR DIARY
or
INTELLIGENCE SUMMARY.

Army Form C. 2118.

Reference Map:
LENS 11 1/10,000
57D Corrected to 20.6.18

Place	Date	Hour	Summary of Events and Information	Remarks and references to Appendices
BIENVILLERS	23/6/18		Lt Col L.J. Brocks (D.S.O.) took over command of Reg.tl Artillery group	fill
"	27.6.18		The batteries co-operated in bombardment of ROSSIGNOL WOOD and assisted in raid by 7th INF. BDE.	fill
"	30.6.18		Batteries located as follows :—	
			A> 10 (6) E 21 a 0 50	
			Hq E 8 c 7. 2. B> 10 (4) B 14 b 39 8 86	
			(2) E 21 c 10 85	
			C> 10 (4) E 26 B 02 91	
			(2) D 30 d 84 35	
			D> 10 (4) E 21 c 65 61	fill
			(2) E 27 c 70 70	
			Total strength Officers 36 Horses 651	
			" " " 714	
			Effective do 35 " 774 " 647	
			Reinforcements received during month 4.60 N.C.O.	
			1 L. Col.	
			Comdg 3rd # Reg. R.F.A.	

CONFIDENTIAL

WAR DIARY

of

210TH BDE. R.F.A.

PERIOD – MONTH OF JULY, 1918

Vol. III

WAR DIARY
or
INTELLIGENCE SUMMARY.

Army Form C. 2118.

Reference Maps
LENS 11 1/10,000
57d [?] 1/20,000

Place	Date	Hour	Summary of Events and Information	Remarks and references to Appendices
BIENVILLERS	4/7/18		Relieved 1st NZ Bde RFA in Right Div II Corps.	A.1
BUS	5/7/18		1st NZ Bde RFA relieved 2nd Bde in Centre Div II Corps	A.2
"	7/7/18		Lt S.H. Cope returned from leave in UK	A.3
"			Lt A.C. Hyslop proceeded on leave to UK	A.4
"	12/7/18		Lt Col D. Mason DSO proceeded on leave to UK. Major St Brutnell assumed command	A.5
"			210th Bde took part in 63rd (RN) Div Raid N of HAMEL (33 prisoners)	A.6
"	15/7/18		Cooperated with II Corps HA in bombardment of PUISIEUX	A.7
"	16/7/18		" with 63rd Div in bombardment of Q 4 & b & d	A.8
"	19/7/18		" " " 9.10 b and 11 a	A.9
"	24/7/18		Fired on 127 Inf Bde on raid on K 28 c	A.10
"	28/7/18		" 135 — on raid on enemy post in K 28 c	A.11
"	24/7/18		" 135 — on raid on enemy trenches in K 34	A.12
"	25/7/18		Lt Col D. Mason DSO returned from leave	A.13

WAR DIARY
or
INTELLIGENCE SUMMARY.

Army Form C. 2118.

Reference Map: LENS 11
57d combined (German)

Place	Date	Hour	Summary of Events and Information	Remarks and references to Appendices
BUS	30/9/18		Assisted V Corps in front attack on Q.H.	
			210th Bde NP J34 d.6.6. J36 d.95.26 A/240	
			J35 c.30.81 B/240	
			J35 c.25.92 C/240	
			J35 a.20.20 D/240	
			Officers ORs Horses	
			37 794 652	
			36 786 640	
			Total Strength	
			Effective	
			Reinforcements received during month	
			Officers ORs Horses	
			1 49 9	

Murr
Lt Col
Comm'g 210th Bde RFA

CONFIDENTIAL.

WAR DIARY

of

210th Brigade, R.F.A.

from 1st August 1918 to 31st August 1918.

VOLUME XX.

****

WAR DIARY or INTELLIGENCE SUMMARY

Army Form C. 2118.

Reference MAPS — LENS 1/10000 / 57th Combined 1/10000 / NE

Place	Date	Hour	Summary of Events and Information	Remarks and references to Appendices
BUS	1/8/15		2/Lieut H.L. Penn returns from leave. Bayn General and Harassing fire on Green & VALLADE Trenches	
"	2/8/15		Carried out RIGHT GROUP O.O. 22 with bombardment of WATLING ST & VALLADE TR in K34	
"	3/8/15		Lieut REES returns from leave	
			Operation order 22 carried out also wire cutting in front of WATLING ST by 4.5" hows	
			Registration of VALLADE, LEGEND & GREEN TRENCHES	
"	4/8/15		O.O. 22 para 6 carried out with intention that the 126th Bde would occupy WATLING ST	
			Our Artillery supports a raid on WATLING ST and carried out concentrations	
"	5/8/15		in accordance with O.O. 22	
"	4/8/15		O.O. 24 700 gas projectors on WATLING ST VALLARD TR Saughbeauhers in which our Companies	
			according to Table A.	
BERTRANCOURT	6/8/15		HQ quarters moved to J36a56. Batteries moved up to prolong K36a56 areas. Harassing fire on ROMAN ROAD & VALLARD. And wire cutting by 4.5" Hows in front of WATLING ST	
"	7/8/15		Lieut FRASER returns from leave. Continued Smoke and gas barrage Q46.B5.y5 — K34 & P033	
"	9/8/15		and wire cutting by 4.5" Hows starting afternoon 17.8"	
"	10/8/15		7.0 AM — 7.15 AM 10th Aug. Gas & Smoke cloudy & wire cutting in rear of WATLING ST	
"	11/8/15		Captain HIGGS proceeds on leave & Capt GREENWOOD reports for duty as as/adjust	
"	12/8/15		2/Lieut BRADFIELD " " and 2/Lieut BOYD proceeds on leave.	
"	17/8/15		Lieut HORNER returns from leave	
			Lieut HUGHES proceeds to the Army Artillery school. Vi Corps	

Army Form C. 2118.

WAR DIARY
or
INTELLIGENCE SUMMARY.
(Erase heading not required.)

Reference Map
LENS 11 10000
FRANCE 57d & 57c 40000

(2)

Place	Date	Hour	Summary of Events and Information	Remarks and references to Appendices
BERTRAN COURT	16/8/18		Bgde's shelled areas in L31 & L32 and carried out usual harassing fire	Att
	17/8/18		Major BIRTWISTLE proceeds on leave	Att
	18/8/18		Harassing fire put down on Slopes in L32a & the Enemy having evacuated SERRE	Att
	19/8/18		Continued fire put down on Enemy parties observed moving about in L32d & Central	Att
CHALK PITS K32.R.41			Capt JACKSON returned from leave	Att
	21/8/18		Lieut STUTTARD proceeds on leave	Att
			Harassed the retiring enemy from our battery position in K34	Att
	24/8/18		Carried out O.O. 28 assisting 7th L.F. and 5th L.F. and 5 MANCHESTERS in their attack on ridge running through L31 L32 & R2	Att
	22/8/18		At 2.30 PM provided a barrage for RIGHT INFY Bde and put down 2 concentrations of gas at 12.30 & 3.30 PM on L35 C	Att
	23/8/18		Majors Bayard mayer times to J.34 d	Att
	23/8/18		Lieut R HARTLEY proceeds on leave	Att
MIRAUMONT	24/8/18		Bgde's moved up to positions in R4 a/b and mayor time moved to Sugar factory in K32d	Att
	25/8/18		Bgde's moved by LOUPART WOOD in G34c & account attacks of G3 dur	Att
	26/8/18		Bgde's remained in G34c	Att

Army Form C. 2118.

WAR DIARY
or
INTELLIGENCE SUMMARY.
(Erase heading not required.)

(3)

Place	Date	Hour	Summary of Events and Information	Remarks and references to Appendices
LOUPART WOOD	26.8.18		Batteries in position in N.2.c & shelled THILLOY all day	AAA
"	27/8/18		Barrage THILLOY in cooperation by attack by 63rd DIV	AAA
"	28/8/18		THILLOY evacuated and headquarters moves to M9a.99, and batteries to N11b & 12a	AAA
			shelled RIENCOURT and moved to "VILLERS au FLOS"	AAA
R.32.a.41	28.8.18		LIEUT DICK wounded	AAA
LOUPART	29.8.18		" G.P.HARTLEY proceeds on leave	AAA
THILLOY	29.8.18		RIENCOURT evacuated by enemy and batteries moves to positions in N3 central	AAA
"	30.8.18		Batteries shelled high ground in N6 from positions in N3 central	AAA
			BEAULENCOURT	AAA
"	31.8.18		At 4.55 A.M. on the 31st at standing barrage in N6d.65.15 to O7a.88 in support 17	AAA
			The 42nd DIV infantry to occupy grounds in N6 - O7	

Total Strength (ration) Officers ORs HORSES
& Helium 32 666 660
" 37 752 636.

Total reinforcements
during month Nil 14 23

WR 20

VOL VII

War Diary

210th Bde R.F.A.

From 1.9.18
To   30.9.18

WAR DIARY
or
INTELLIGENCE SUMMARY.
(Erase heading not required.)

Army Form C. 2118.

Reference Maps
1/100,000 LENS & 57c Combined.

Instructions regarding War Diaries and Intelligence Summaries are contained in F. S. Regs., Part II. and the Staff Manual respectively. Title pages will be prepared in manuscript.

Place	Date	Hour	Summary of Events and Information	Remarks and references to Appendices
THILLOY	1/9/18		Brigade in action in N 3 a and N 3 a. Fired barrage in support of 21st Div. attack on BEAULENCOURT and also in support of attack by N.Z.Div. Ammn. Exp 3476 Rds	
do.	2/9/18		Moved to positions in N 5 c and d N.W. of REINCOURT. C/210 had captured 77mm in action. Ammn Exp N11	
do.	3/9/18		Moved to positions on O 14 b and 15 a S.E. of MILLERS AU FLOS and came into action in support of 125 Inf Bde, up to which time it had been supporting 126 Inf. Bde. In the afternoon moved to positions in O 18 c and 23 b (W of BUS) with H.Q at BARASTRE. Ammn Exp 400 Rds	
BUS	4/9/18		Bde. moved to P 19 b (N.W. of YTRES) and came into action there in support of attack on NEUVILLE BOURJONVAL. Ammn Exp 1729 Rds	
YTRES	5/9/18		Brigade transferred to 42nd Div. on relief of N.Z Div and was attached to 2nd Bde N.Z Div. H.Q 210 moved to P 19 b. Ammn Exp 2945 Rds	
do	6/9/18		Bde moved to positions in P 21 d and came into action near Brickyard E of YTRES. Ammn Exp 978 Rds	
do	7/9/18		Bde moved to Q 25 c and P 30 b with H.Q. at P 25 a 3 3. Wagon Lines in VALLULART WOOD. Group commanded by Lt.Col McQuarrie M.C. of N.Z Div. Expenditure 1734 Rds.	
METZ-EN-COUTURE	8/9/18		Fired during day on Q 33 b, Q34 a Q 28 c and Q 28 d. Expenditure 1099 Rds	
	9/9/18		At 4.a.m. fired barrage in support of attck by N.Z Div. Fired repeatedly during the day at request of Inf. Comdr. on roads and trenches in Q 29 c and Q 35 a. Enemy artillery active throughout whole day on battery positions. Expenditure 4657 Rounds.	
do	10/9/18		Fired Counter Preparation from 4.30 to 5 a.m. on Q 29 b and d, Q 30 a and c, and Q 35 b Major H.B. Eccles C/210 wounded but remained at duty and Lt Bowles M.C.,M.M. killed. Fired throughout the day ar request of Inf Comdr. on Q 35 a and c and Q 29 d. At 5.35 p.m. put down annihilating fir to prevent enemy counter attack. Battery positions shelled intermittently throughout the day. At 8 p.m. only B/210 carried on, other batteries unable to approach guns. Expenditure 1806 Rounds.	
do	11/9/18		Fired on Q29 a and c at irregular intervals. Expenditure 1299 Rounds. B/210 Officers Mess knocked out by 8" Lieut Carrick (attached from T.M's) killed, Capt G.W.Greenwood Lts. Collins (attached from T.M's) and Higham wounded. H.Q moved to P 28 c 6.8	
do	12/9/18		Fired creeping barrage in support of attack by N.Z Div and during the day on Q35 b,Q29 d at request of Inf. Comdr. Expenditure 4728 Rounds.	
do	13/9/18		Fired throughout day on Q 35. Expenditure 2210 Rounds. Received orders to withdraw from positions at 9.0 p.m. and retire to Wagon Lines in VALLULART WOOD.	

Army Form C. 2118.

WAR DIARY
or
INTELLIGENCE SUMMARY.

(Erase heading not required.)

Reference Map - LENS 1/1000,000 57c and 57b.

Instructions regarding War Diaries and Intelligence Summaries are contained in F.S. Regs., Part II. and the Staff Manual respectively. Title pages will be prepared in manuscript.

Place	Date	Hour	Summary of Events and Information	Remarks and references to Appendices
YTRES	14/9/18		Remained in Vallulart Wood. Came under 42nd D.A.	Mr.
"	15/9/18		At 4.30 a.m. received orders to be ready to move at 5.30 a.m. to cover Corps Reserve Line E. of YTRES. Did not move.	Mr.
"	16/9/18		Remained in Vallulart Wood until 4 p.m. 22xx 26th Sept.'18.	
TRESCAULT.	26/9/18		H.Q moved to Q.10 central. Batteries in Q.3.d and Q.9.a. Group consisting of 210th and 211th Bdes. under Lt.Col D.J.Mason D.S.O.	23rd Mr.
"	27/9/18.		Fired creeping barrage in support of 125 Inf.Bde at 5.20 a.m. and again at 6.30 p.m. 10163 rds. (expended)	Mr.
"	28/9/18.		Group consisted of 210th 211th and 123 Bdes. all in R.3b and d. Lt M.H.R.D Wounded 1392	Mr.
"	29/9/18		H.Q. moved to R.7.b. Batteries to R.1 and R.7. Came under orders of N.Z.D.A. Batteries moved forward to R.9a. and c. and R.11.b. with H.Q. at R.3.8.0.0.	Mr.
COUILLET WOOD.	30/9/18		Fired creeping barrage in support of N.Z.Division. Expenditure - 1052 rounds. Batteries in R.9a and c.	

	Off.	O.R.	Horses	Mules.
Total Strength	30	745	612	10
Effective Strength	29	741	601	10

Reinforcements received during month- 81 other ranks.
20 Horses.

[signature]

Lieut-Colonel.
Cdg. 210th Bde. R.F.A.

Vol 21

CONFIDENTIAL

WAR DIARY
of
210th Bde R.F.A.

PERIOD — Month of Octr 1918

Vol. VIII

Army Form C. 2118.

WAR DIARY
or
INTELLIGENCE SUMMARY.

(Erase heading not required.)

Reference Maps. LENS 11 1/100,000
VALENCIENNES 12 1/100,000
57 B and 57 c 1/40,000

Instructions regarding War Diaries and Intelligence Summaries are contained in F.S. Regs., Part II. and the Staff Manual respectively. Title pages will be prepared in manuscript.

Place	Date	Hour	Summary of Events and Information	Remarks and references to Appendices
VAUCELLES	1/10/18		Right Group consisting of 123, 210 and 211 Bdes. under Lt.Col Mason, D.S.O. supported the N.Z. Division with H.Q of Group at R 11 d 5.7 and Batteries of 210 Bde in M 8 a and c with Wagon Lines in L 33 and 27. Our Infantry hold West bank of Canal St. Quentin. All batteries fired on captured German guns. One section of each Bde. pushed forward to engage enemy movement. Expenditure 864 Rounds. The 3rd N.Z.F.A.Bde releived the 123rd Bde night 1/2 Oct 1918.	
do.	2/10/18		Batteries reconnoitered for positions to cover canal crossings and bridges. Movement fired on during day. Expenditure 160 Rounds.	
do.	3/10/18		Lt.Col. McQuarrie 3rd N.Z.F.A.Bde took over command of Group. Enemy movement fired on throughout day. Expenditure 169 Rounds.	
do.	4/10/18		Signs of enemy retirement. Many aerial calls on movement. Expenditure 366 Rounds.	
do.	5/10/18		Our Infantry crossed Canal and occupied line CHENEAUX WOOD - LE BOSQUET.Batteries moved forward to M 2 b and c and continued firing on movement. Expenditure 1481 Rounds.	
do.	6/10/18		Wire cutting by 4.5 Hows. on BEAUVOIS-LEZZE MASNIERES line and continued firing on enemy movement. Expenditure 1236 Rounds.	
do	7/10/18		Batteries moved to M 10 c and M 16 b and c with H.Q at M 16 a 9.7	
do	8/10/18		Fired barrage in support of attack by N.Z. Division on LONGSART, after which Batteries moved forward to N 1 b 2.3. Expenditure 4178 Rounds.	
LONGSART	9/10/18		Batteries moved forward to H 30 b and I 19 and 25 with H.Q. at H 36 b 9.5, and fired 100 rounds harassing during night 9/10 Oct. 1918. Expenditure 400 Rounds.	
FONTAINE	10/10/18		Batteries move forward to FONTAINE and remained in a position of readiness but did not come into action. Bde remained in Reserve until 1500 12th when it took over positions of 124th Bde in D27c and d with H.Q. at J 3 a 8.0. At 1800 fired a barrage in support of N.Z. Division on BELLE VUE FARM. Expenditure 1563 Rounds.	
VIESLY	12/10/18		Fired harassing fire during night.	
do.	13/10/18		Fired during day on movement. at 1619 S.O.S went up . Enemy retook BELLE VUE FARM. Expenditure 1326 Rounds.	
do.	14/10/18		Considerable enemy movement and M.G's fired on during day. Desultory shelling by enemy. Expenditure 1139 Rounds.	
do.	15/10/18		Fired considerable amount of ammunition on enemy movement and M.G's. D/210 fired gas concentration at 2100 on Favine in E13d and F19 a. Batteries shelled all day. A/210 had two guns knocked out. Expenditure 917 Rounds.	
do.	16/10/18		Fired Counter Preparation for five minutes at 0525	

WAR DIARY or INTELLIGENCE SUMMARY

Army Form C. 2118.

Place	Date	Hour	Summary of Events and Information	Remarks and references to Appendices
PRAYELLE	17.10.18	0420 / 2330	Fired 5 minutes intense on railway E 136 r.c. and naval harassing fire. Expended 830 rds	
do	18.10.18	0445	" " " " Harassing fire on Railway triangle SOLESMES. Expended 762 rds	
do	19.10.18		Fired on Rly line E 13 b & E 13 c during day. Batteries moved to D 22 a v c. Expended 409 rds	
BRIASTRE	20.10.18	0200 / 1530	Area barrage in support of attack by 126 & 127 Inf Bdes. Fired standing barrage — E 35 9.9 – W 27 d 9.4 for 15 minutes. S.O.S. at 1311 fired on	
		2/10	Fired 15 mins. Intense on sunken road E.3b. Expended 6978 rds	
SOLESMES	21.10.18		Btys moved to E 7 b+d and E 6 a with HQ at E 7 b 5.9 and Wagon lines at E 30 a v c. Expended 1497 rds	
do	22.10.18		Usual harassing fire all day. Expended 1317 rds	
do	23.10.18	0031 / 0320	SOS fired on and creeping barrage in support of attack by 125 Bde + NZ Div. A 210 sent forward in advance battery and went into action at E 3 b.	
ROMERIES	23.10.18		Remaining Bty's moved up during afternoon to W 22 d, V 23 c. with HQ in ROMERIES. Expd 7360 rds	
do	24.10.18		Came into Group under Lt Col. McQUARRIE M.C. Remained in W.L. Expd Nil	
BEAUDIGNIES	25.10.18		Moved into action in R 31 d with HQ in BEAUDIGNIES. Fired continuous harassing all day.	
	26.10.18		Batteries moved forward to R 16 b, 17 a v c. Fired harassing all day.	
	27.10.18		Many aerial calls answered by D 210. Fires harassing fire. Expended 471 rds.	
	28.10.18		Moved back to positions in R 31 d each Bty leaving 1 forward section in action forward with 4 guns per Bty in mean. Expended 306 rds	
	29.10.18		Forward sections moved to rear positions in R 32 a, 1.26 d. Usual harassing. Exp'd. 468 rds.	

Army Form C. 2118.

WAR DIARY
or
INTELLIGENCE SUMMARY.
(Erase heading not required.)

Instructions regarding War Diaries and Intelligence Summaries are contained in F. S. Regs., Part II. and the Staff Manual respectively. Title pages will be prepared in manuscript.

Place	Date	Hour	Summary of Events and Information	Remarks and references to Appendices
BEAUDIGNIES	30.10.18		Ineffectual harassing fire. Extended Rests-es. Orders received to move on 31.10.18.	F.9.44
	31.10.18	0330	Assisted NZ Div in raid and fired creeping barrage for 30 minutes. on R 29 c 00 80 - R 29 a 00.00 Relieved by 211 Bde R.F.A. Relief complete 1700. Moved back to rear of VERTIGNEUL. Expd. 1807 r.d.s. Location HQ. W 5 c 2 8. C 210 W 27 c 66 A 210 W 27 d 86 D 210 E 4 a 75 B 210 E 4 c 55	29.44

			Effective Strength . 29 O OR Horses Mules
			                                 711 546 56
			Total Strength . 30 715 557 56
			
			Drafts received during month -
			           Officers OR
			             4 51	

[Signature]
MAJOR
Cdg. 210th Bde R.F.A.

98/22

Confidential

War Diary

of

216th Brigade R.F.A.

Nov 1918

WAR DIARY
or
INTELLIGENCE SUMMARY

Army Form C. 2118.

Place	Date	Hour	Summary of Events and Information	Remarks and references to Appendices
Vertigneul	1/11/18		Bde in rest. Positions in R.20.b & d (57H SE) reconnoitred and ammunition dumped by midnight 3/4 for forthcoming operations	
"	2/11/18		Still in rest. Parties for burying sent forward at night	
Ruesnes	3/11/18		Positions occupied. Barrage prepared. HQ at R.20.b.15.60. Bde under Le Groot (Lt Col McSwiney M.C.)	
	4.11.18	0530	Arts Barrage in support of attack by N.Z. Div.	
		0615	Positions reconnoitred in R.22.b. la coln advance from Green line to Red line	
		0951	Battalions moved forward and occupied positions in R.22.b. with HQ at R.21.a/9.	
		1500	Positions reconnoitred in M.22.b. & D.	
		2300	Orders received to come under Command 151st Bde. N.Z.P.A. from 0600 5th inst. Brigade to take up position to cover defensive flank. LE CULOT - FORESTERS HOUSE	
Herbignies	5/11/18	0530	Advance resumed. Positions occupied A.20. M.30.b.28. B.20. M.30.a. 95.80. C.20. M.29.b. 81.98. D.20. M.30.a. 19.00.	
		1200	Orders received from 42nd Div. to follow 127 Bde. in close support of attack by 126 Bde.	
"	6/11/18		Advance resumed by 126 Bde. Moved in rear of 127 Bde to MAISON ROUGE & road N.31.c & d. FORÊT DU MORMAL. 126 Bde got first objective after rough fighting. Awaiting further orders	
	7.11.18	0600	Advance resumed 126 Bde advancing Coys flank to HARGNIES. 125 Bde relieved by 127 Bde	

Army Form C. 2118.

WAR DIARY
or
INTELLIGENCE SUMMARY.
(Erase heading not required.)

Instructions regarding War Diaries and Intelligence Summaries are contained in F. S. Regs., Part II. and the Staff Manual respectively. Title pages will be prepared in manuscript.

Place	Date	Hour	Summary of Events and Information	Remarks and references to Appendices
HERBIGNIES	9/11/18	0700	Brigade advanced through FORET DE MORMAL to VIEUX MESNIL. Ponton Bridges at BOUSSIERES & PONT-SUR-SAMBRE were reconnoitred to enable River Sambre to be crossed when ordered	
"	10/11/18		Battery position, wagon lines, locomotives in neighborhood of HAUTMONT to own men line of resistance — Rd from JOUVROL in Q14C to Q31b.	
"	11/11/18	0900	Brigade advanced to HAUTMONT.	
		0910	News received from H2 DA that hostilities would cease at 11.00 today. Troops to stand fast on lines occupied. Locations HQ P23d 34. B210 Q13c 00 00 A210 P27d 57. C210 Q14d 76 D210 Q14d 05.	
	12/11/18 to 30/11/18		Brigade engaged upon military and Recreational Training	

Effective Strength
O 29 OR 757 Horses 637
Total Strength 30 759 650

Reinforcements received during month
3 Officers
169 Other Ranks
80 Horses

J. M[?]ller Major
Cdg 210 H. Bde R.F.A.

WD 23

CONFIDENTIAL

WAR DIARY
- OF -
201 BRIGADE RFA

FOR THE MONTH
OF
DECEMBER 1916.

WAR DIARY
or
INTELLIGENCE SUMMARY.
(Erase heading not required.)

Army Form C. 2118.

Place	Date	Hour	Summary of Events and Information	Remarks and references to Appendices
HAUTMONT	19/3/18 to 23/4/18		Brigade engaged in Military and Advanced Duties. Left for new area.	
JEUMONT	24/4/18		Brigade moved by route march to JEUMONT	
THUIN	25/4/18		Brigade moved by route march to THUIN	
	26/4/18 to 29/4/18		Brigade Resting	
MONTIGNES SUR SAMBRE	30/4/18		Brigade moved to final destination — MONTIGNES-SUR-SAMBRE (CHARLEROI). Arrived in billets and horses in gardens.	
	1/5/18 to 31/5/18		Military and Ceremonial Training	

Strength:
	O	OR
8/Durham L.I.	27	693
1st K.R.R.	28	697
	631	
	644	

Reinforcements received during month 66 OR

W.J. Nisbet
Brig. Gen. the Brigade

CONFIDENTIAL.

WAR DIARY.

- OF -

210th BRIGADE, R.F.A.

From 1st January 1919.   To 31st January 1919.

VOLUME XXV

Army Form C. 2118.

WAR DIARY
or
INTELLIGENCE SUMMARY.
(Erase heading not required.)

Instructions regarding War Diaries and Intelligence Summaries are contained in F. S. Regs, Part II. and the Staff Manual respectively. Title pages will be prepared in manuscript.

Place	Date	Hour	Summary of Events and Information	Remarks and references to Appendices
Montignies sur Sambre.	1-1-19 to 31-1-19.		During the month the Brigade was quartered in and around this town and has devoted the time to Military, Educational, and Recreational Training. Demobilization has proceeded steadily throughout the month as shewn below,	
			Date Officers. O.Rs. Total.	W.L.S.
			Jan. 9 1 1	
			10 3 35 38 2/Lt.Bradfield W.H.,2/Lt.Boyd W.,2/Lt. Brown W.	W.L.S.
			11 2 2	
			13 1 4 5 Lieut. Mackrell C.	W.L.S.
			14 16 16	
			18 15 15	
			21 19 19	W.L.S.
			26 23 23	W.L.S.
			29 29 29	
			TOTAL 4 144 148	W.L.S.
			Off. O.Rs.	
			EFFECTIVE STRENGTH 21 532	
			TOTAL 21 530	
			LEAVE.	
			Lt. Cooper C.H. from 14-1-19 to 24-1-19.	
			Lt. Horner R.H. " 13-1-19 to 27-1-19.	
			Re-inforcements received during the month.	
			NIL.	

W. L. Shephard
Lieut. Colonel.
O.C. 210th Brigade,R.F.A.

CONFIDENTIAL.

WAR DIARY.

of

210th Brigade R.F.A.

VOLUME XIV

From 1st February 1919.

To 28th February 1919.

Army Form C. 2118.

WAR DIARY
or
INTELLIGENCE SUMMARY.
(Erase heading not required.)

Instructions regarding War Diaries and Intelligence Summaries are contained in F.S. Regs., Part II. and the Staff Manual respectively. Title pages will be prepared in manuscript.

Place	Date	Hour	Summary of Events and Information	Remarks and references to Appendices
Montignies-Sur-Sambre.	1.2.19. to 28.2.19.		During the month the Brigade was quartered in and around this town and has devoted the time to Military, Educational, and Recreational Training. Demobilization ceased after 8.2.19. on account of orders to maintain "B" Cadre strength with the exception of men with A.F. Z.32 and A.F. Z.56. Number demobilized during month :-	

Number demobilized during month :-

Date.	Officers.	O.Rs.	Total.
Feb.1st	1	-	1
" 3rd	1	38	39
" 6th	1	-	1
" 7th	1	25	26
" 8th	1	3	4
" 22nd	-	5	5
	5	71	76.

	Offrs	O.Rs
Effective strength	17	442
Total -do-	18	442

Officers Demobilized

Lieut. H.B. HORNER M.C.
Lieut. T.A. STUTTARD.
Capt. F.J.G. JACKSON M.C.
Lieut. N. PEACOCK.
Lieut. R. COOKE M.C.

Lt. Col. D.J. MASON, D.S.O. Retd. from leave 23.2.19.

LEAVE

Major. R. YATES 23.2.19. to 9.3.19
2/Lieut. M.J. BARRETT.

HOSPITAL

2/Lieut. F.C. CAWTHORNE 26.2.19.

POSTINGS.

2/Lieut. McIntyre from 42nd Div. Sig. Coy.

Reinforcements received during the month 1.

[signature]
Capt. & Adjt for
Officer Cmdg 210th Bde., R.F.A.

Vol 26

CONFIDENTIAL.

War Diary

of

210th Brigade R.F.A.

Volume XXVI.

From 1st March 1919.   To 31st March 1919.

Army Form C. 2118.

WAR DIARY
or
INTELLIGENCE SUMMARY
(Erase heading not required.)

Place	Date	Hour	Summary of Events and Information	Remarks and references to Appendices
Ontignies-Sur-Sambre.	1/3/19 to 31/3/19		During the month the Brigade was quartered in and around this Town and has devoted the time to Military, Educational, and Recreational Training. Number demobilised during month:- Date. Officers. O.Rs. Total. 6/3/19 5 5 19/3/19 30 30 25/3/19 3 3 ------------------------------ 38 38 Effective strength. Offrs. 15 O.Rs. 229 Total strength. 15 244 LEAVE. Major.F.Yates. returned form Leave Date. 26/3/19. Lieut.M.G.Barnett. " " " 16/3/19. 2/Lieut.Goldsborough. " " " 24/3/19. Capt.H.Lord. (R.A.V.C.) " " " LEAVE. Lieut.C.P.Humphrey. 22/3/19. to 5/4/19. Capt.H.Lord. (RAVC) 9/3/19 " 23/3/19. 2/Lieut.F.C.Cawthorne 13/3/19 " 27/3/19. POSTINGS. 2/Lieut.Goldsborough. from 42nd.D.A.C. 14/3/19. Lt. Walmsley T.H. " " 14/3/19. 2/Lieut.Cawthorne.F.C. " to 86 AFA 25/3/19. Lieut.Rees.C.G. M.C. " " 25/3/19. Lieut.Hamilton.H.A. " " 25/3/19. Lieut.Humphrey.C.P. " " 25/3/19. 2/Lieut.McIntyre. " 42nd Div.Sigs. 18/3/19. Major C.R Brown " 211 Bde RFA 14/3/19 Reinforcements received (Retainable personnel) during the month 79. Retainable personnel posted from the Brigade 218. T.F. Penn Capt.& Adjt for Officer Commanding 210th.Bde.R.F.A.	Nil Nil Nil

Army Form C. 2118.

WAR DIARY
or
INTELLIGENCE SUMMARY.
(Erase heading not required.)

Place	Date	Hour	Summary of Events and Information	Remarks and references to Appendices

Montignies -sur- Sambre.	1/4/19. to 11/4/19.		During the period the remaining personnel of the Brigade was quartered in and round this Town, and the time has been devoted to clearing up and demobilizing the Releasable Personnel. The Retainable Men were all transferred to 42nd Divisional Details on 10/4/19.
			
			Effective strength:- NIL.
			
			LEAVE. Major W.T.Highet, M.C. 11/4/19 to 25/4/19.
			
			POSTINGS.
			  Lieut. C.P.Humphery to 2nd.Army Area.
			  Lieut. M.G.Barnett to 2nd Army Area.
			  2ndLieut. P.Chapman to 86th A.F.A. Bde.
			  Lieut. G.H.Cooper to 42nd D.A.C.
			
			OFFICERS DISPERSED.
			  Capt. G.P.Hartley, 10/4/19.
			  Capt. H.L.Penn, 11/4/19.
			  Major R.Yates, 10/4/19.
			  Capt. A.E.Birtwistle 10/4/19.
			  Capt. H.H.Lord, R.A.V.C. 10/4/19.
			
			POSTING.
			  2nd/Lieut. J.Aitkin. to 42nd D.A.C.
			
			             Capt. & adjt. for
			      Officer Commanding 210th Bde. R.F.A.	

www.ingramcontent.com/pod-product-compliance
Lightning Source LLC
Chambersburg PA
CBHW080844010526
44114CB00017B/2369